STAND AND DELIVER

MERTHYR TYDFIL PUBLIC LIBRARIES

STAND AND DELIVER

by
PATRICK PRINGLE

DORSET PRESS
New York

This edition published by Dorset Press,
a division of Marboro Books Corporation.
1991 Dorset Press

ISBN 0-88029-698-4

Printed in the United States of America
M 9 8 7 6 5 4 3 2 1

CONTENTS

Chapter		Page
	INTRODUCTION	7
I	THE FATHER OF HIGHWAYMEN	13
II	THE MAN FROM DUNSTABLE	16
III	AMATEURS AND PROFESSIONALS	21
IV	STRICTLY BUSINESS	28
V	GAY CAVALIERS	35
VI	THE PRINCE OF PRIGS	42
VII	WICKED LADIES	54
VIII	THE BROAD HIGHWAYS	62
IX	RESTORATION	73
X	CONFESSIONS OF A HIGHWAYMAN	81
XI	A VERY GALLANT GENTLEMAN	98
XII	THE GOLDEN FARMER	109
XIII	OLD MOB	117
XIV	THE YORKSHIRE ROBBER	123
XV	WHO RODE TO YORK?	135
XVI	WAR CRIMINALS	145
XVII	IN OLD NEWGATE	155
XVIII	"SO YOU WON'T TALK?"	163
XIX	CONCERNING THE ORDINARY	173
XX	THE ROAD TO TYBURN	182
XXI	JONATHAN WILD THE GREAT	195
XXII	THE REAL DICK TURPIN	207
XXIII	GENTLEMEN OF THE ROAD	220

Chapter		Page
XXIV	The Arm of the Law	231
XXV	William Page and the Weston Brothers	243
XXVI	Sixteen String Jack	251
XXVII	Jerry Abershaw and Galloping Dick	258
XXVIII	The Last of the Highwaymen	265
	EPITOME	269
	BIBLIOGRAPHY	274
	INDEX	279

INTRODUCTION

THE first chroniclers of the highwaymen—who wrote about two hundred years ago—were a very apologetic crowd. They seemed to think that the choice of such a low subject could only be justified by a profession of very high motives. So they usually began their books with long screeds on crime-does-not-pay lines, assuring their readers that their only object in writing was to show up these scoundrels for what they really were. They tacitly assumed that their readers were at least potential criminals, and expressed pious hopes that these books would make them see the light and resign themselves to living honestly. The books themselves were written in the same strain, the authors always taking care to say how repugnant it was to them when they went into gruesome details that were in fact quite unnecessary.

I don't suppose the reader was fooled. These genteel chroniclers were just observing a convention set by writers of the older smut-hunter's classics. But to-day it seems that such apologies are no longer fashionable. Freud and Co. have knocked the bottom out of that bit of hypocrisy. We all know now that I am only writing about highwaymen for the vicarious gratification of my base, society-thwarted lusts for adventure, cruelty, murder, plunder, rapine (and rape)—and that you are reading this book for the same unworthy motives. So much the better. That means that I haven't got to keep telling you I don't enjoy it when I do, and you haven't got to pretend to be shocked.

Nor shall I make the claim of some modern purveyors of vicarious violence that such wares benefit society by satisfying the consumers' criminal desires. It is a contemporary hypocrisy that murder books and films are sanative provided the villain is caught out in the end. The same theory does not seem to extend to sex, whatever the ultimate triumph of virtue over vice; but then, there is a quaint idea that human destruction is a more wholesome subject for entertainment than human procreation.

The old chroniclers had another convention that we are going to ignore. After they had solemnly expatiated on the evils of highway robbery, they issued equally solemn warnings to the reader to have no truck with the unscrupulous novelists who made heroes out of the villains of the road. This attitude persisted well into the nineteenth century, and Harrison Ainsworth—on whose behalf we shall put up a spirited defence later in this book—came in for a lot of slanging on this count. It was all rather petty. You don't damn Shakespeare because he put Bohemia by the sea, and you don't go to a historical novel when you want to learn history. The Harrison Ainsworths were only trying to entertain, and did not pretend that their books were historically accurate. And, ironically, even a superficial examination of the serious works of the I-can-give-you-the-truth merchants makes it clear that their accounts were often as wide of the mark as those of the novelists!

The true story of the highwaymen has never been written, nor can it be. The chroniclers were slavishly faithful to their authorities—flatteringly so, in fact; for these authorities consisted of a lot of chapbooks, broadsheets, penny-dreadfuls and twopenny bloods, " dying confessions " that had come in for a good deal of posthumous editing, and the contemporary gutter Press—which was even more unreliable then than it is to-day. Many of these ' authorities ' were so contradictory that the truth-at-all-costs chroniclers left out some of the best bits of highway lore in their vain attempts to keep faithful to their ridiculous principles.

Our own ambition is more modest. We have not sought the El Dorado of absolute truth. We have gone back to the same sources that the chroniclers used—and we have taken pains to ignore the latter gentlemen whenever contemporary reports are still extant. We have not moralized, like the chroniclers, nor have we embellished, like the novelists. We have added nothing—but we have taken away a good deal. We have tried to use our discretion in selection, and our judgment in discrimination between contradictory versions of the same events. Since it was impossible to be faithful to the letter, we have tried to recapture the spirit of the Age of Highwaymen.

All the dialogue is authentic. That doesn't mean that it is

what the highwaymen themselves said, of course. If we had confined ourselves to that there wouldn't have been any dialogue at all—and that, as Alice shrewdly observed, would have made it a dull book. But it is authentic in the sense that the words were put into the mouths of the highwaymen by their contemporary biographers. To repeat them now is a natural development of our plan to try to observe the spirit of the times. The dialogue has not been doctored, although we have (regretfully) had to omit some of the very speeches that seemed most likely to have been uttered by the highwaymen themselves because the *Oxford English Dictionary* has since condemned a lot of their favourite words as " not in decent use." (This scarcely justifies the suggestion of one chronicler that " Nature spoiled them in the making by setting their mouths at the wrong end of their bodies.")

The spelling in the dialogue and other quotations has been modernized, exceptions having been made where the original form was thought to make for added interest without putting too much strain on the reader's eyes.

STAND AND DELIVER

CHAPTER ONE

The Father of Highwaymen

THERE are highwaymen of sorts in the Old Testament. All crime has a common ancestry; and the true Father of Highwaymen was the wily old serpent in the third chapter of Genesis.

But our history is of English highwaymen; and their Father was a much more likeable fellow, although his existence was almost as apocryphal as that of the serpent.

Robin Hood has been the subject of a large number of learned treatises, and out of a sense of duty we have read some of them. They are dreary and unconvincing. If Robin Hood ever existed it was probably some time during the twelfth or thirteenth century. Some historians talk of his having been visited and pardoned by King Edward I; others suggest that he was the rival of King John for the hand of Maid Marian. (The latter, however, was almost certainly an importation from France, where Robin's deeds were sung in motets as early as the thirteenth century.) A considerable stir was raised in the nineteenth century by the discovery of a document dated 1324 which included an entry of payment by the Royal Household of the sum of five shillings to a "vadlet" named "Robyn Hode"; at once a learned scholar wrote a treatise proving that our hero was an adherent of the Earl of Lancaster in the insurrection of the previous year. But this theory fell into discredit after the disappointing discovery that "Robyn Hode" was a common name in the fourteenth century. A more popular theory was that Robin was the grandson of Ralph Fitz-othes, or Fitzooth, a companion of William the Conqueror. It is interesting to note that Robin was not raised to the peerage as the Earl of Huntingdon until the sixteenth century, when peers were apparently less in disfavour than formerly.

To-day, Robin Hood is always associated with Sherwood

Forest, but in the Middle Ages he was a more truly national hero. If place-names are any guide he was a ubiquitous fellow. Robin Hood's Pricks or Butts exist in Yorkshire, Shropshire, and Somersetshire; there are Robin Hood's Hills in both Gloucestershire and Derbyshire; he has a Bay near Whitby, a Tor near Matlock, a Leap at Chatsworth, and Wells in Nottinghamshire, Yorkshire, and Lincolnshire; a Chair in Derbyshire, a Stable in Nottinghamshire, and a Bed in Lancashire; and Oaks all over the country.

Robin appeared in print as soon as printing was invented. The earliest recorded literary allusion to him is in Langland's *Piers Plowman* (*c.* 1362), in which Sloth the priest excuses his ignorance of the paternoster by saying, "But I can ryme of Robin Hode." The context makes it clear that his was already a household name. Yet he was ignored by Chaucer, and he next appears in Wyntoun's *Chronicle of Scotland* (*c.* 1420):

> Lytill Ihon and Robyne Hode
> Waythemen ware commendyd gude.

The first "biography" of Robin appeared in 1495, in the form of a collection of ballads with the title *A Lytell Geste of Robyn Hoode*, printed by Wynkyn de Worde. Clear evidence of his popularity in Scotland is the fact that the second ballad anthology was published in Edinburgh only thirteen years later. After that there was a positive spate of Robin Hood literature, which persisted throughout the sixteenth century. Then the Elizabethan dramatists adopted him, notably Anthony Munday, who wrote a highly successful play co-starring Robin Hood and Maid Marian, who was raised to the same social status as the noble hero by being identified with Mathilda, daughter of Robert Fitzwalter.

The psychology of Robin Hood is very plain. There was no Robin Hood, so it was necessary to invent one. His creation was simply a wish-fulfilment. His creators were the common people of England in the Dark Ages—the England of serfdom and oppression. The three powers in the land—King, Barons, and Church—were for ever warring among themselves, and the common people were their common ammunition. Most hated of the three were the oppressive Barons.

The Barons were rich, the people were poor. The people wanted a redistribution of wealth; Robin Hood got it for them. The people wanted to see the arrogant nobles humiliated; Robin Hood did this for them, too. . The people wanted the hated Sheriffs to be outwitted; Robin Hood fooled them as well. Other, less topical wishes Robin fulfilled for the people—the wishes of which heroes of all ages and all lands are the fulfilment. He was strong, healthy and handsome, a fine physical specimen; he was chivalrous and a great lover; he was utterly fearless; and he was the embodiment of the more insular virtues of sportsmanship and sense of humour.

Robin Hood shot the King's deer and ate venison because the people's mouths were watering for these deer every day. Robin Hood won every archery competition because archery was the national sport. Robin Hood rescued the widow's sons from execution because the country was full of widows with condemned sons. Robin Hood slew Guy of Gisborne because Guy of Gisborne was as common a figure as the distracted widow. Robin Hood made a fool of the Bishop of Hereford because Bishops were hated almost as much as Sheriffs. Robin Hood was a Royalist because the common people clung to a naïve hope that the King, more remote than the Barons and Bishops, would free them from oppression if he only knew how things really were. Above all, Robin Hood was a leader because the common people craved for leadership.

The oppression continued, and Robin Hood fulfilled the same wishes in succeeding generations. Because all belief is wishful, his existence was believed in as long as the belief was necessary. Moreover, prophecy—another of desire's numerous children—promised his rebirth. The advent of a new Robin Hood was looked forward to with almost Messianic fervour. This goes some way to explaining the enormous popularity robbers enjoyed until comparatively recent times. Robin Hood was not only the Father of Highwaymen; he was also their Patron Saint.

CHAPTER TWO

The Man from Dunstable

IN the title of the previous chapter we paid Robin Hood a doubtful compliment. If, as is the fashion these days, the sins of the children are to be visited upon the fathers, then he has got a lot to answer for. We have made him the first of a long line of scoundrels, few of whom had many of his redeeming characteristics. They robbed the rich all right, but showed little concern for social justice. There were exceptions, as will be seen, but they were the minority. We may as well state now that highwaymen generally were a tough crowd.

The answer to this is that besides a Father, the highwaymen had a wicked Uncle. His existence may have been as apocryphal as that of Robin, but some pretty serious biographies of him were turned out a few hundred years ago, and they are nothing if not good copy. Thomas Dun was his name. He did not come from Dunstable, but Dunstable, it is said, came from him. More of that later. Dun hailed from Bedfordshire, and from most accounts he appears to have practised his trade— it was not a profession in those days—about the end of the eleventh century. He was a precocious child, it seems, being noted at an early age for his cruelty and pilfering habits— "whatsoever he touched stuck to his fingers like birdlime."

Life was cheap in the days of Henry I, and Dun had a few murders to his credit while still a youngster. One of his earliest exploits was the holding up of a wagon laden with corn on the way to Bedford market. Dun called out a friendly greeting, and managed to engage the wagoner in conversation. While they were thus passing the time of day Dun suddenly whipped out a dagger and stabbed the man through the heart. Then, after burying the body, he boldly drove the wagon into Bedford, sold the corn and the wagon and horses, and then disappeared.

This is a pretty banal story, but it is instructive for two reasons. First of all, we can see quite clearly why the real Age of Highwaymen did not begin much earlier than the sixteenth century. Note that there was none of the stand-and-deliver stuff about Thomas Dun. How could there be, when he had only a dagger to threaten with? Perhaps we may say, then, that the true Father of Highwaymen was the inventor of firearms.

The other point of interest is that Dun did not threaten his man at all, but just killed him. Two reasons can be found for this. First, threatening with a dagger, as we have said, was not so safe as with a pistol; second, by killing his man the thief was not putting himself in any fresh danger from the law. If he was caught they could only kill him. They would do that anyway, merely because he stole the corn. By killing the wagoner he was both guarding against the hue-and-cry being raised before he disposed of the stuff, and also eliminating the only actual witness of the theft.

Looking at it this way, we may wonder why there were not many more highway murders in later years. As long as highway robbery was a capital crime—that is, throughout the whole of the Highwayman Era—murder thrown in made no difference to the highwayman's future if he was caught. Yet the vast majority of the victims of hold-ups never suffered so much as a scratch. Why? There was no real problem about disposal of the body. The highwayman could just throw it in a ditch—which was probably all the " burial " Dun gave his wagoner. The highwayman was probably already an outlaw with a price on his head, so he did not have to worry about covering up his tracks. Nor is the suggestion that murder would rouse the authorities to more strenuous efforts than they took against simple robbery very convincing. So we are left with only one explanation: that the highwayman was not such a bloodthirsty fellow as the debunkers would have us believe. He may not have been the glamorous hero the novelists have made him, but at least he had a strong aversion to killing in cold blood. If he did not maintain the counsel of perfection established in Sherwood Forest, then at least he inherited something from Father Robin as well as from Wicked Uncle Tom.

We left Uncle Tom making his getaway from Bedford. His next adventure shows him in a more attractive light—even somewhat in the Robin Hood tradition. The scene was again Bedford. A dozen or so lawyers arranged to have dinner at an inn there, and Dun got advance information about it. An hour before dinner was due to begin, therefore, he entered the inn in great haste, bustling about importantly, summoned the landlord, and ordered him to get on with the preparations at once. The landlord took him for a servant of the lawyers, and did as he was bidden. When the lawyers arrived Dun continued to bustle about the place, and they took him for one of the staff of the inn. He kept up the double rôle all through dinner. Naturally both parties regarded him as the natural intermediary for the payment of the bill, and it was only when the lawyers began to get impatient about their change that the trick was discovered. Dun had made a thorough job of it, for the lawyers found their hats and cloaks had gone, while the landlord was short of some of his best silver.

That story is a pretty typical legend not so much of Dun as of the period. We can take it as almost certain that it was fathered on Dun after his death. It was, of course, just another wish-fulfilment tale. We see in it the same elements that inspired the majority of the Robin Hood ballads. Lawyers were a hated class in the Middle Ages, and stories against them were as popular as those at the expense of the Sheriff of Nottingham.

The next story about Dun is in a similar vein, and his victim this time was the Sheriff of Bedford. It seems that Dun had collected a band of over fifty desperadoes, all mounted, who differed from the Sherwood Foresters only in that they gave nothing to the poor. The Sheriff of Bedford resolved to put down this gang, and he sent quite a considerable force against them. There was a pitched battle in the woods, which ended in a complete victory for Dun and his men. The enemy were routed, and eleven prisoners taken. At Dun's orders these were hanged on the battlefield, as a solemn warning to the rest of the Sheriff's men. They were not hanged in their clothes, though. Dun needed these.

Shortly after this event a party of the Sheriff's men appeared at the gates of a near-by castle. Their leader asked for admission in the Sheriff's name, as he had reason to believe that the notorious Thomas Dun was in hiding within. The mere thought of such an unwelcome guest was enough for the servants, and the Sheriff's men were admitted without delay. They made a thorough search of the castle and grounds, but could find no trace of Dun. Their leader was positive, however, and he asked for the keys of the trunks, where he suggested Dun might have hidden. (How Dun could have locked the trunks from the inside and then put the keys back is not explained, but no one asked that awkward question.) The keys were handed over, and the trunks were searched. Then Dun and his men—don't tell me you hadn't guessed—rode out of the castle with a good amount of loot.

There is a sequel to this remarkable story. The lord of the castle, upon hearing of the affair, "found himself not a little moved." He lodged complaints with the King and Parliament, and the Sheriff of Bedford got a severe rep. No one, it seems, even suspected that Dun was at the bottom of it, for all the Sheriff did was to have one of his own officers hanged on suspicion of having taken part in the affair!

These last two stories, though more entertaining, were much less typical of Dun than the account of the murder of the wagoner. It was not the Sheriff who got him in the end, but the common people. His mistake of alienating the peasant folk proved literally fatal. The cruelties and senseless killings committed by his men roused the whole countryside against him, and one night the hated Sheriff's men were tipped off. Only a bare half-dozen of them went after Dun, but they were assisted by scores of the Bedford townsfolk. Dun's followers melted away, and he himself had to run for it. He took refuge in an inn, which was quickly surrounded. Game to the last, he fought his way out, killing a couple of the besiegers as he went, and wielded his sword with such vigour that he managed to get clear of the mob. Without his horse he had to take to his heels over the country, and he very nearly gave his pursuers the slip in a field of standing corn. But they caught up with him again, and their numbers had now swelled to some three hundred. Dun went on till he got to a river. With his sword between his teeth he plunged in, and swam to an island in the middle. His pursuers launched boats, but he managed to hold them off. Finally, leaving his temporary refuge, he swam for another part of the bank. But the mob was there first. They battered him unconscious with oars and other weapons, and he was carted off to Bedford Gaol. When he recovered consciousness he was brought before a magistrate, who dispensed very summary justice. Dun was taken to the market-place for execution the same day.

Dun fought his executioners furiously, beating them off nine times in succession. Then they overpowered him. There was no Jack Ketch for Thomas Dun. Whatever crimes he had committed in his lifetime were fully repaid by the manner of his execution, of which a very graphic description has come down to us:

" He yields, and the executioners chopping off his hands at the wrists, then cut off his arms at the elbows, and all above next, within an inch or two of his shoulders; next his feet were cut off beneath the ankles, his legs chopped off at the knees, and his thighs cut off about five inches from his trunk, which, after severing his head from it, was burnt to ashes. So after a long struggle with Death, as dying by piece-meal, he put a period to his wicked and abominable life."

Here is a footnote to the story of Thomas Dun.

" King Henry the Fifth," one of the old chroniclers tells us (he means the First), " founded the town of Dunstable in Bedfordshire, to hinder the outrageousness of this Dun, from whom the aforesaid place takes its name."

There may be a grain of truth in this. Dunstable was certainly founded in the reign of Henry I, and the King himself had a house built there. According to the etymologists, however, the name of the town comes from a combination of the words " dun," meaning hill, and " staple," meaning market. But you can still see the spot where Dun is said to have stabled his horse!

CHAPTER THREE
Amateurs and Professionals

PROPERLY speaking, they were all professionals. True, there were some gay young sparks who took a purse for the fun of the thing—but they never returned the purse. Even Robin Hood, for all his philanthropy, kept enough to provide himself and his followers with the necessities of life. However, the amateur highwayman is a dearly cherished character in our national literature, and cannot be passed over merely because he did not exist.

We have only very scanty records of highwaymen before the beginning of the seventeenth century, but there is no doubt about their existence. Moreover, their reputation in Elizabethan times was probably higher than at any period before or since. Shakespeare's attitude to the profession is astonishingly tolerant. In *Henry IV, Part I*, highway robbery is treated as a fair sport. The dialogue following Falstaff's suggestion that Prince Hal should join in a robbery on Gad's Hill is typical:

PRINCE HAL. Who, I rob? I a thief? Not I, by my faith.

FALSTAFF. There's neither honesty, manhood, nor good fellowship in thee, nor thou camest not of the blood royal, if thou darest not stand for ten shillings.

PRINCE HAL. Well then, once in my days I'll be a madcap.

FALSTAFF. Why, that's well said.

And so, apparently, thought the audience. A gentleman who donned a black crêpe mask and packed a pistol in order to rob an innocent traveller was no worse than a madcap.

Shakespeare is even kinder to highwaymen in *Two Gentlemen of Verona*. The scene is in Italy, but the characters could scarcely be more typically English. Valentine, banished from Milan, is waylaid by outlaws.

"Stand, sir, and throw us that you have about you," says one of the outlaws.

"If not, we'll make you sit and rifle you," he continues bluntly.

Valentine explains his plight, and the outlaws change their attitude. He is an outlaw, too—and a gentleman into the bargain! In one of the most unconvincing passages in Shakespeare's plays the outlaws ask Valentine to join them and to become their captain—adding, "But if thou scorn our courtesy thou diest." Valentine gives a conditional acceptance, which is in the true Robin Hood tradition:

> I take your offer and will live with you,
> Provided that you do no outrages
> On silly women or poor passengers.

"No; we detest such vile, base practices," is the quick reply.

In the last scene of the play, when Valentine is returned to favour, he brings the outlaws with him to the Duke of Milan, confident of securing their pardon. Here is his description of them:

> These banished men that I have kept withal
> Are men endued with worthy qualities . . . .
> They are reformed, civil, full of good
> And fit for great employment . . .

—which, of course, they are duly given.

That Shakespeare's plays were written for the gallery tells us nothing. How had highwaymen acquired this enviable reputation? Who were the prototypes of Gadshill and Valentine and his outlaws? We know that John Gay's *Beggar's Opera* of a century later was partially based on fact; Captain Macheath, although of exaggerated virtue and certainly not typical, could be identified with more than one gallant highwayman of the Commonwealth period. But we have no clue to the sources of Shakespeare's genteel highwayman, nor does the literature of his contemporaries and predecessors give us any help. In the *True and Honourable History of the Life of Sir John Oldcastle* (1600), generally attributed to Anthony Munday and his collaborators, we get the same tolerant attitude. Sir John Oldcastle—who is believed to have been the original of Sir John Falstaff—introduces himself as "in plain terms, a thief; yet, let me tell you, too, an honest thief."

The few facts we know about pre-Elizabethan highwaymen give a very different picture. There was Sir Gosselin, or Jocelyn, Denville, for example, who lived some three centuries after Thomas Dun. There are numerous chronicles of his career, all very unreliable; but the interesting point is that not one of them is at all favourable to him.

Gosselin Denville was the fourth of five children, his seniors all being girls. They came from a religious family, and the young ladies all went into a convent. Gosselin and his younger brother, Robert, were intended for the Church. However, their father died while they were still at Cambridge, and they lived according to their own desires, which were pretty low. They had inherited an estate worth £1,200 a year, which a chronicler describes as " a considerable fortune in those days." Not considerable enough for Gosselin and Robert, though. They got through most of it in three years—mainly by gambling—and only when it was nearly all gone did they think of taking up a profession. As they had both wasted their time at Cambridge, and were disinclined to serious work, they adopted the profession of the road.

At first the Denvilles joined a gang of ruffians led by one Middleton, and committed a number of robberies, mostly with violence. Gosselin himself was described as " of a very desperate and bloody disposition," and soon had several murders to his personal credit. The same chronicler reveals a cynical sense of values in his next sentence: " Breaking into nunneries, Sir Gosselin would not only take what was most valuable, but also ravish the nuns."

Eventually the pair quarrelled with Middleton, and expelled him from his own gang. Their numbers now ran into hundreds, and Gosselin's crowning achievement, we are told, was the robbery of King Edward II himself. After this a reward of 1,000 marks was offered for the capture of Gosselin, and 500 marks for Robert, dead or alive. The reward for the capture of any other member of the gang was 100 marks. " These premiums," continues the chronicler, " made honest people to watch their waters very narrowly." So narrowly, he goes on, with a nice show of accuracy, that within six months fifty-nine of the gang had been apprehended.

A story in a lighter vein tells how Gosselin once held up a Dominican monk named Andrew Sympson. The monk was almost penniless at the time, so Gosselin bade him climb into a tree and preach a sermon in lieu of delivering his purse. The monk had no choice but to obey, and he made the best of it. His text was taken from the Gospel according to St Luke: "A certain man went down from Jerusalem to Jericho, and fell among thieves." This and the sermon that followed so tickled Gosselin that he organized a collection among his followers, and contributed generously himself. It must be pointed out that the story of a highwayman making a clergyman preach an extempore sermon is a recurrent theme among the chroniclers, and to be treated with the strictest reservation. However, to Sir Gosselin goes the honour of being the first to be credited with the story.

Sir Gosselin was eventually betrayed by the wife of an innkeeper, and a company of some six or eight hundred Sheriff's men were sent to capture him. His gang, surrounded, put up a stiff and bloody fight, casualties on both sides being estimated at two hundred killed. Denville and twenty-three other leading members of the gang were arrested and taken to York, where, "without any trial, or other proceedings had upon them, they were executed, to the joy of thousands, the satisfaction of the great, and the desire of the common people."

Somewhat nearer to Shakespeare's conception of a highwayman was Sir John Popham, who graduated from the road to become Lord Chief Justice of England. There is nothing apocryphal about his story, which is taken from the most reputable authorities. Popham was born at Huntworth, in Somersetshire, in 1531, and educated at Balliol College, Oxford. He was put to study law, and didn't like it. He got in with a rakish set of undergraduates, and among their amusements they included waylaying travellers on the highway and robbing them of their purses. (Just for the fun of it, of course.) Popham married at the age of twenty—"a respectably inclined wife"—but showed no signs of settling down. He followed the highway profession for another ten years before she at last succeeded in persuading him to give it up and resume his studies, saying that "he could, with application, make as much money by the Law as by highway robbery." He did, too. He entered the Middle Temple, was elected to Parliament, and created a Privy Councillor in 1571. Eight years later he was appointed Solicitor-General, and two years after that Attorney-General, holding the latter office until 1592, when he was knighted and created Lord Chief Justice. In this capacity he presided at the trials of the Earl of Essex, Sir Walter Raleigh, and Guy Fawkes.

The financial argument attributed to Popham is probably the invention of a later writer, but it is an interesting commentary on the status of these so-called amateur highwaymen. The facts about Sir John Popham's early life rest on sounder foundations. Dr Fuller, in his *Worthies of England*, states that " in his youthful dayes he was as stout and skilful a man at sword and buckler as any in that age, and wild enough in his recreations." Aubrey's *Letters by Eminent Persons* are more explicit, and the influence of Popham's wife is described in a more credible manner:

" For severall years he addicted himselfe but little to the studie of the lawes, but profligate company, and was wont to take a purse with them. His wife considered her and his condition, and at last prevailed with him to lead another life, and to stick to the study of the lawe, which, upon her importunity, he did, being then about thirtie yeares old."

According to Aubrey, when Popham agreed to quit the highway he persuaded his wife " to provide a very good entertainment for his camerades to take his leave of them. . . . And after that day fell extremely hard to his studie, and profited exceedingly." They did not profit, however, as Fuller tells us.

" In the beginning of the reign of King James," says Fuller, " his justice was exemplary on theeves and robbers." The writer continues with a description of the influence of demobilization on the incidence of crime, which is a recurring theme in the history of highwaymen, and which makes interesting reading to-day. " The land then swarmed with people which had been souldiers, who had never gotten (or else quite forgotten) any other vocation. Hard it was for Peace to feed all the idle mouthes which a former War did breed; being too proude to begge, too lazy to labour. Those infested the highwayes with their felonies."

Set a thief to catch a thief. Fuller goes on to say that Popham " possessed King James how the frequent granting of pardons was prejudicial to justice, rendring the Judges to the contempt of insolent malefactors; which made His Majesty more sparing afterward in that kind. . . . Travellers," concludes Dr Fuller, " owed their safety to this Judge's severity many years after his death, which happened anno Domini 1607."

For all his severity, however, the ex-highwayman judge was quite open about his past. On one occasion he had to preside over the trial of an " upper-class " highwayman who moved in the same circles as he himself had in former years. When the jury retired to consider their verdict—which was a foregone conclusion—his Lordship asked the prisoner if he knew what had happened to any of the old crowd. The prisoner replied:

" All the villains are hanged, my lord, except you and me."

Two years before Popham's death a London publisher brought out what is believed to have been the first full-length biography of a highwayman. The book was entitled *The Life and Death of Gamaliel Ratsey*, and a copy is preserved in the Bodleian Library. It was brought out with a portrait of Ratsey as a frontispiece, but unfortunately this has been lost. The text is dull and not very informative, and its only real interest is its antiquity.

Gamaliel Ratsey was apparently the son of a well-to-do gentleman of Market Deeping, Lincolnshire. His date of birth is not stated, and the first we hear of him is in 1600, when he served under Sir Charles Blount (later the Earl of Devonshire) in Ireland. He returned to England three years later, and soon afterwards was arrested for stealing £40 from the landlady of an inn at Spalding. The death-sentence was almost a certainty; but before his trial Gamaliel escaped from prison—wearing only a shirt—and rode off into Northamptonshire. There he fell in with two hardened rogues named Snell and Shorthose, and the three took to the road for a living. They were a bold trio, and once held up a company of nine travellers.

Gamaliel himself always wore a special mask which covered his whole face, and on which were painted features of an especially repulsive appearance. An idea of his contemporary notoriety can be got from a passage in Ben Jonson's *The Alchemist* (1610) in which a character is described as having a " face cast worse than Gamaliel Ratsey's." He was a daring fellow with a rather crude sense of humour. According to his biography, he followed Sir Gosselin Denville's example in making his victims give of their professional talents if they had no gold. Thus a penniless actor was forced to recite a scene from the popular *Hamlet*, while a poor Cambridge scholar had to deliver a learned oration. These stories are as unlikely as the constantly repeated assertion that Ratsey was always giving away money to the poor.

Snell and Shorthose were caught in the beginning of 1605, and in an attempt to save their own skins they turned King's evidence. On their information Ratsey was discovered and arrested, and he was hanged at Bedford on March 26. His *Life and Death* was published on May 2, and at the end of the same month another publishing house brought out a sequel entitled *Ratseis Ghoaste ; or, the Second Part of his Madde Pranks and Robberies*. As the " official " biography included all Ratsey's known pranks and robberies, this second volume was almost entirely fictitious.

CHAPTER FOUR

Strictly Business

THE Age of Highwaymen properly begins in the seventeenth century. For this there were two main reasons: the increase in traffic on the roads, and the improvements in design of portable firearms. Thus it was during the reign of Charles I that the first real "knights of the road" appeared, complete with cocked hats and lace, crêpe masks, pistols, and prancing steeds.

These early seventeenth-century highwaymen were, for the most part, what were called gentlemen. (This was a reference to their parentage rather than their conduct.) It is not implied by this that the practice of crime at the time was largely in the hands of the upper classes. Far from it. But the majority of the poorer criminals were as yet still operating on a smaller scale, as pickpockets, house-breakers, and common footpads. Between the footpad and the highwayman there is one big difference, as the *Oxford English Dictionary* will tell you. The difference is: a horse.

These gentlemen highwaymen were spiritual descendants of the Gamaliel Ratsey type rather than of the amateurs like Judge Popham. Indeed, it was they who made the vocation a profession. They did not take to the roads because of any zest for adventure or other high-spirited nonsense. Their attitude was strictly business. They turned to highway robbery simply because they could see no other way of paying their debts, especially those incurred by gambling.

It is noteworthy that scarcely any of these highwaymen came from impoverished gentry. This class was to provide many recruits at a later stage in our history, but not in the period before the Civil War. Almost without exception these gentlemen professionals were young men of ample means.

Typical of the class was John Clavel, nephew and heir of Sir William Clavel, a Dorsetshire squire. We know little about his career, except that it ended when he was only twenty-three. He was arrested in the company of a common soldier whom he had taken as a partner in crime. That was in 1626. Despite his youth he was described by a contemporary as " a great highway robber," and it seems that he specialized in holding up the mail.

Clavel and the soldier admitted their guilt, but pleaded that they had never committed robbery with violence. This claim seems to have been borne out, but it did not save them from being sentenced to death. Both appealed, and Clavel begged the King's pardon in verse:

> I that have robbed so oft am now bid stand,
> Death and the Law assault me, and demand
> My life and means. I never used men so,
> But having taken their money let them go.
> Yet must I die? And is there no relief?
> The King of Kings had mercy on a thief.
> So may our gracious King too, if he please,
> Without his council, grant me a release.
> God is his precedent, and men shall see
> His mercy go beyond severity.

Whether the flattering analogy pleased Charles, or whether his council was bribed by John Clavel's influential relatives, a reprieve was granted—not only for Clavel, but for the soldier as well, which was a remarkable thing in those days. Both sentences were commuted to imprisonment.

Possibly because he prided himself on the success of his first literary effort, John Clavel occupied his time in prison by writing his autobiography. It is a curious document, entitled *Recantation of an Ill-led Life*, and mostly in verse. It was dedicated to the King, the Queen, the Court, the Privy Council, the Judges, and practically everyone else of any importance, with a special address to " the Right Worshipful, his ever dear and well-approved good uncle, Sir William Clavel, Knight Banneret:

> if again
> I ever take a course that shall be vain,
> Or if of any ill I faulty be,
> O then for ever disinherit me."

The last line loses its point, as Sir William had already done so.

As an autobiography it is pretty dull stuff. Clavel tells us hardly anything about his adventures on the road, beyond the fact that his favourite haunts were Gad's Hill and Shooter's Hill. But the book was not intended as a personal memoir. It was, rather, a sort of guide on how to travel without being robbed, as the sub-title suggests—" A Discovery of the Highway Law, with vehement dissuasions to all offenders, as also many cautious admonitions and full instructions how to know, shun and apprehend a thief, most necessary for all honest travellers to peruse, observe, and practice."

Clavel's " Discovery " was scarcely original. After a brief sermon to his former colleagues on the wickedness of highway robbery, he devotes the bulk of his tract to advice to travellers. It is all very obvious stuff, and one wonders why Clavel bothered to write it. The answer comes at the end. He wants to get out of prison, and offers his services in the war against France in exchange for his release.

Eventually Clavel was released, although whether he did in fact serve in the Army is not known. The only clue to his subsequent history is contained in a cryptic publisher's note that was added to the third edition of the *Recantation* (undated):

" The late and general false report of his relapse and untoward death made me most willing again to publish this work of his, to let you know he not only lives, but hath also made good all these his promises and strict resolutions; insomuch that it has become very disputable amongst wise men whether they should most admire his former ill-ways, or his now most singular reformation, whereat no man outjoys his friend and yours.— RICHARD MEIGHEN."

The case of John Clavel was exceptional. The number of highwaymen—gentlemen or players—to be reprieved in the seventeenth and eighteenth centuries together was very small.

Our next gentleman of the road is one Isaac Atkinson, son of a Berkshire squire. Isaac was educated at Oxford, and he apparently had a good future. The family estate was big enough to keep him in comfortable circumstances for the rest of his life. But young Isaac got on the wrong side of his father at an early age. He had a strong liking for what the chroniclers call the bad things of life—we call them the good things. But it must be admitted that Isaac carried matters too far, especially where women were concerned. "Not a maidservant could live with the old gentleman for the son's importunities, unless she gave up her honour to his desires," wrote his biographer. "Not a handsome wife or daughter in the neighbourhood but either submitted to his pleasure or complained of him to his father."

His father got it both ways. If they didn't complain they produced babies, and the number of his grandchildren became embarrassingly large. He gave his son several warnings, but the birth-rate didn't go down. Finally Isaac was disinherited and kicked out of the family homestead.

He took to the road. And, believe it or not (I don't), in less than eight months he had held up no fewer than one hundred and sixty attorneys in Norfolk alone, with a gross bag of £3,000. That was pretty good going for a novice, especially when we consider the time he must have had to set aside for the satisfaction of his excessive amorous instincts. But why did he have such a down on lawyers? Well, that seems to have been a common characteristic among these early highwaymen. In fact, so many lawyers were robbed and discomfited in so many ways, and so improbable are the majority of these stories, that we are bound to suspect that our early historians themselves had a bit of a down on lawyers. But we promised not to inquire too closely into the facts that have come down to us—they're all we've got, anyway—so we must let this pass.

On one occasion, we are told, Isaac rode up to no less a personage than Noy, Attorney-General to the King.

"Sir, I have a writ of Capias ad Computandum against you, which requires an account of all the money in your pocket," he said.

Noy did not get his meaning at once, and asked for his authority. Isaac produced it—both of them, one in each hand. The Attorney-General rendered the required account.

Young Isaac's brief career came to an inglorious end. He was caught after stealing a bag of halfpence from a market-woman on Turnham Green—although in his defence it must be said that he thought the bag contained gold. He reached the scaffold at the age of twenty-four. His dying speech was brief and pointed.

"Gentlemen," he told the crowd, "there's nothing like a merry life, and a short one."

Our last gentleman highwayman of this period was written up much better than either Clavel or Atkinson. His name was Walter Tracey, and he was the younger son of a Norfolk gentleman whose estate was worth £900 a year. Like Atkinson, Walter went to Oxford, and his father wanted him to enter the Church. But he got into bad company at the University, and was sent down in disgrace. His father took much the same line as Mr Atkinson senior had done with Isaac, and Walter had to seek his own fortune in the world. At first he lived honestly enough, working for a grazier. Like Isaac Atkinson, he had a bit of a roving eye, and his good appearance, charming manners, and musical accomplishments gained him many conquests. One of his biographers tells a story of his remarkable performance on a "musical instrument" which is, alas, all too easily recognizable as a copy of Boccaccio's delightful tale about "putting the Devil in Hell" (omitted from the more respectable English translations).

Tracey married the grazier's daughter, who had been one of his earliest conquests, and got a comfortable dowry. However, he soon tired of the simple pleasures of the country. He persuaded his father-in-law and the rest of the family to accompany him to London, and on the way he fell in with some of his associates of undergraduate days. They celebrated the reunion, and from that moment Tracey resolved to seek more sophisticated pleasures. He got up early the next morning, stole his father-in-law's wallet and a few other trifles, and took to the road.

Going to Coventry, Tracey entered an inn and heard sounds of argument from upstairs. He listened, and gathered that it was the innkeeper and his wife who were quarrelling. The former was an oldish man, and he had just discovered that his newly wed wife had married him for his money. Her complaint was that she was not getting it. Tracey appointed himself arbitrator, and delivered judgment with the wisdom of Solomon.

"Money," he declared, "has been the cause of this confusion. Without it you may live in peace and quietness; so, for your own sakes, hand me at once the money you possess." He enforced his ruling at the point of a pistol, and the innkeeper parted up with eighty-five guineas.

On the very next day Tracey became a real highwayman. Travelling southward, he fell in with an Oxonian, who was carrying a valise with him. This article aroused Tracey's newly acquired professional instincts, and he made several careless remarks about it in the hope of finding out what was inside. Whether he overdid it, or whether his companion had been reading Clavel's *Recantation*, his suspicions were aroused. All the same, he continued to travel with Tracey, and after a halt at an inn he remarked casually that he was going to the University to take his M.A. degree, and in his valise he had sixty pounds for his expenses.

Tracey wasted no time on finesse.

"Have you so?" he said pleasantly. "That is very convenient for me at this time, for I want to borrow just such a sum, and you could not lend it to a better person than myself."

The student was heart-broken. His whole career depended on his getting his M.A., he said, and the sixty pounds had been borrowed on that security. He pleaded with the highwayman to let him have at least part of it.

Tracey gave him four pounds out of his own pocket, and thought he was being very generous. Actually he was. Bidding his companion farewell, he rode off with the valise, and opened it at his leisure. In it he found not sixty pounds, but a miscellaneous collection of two old shirts, half a dozen dirty collars, a student's threadbare gown, a pair of stockings without any feet, a pair of shoes with only one heel, and " some other old trumpery."

It is not often that we find stories told against the highwaymen, and there is certainly no reason to be sceptical about this one. Nor can we doubt the biographer's statement that Tracey fell to " a-swearing and cursing like a devil."

But that was Tracey's first exploit as a highwayman, and he had to learn. Compare this with his famous encounter with

Ben Jonson, who thought to discomfit the highwayman by a bit of impromptu verse:

> Fly, villain, hence, or by thy coat of steel
> I'll make thy heart my leaden bullet feel,
> And send that thricely thievish soul of thine
> To Hell, to wean the Devil's valentine!

But Tracey had been first on the draw, and he called the poet's bluff in a similar manner:

> Art thou great Ben? or the revived ghost
> Of famous Shakespeare? or some drunken host
> Who, being tipsy with thy muddy beer,
> Dost think thy rhymes will daunt my soul with fear?
> Nay, know, base slave, that I am one of those
> Can take a purse as well in verse, as prose;
> And when thou art dead, write this upon thy hearse,
> "Here lies a poet who was robbed in verse."

To which we are told Ben could find no reply in rhyme or otherwise.

That was a bad day for Ben, for after leaving Tracey he was attacked by a band of footpads who stole his horse and bound him hand and foot. He was left in a field with other victims of this band, and they had to stay there until rescued by some reapers. Before then Ben heard a voice lamenting that they were undone; to which one of the other captives remarked, "Pray, if you are all of you undone, come and undo me." Ben knew good copy when he heard it, and later described the incident in verse.

Walter Tracey was a fairly successful highwayman, and, apart from his amorous inclinations, of a less extravagant nature than most of his contemporaries. He managed to save enough from his earnings to guarantee himself a decent income, and then retired. But he was out of luck. His investments went wrong, and he was swindled out of the lot. Tracey was forced to return to the road, and soon afterwards he was caught when holding up the Duke of Buckingham. He was executed at the age of thirty-eight.

CHAPTER FIVE

Gay Cavaliers

WHEN Civil War broke out the highwaymen stood by King Charles almost to a man. Many of them were sincere Royalists, especially those who graduated from the upper classes. Others supported the King for more cynical reasons. They may be compared with the American gangsters who supported prohibition. Puritanism was bad for trade. Highway robbery flourished when the roads were filled with the carriages of a rich and dissolute aristocracy. Half-drunk peers and their bejewelled girl-friends were easy game.

When the War was over the highwaymen went back to the roads and had to make the best of it. Some of the old-timers had been killed fighting for the King, but their ranks had been greatly increased as a result of the War. Not only did many disbanded Royalist soldiers turn to the road as the only means of making a livelihood, but there were ex-officers among them too. Dispossessed and often with a price on their heads, many a gallant Captain—and even higher ranks—spent the time waiting for the Restoration as knights of the road. These officers made full use of their experience of military leadership, and in the early days of the Commonwealth the roads were infested with armed and well-organized bands of highwaymen. Things got so serious that General Fairfax had to issue proclamations offering high rewards for their apprehension.

Typical of the new brand of highwayman was Captain Reynolds, who " was of the King's party in Cornwall, at the disbanding of the Lord Hopton's Army at Truro." When he was taken to Tyburn for his execution " his carriage was very bold, and, as he was going to be turned off, he cried, ' God bless King Charles! Vive le Roi! ' "

Another Cavalier highwayman of this period was Captain Philip Stafford, only son of a gentleman farmer of Newbury.

He was happy enough on the farm till war broke out. Then, only twenty years of age, he volunteered for service, and was soon commissioned. As a result of the part he played in the War his patrimony was sequestrated, and he was left pretty well penniless. So he took to the road.

Stafford had a special dislike for nonconformist ministers, and one of his earliest exploits was the robbing of forty guineas from a clergyman, whom he left bound to a tree. Later he was himself ordained a minister, apparently by popular demand, and as such he "acquitted himself to the entire satisfaction" of the congregation. He left suddenly, and the congregation were less satisfied when they found he had taken the sacramental plate and linen with him.

Stafford's career came to an end after he had robbed a farmer of £33 on the Reading road. He was caught within an hour, and stood his trial at Reading Assizes. After an unsuccessful attempt to escape he was taken to Reading for execution. Dressed in "a fine light suit of clothes," and "with a nosegay in his bosom," he looked, we are told, more like a bridegroom than a man condemned to death. On the way to the gallows he stopped the cart at a tavern, and had a last drink—promising to pay on the way back. In later years this joke became almost a ritual among travellers to Tyburn.

Apart from his behaviour on the day of his execution Captain Stafford did not cut a very fine figure. Clergymen and farmers were poor game for an officer and gentleman of His Majesty's Army. Captain Zachary Howard, who reached the road by a similar route, shows up much better. He lived in Glamorganshire before the War, and his father died just before the fighting broke out. Zachary inherited an estate worth £1,400 a year, which he immediately mortgaged for £20,000 and used the money to raise a troop of horse for the King. At the end of the War he was dispossessed and went into exile. He returned to England with Charles II, and fought at the Battle of Worcester; then, with a price on his head, he went underground.

Zachary became a highwayman, but he was particular about whom he robbed. He would not take the purse of anyone but known supporters of the Commonwealth. And he aimed high. One of his earliest victims was the Earl of Essex, a former C.-in-C. of the Parliamentary forces. Single-handed Captain Howard waylaid him on Bagshot Heath. The Earl had five or six men in attendance, but the Cavalier got away with no less than £1,200.

A little later Howard held up " the factious Earl of P——," who was attended only by a footman. How Captain Howard greeted the nobleman is not recorded, but we can get an idea from the Earl's reply.

" You seem by your swearing to be a ranting Cavalier," he said sternly. " Have you taken a lease of your life, sir, that you dare venture it thus against two men? "

" I would venture it against ten men, with your idol Cromwell at the head of you," retorted Captain Howard.

He collected a purse of gold and a fine diamond ring on this occasion, and he decided to teach the haughty Parliamentarian a lesson. He made him dismount from his horse and, at the pistol point, climb on to the horse of his footman. Captain Howard made the pair sit back to back—with the Earl facing the horse's tail. Then he bound them securely together, and gave the beast a crack of his whip. And that was how the Earl rode into the next town.

On another occasion Zachary Howard got to hear that General Fairfax was sending a consignment of plate to his wife. The highwayman laid an ambush for the transport, and stole the plate and a letter addressed to Lady Fairfax. Then, putting the plate in a safe place and making the necessary arrangements to ensure that he would not be followed for a little while, he went on to the Fairfax ménage. There he handed over the letter.

Lady Fairfax, taking him for the messenger mentioned in her husband's letter, asked what he had done with the plate. Glibly he explained that he had lodged it with a neighbouring innkeeper for fear of highwaymen, and would collect it in two days' time. Her ladyship had no reason to doubt his word. If he had been dishonest and stolen the plate, obviously he would not have come to deliver the letter. She invited him to stay the night. Zachary accepted the invitation with pleasure, and was taken to the servants' quarters.

In the middle of the night the bold highwayman got up,

tied all the servants to their beds, and gagged them. Proceeding upstairs, he served Lady Fairfax and her daughter in the same manner. "Then," says his biographer casually, "he ravished them both, beginning with the daughter." Getting back to business, he helped himself to a variety of valuables, and left by the front door.

As a result of this General Fairfax issued a proclamation offering a reward of £500 for the apprehension of the highwayman—a sum which doubtless appeared insultingly small to his wife and daughter. Zachary left the country, going to Ireland. He stayed there until the hue and cry had died down, and then returned to England. More ambitious than ever, he contrived to put up at Chester at the same inn as Oliver Cromwell himself. Greatly daring, he succeeded in ingratiating himself with the Protector, who later invited him to join him in prayers in his bedroom. Zachary was delighted to accept, with the result that Cromwell's prayers that evening were shorter than usual and certainly not answered. Captain Howard brought the session to an abrupt close by pointing a pistol at Cromwell's head, and he soon had the Protector gagged and bound. He made a rapid selection of Cromwell's belongings, and then once again indulged that whimsical sense of humour of his. His pro-Royalist biographer tells the story with relish: "Taking the pan out of a close-stool that stood in the room, which happened to be pretty well filled [not the room], he clapped it on the head of the rebel, crowning him in such a manner as he deserved."

These last words are typical of the partisan attitude of nearly all the old chroniclers, who were at least as staunch supporters of Charles I as the subjects of their biographies. (We fear that this may have something to do with the extraordinary number of stories told against Cromwell, Fairfax, and other Commonwealth leaders.)

Captain Howard was finally caught at Blackheath, where he attacked six republican officers together. After a fierce struggle he was overpowered and taken to Maidstone Gaol. While he was in prison he was visited by Cromwell himself, and it is a matter of deep regret that their conversation was not recorded. Zachary Howard was executed in 1652.

Of less exalted parentage than either Philip Stafford or Zachary Howard, but none the less ardent in his allegiance to the Crown, was John Cottington, known in the profession as " Mulled Sack." He was the son of a Cheapside haberdasher who drank himself to death, and didn't leave so much as the price of a decent funeral. His descendants, who numbered fifteen girls and four boys, were all broke at the time, and the haberdasher had to be buried by the parish. We can't blame John for this, as he was the youngest of the nineteen.

At the age of eight John was apprenticed to a chimney-sweep, in which honest employment he remained for five years. Then he took up the more lucrative trade of pickpocket, and did so well at it that he earned " almost enough to have built St Paul's Cathedral." But easy come, easy go; young John inherited his father's taste for the bottle, and especially for a bottle of mulled sack—hence his trade-name.

Even in the lowly trade of pickpocket Cottington showed himself a staunch Royalist. He only picked Roundhead pockets. Lady Fairfax was one of his victims, although her loss to him was not so great as that which she had been forced to surrender to Zachary Howard. It happened on Sunday morning outside St Martin's Church, Ludgate, whither her ladyship was bound to hear an eminent preacher. Cottington was dressed in his Sunday best. Lady Fairfax's carriage drew up outside the church, and her ladyship prepared to alight. Just as she was stepping on to the pavement the carriage lurched sideways and threatened to topple over. Many gentlemen hurried forward to assist her to alight safely, but Cottington was first. He had the advantage of foreknowledge, as the axle-pin of the carriage had been removed by accomplices working under his instructions. For his chivalry he was rewarded with a smile and a fine gold watch encrusted with diamonds, which he obtained by snipping the chain with a pair of sharp scissors specially made for the purpose. He escorted her ladyship to the door of the church, raised his hat and bowed, and went on his way.

The preacher's eminence rested largely upon his staying power. During the sermon many of the congregation cast furtive looks at their watches—and it was in this way that Lady Fairfax discovered her loss.

It was fitting that Cottington's last job as a pickpocket was an attempt on Oliver Cromwell himself. He sought the Protector's pocket in the shadow of the Houses of Parliament, but was out of luck. He was caught in the act, and narrowly escaped being sentenced to death. After that he gave up the trade, and became a professional highwayman.

Hounslow Heath became his favourite hunting-ground, and he formed a partnership with a veteran named Tom Cheney. One day the pair spotted the Roundhead Colonel Hewson, a ranker and ex-cobbler, riding at the head of his regiment. The rank and file were well behind, but within sight. Daringly Cheney and Cottington held up the Colonel and robbed him of his purse. The troops were soon after them, and Cheney, badly wounded, put up a strong fight against eighteen soldiers before he was taken prisoner. Cottington got away.

Tom Cheney asked for a postponement of his trial on medical grounds, as he was gravely ill. The authorities took an opposite view and speeded up the Law. It would never have done if the culprit cheated them by dying of his wounds! In Court they " caused a chair to be brought for him to sit in." He was sentenced to death at 2 p.m., and executed at Tyburn the same afternoon.

Cottington found another partner in an ex-Captain named Horne, but he too was caught and executed. After that Cottington worked alone. He was very successful. According to one writer, " he constantly wore a watchmaker's and jeweller's shop in his pocket, and could at any time command a thousand pounds."

Cottington's most famous exploit was when he held up the Army pay-wagon on Shotover Hill. It was a very bold act, as the wagon was always under armed escort; but he had the soldiers covered before they realized what was happening. His haul on this occasion was £4,000. Thinking that the removal of such a large sum called for some explanation, he made a little speech before riding off.

" This that I have taken," he told the terrified wagoner, " is as much mine as theirs who own it, being all extorted from the public by the rapacious members of our Commonwealth to enrich themselves, maintain their janizaries, and keep honest people in subjection."

Accounts of the later life of John Cottington are confused. According to one biography he was only twenty when he robbed the Army pay-wagon; but the same authority states that he was executed in 1656 at the age of forty-five—which would have made him twenty in 1631, or eighteen years before the Commonwealth. We have it on the same bad authority that Cottington went to the Continent, got into the Court of the exiled Charles II, and stole some plate from him. This sounds very unlikely. However, the date of his execution is confirmed by another source. He was convicted of murder as well as highway robbery, although the details of the charges are not known. The execution took place at Smithfield.

John Cottington was fairly representative of one class of highwaymen which practised under the Commonwealth, just as Zachary Howard was the prototype of the other main class. The two together provide an adequate cross-section of the highwaymen of this period. But the interest is always in exceptions rather than types, and easily the most colourful figure on the roads at the time was a man who came into neither class, but stood head and shoulders above all his colleagues. His name was James Hind, and he carried the rank of Captain; and he may be said to be the first really important figure in our history.

Therefore we shall give him a chapter to himself.

CHAPTER SIX

The Prince of Prigs

HISTORIANS should not show preferences, but they nearly always do. Even the great Mommsen did not conceal a strong penchant for Cæsar. So we may as well be frank, and admit that we have our favourite highwayman—our Cæsar of the Road. Actually his conquests were more in the tradition of Casanova than of Cæsar, which perhaps accounts for our admiration. It was Captain Hind who set the fashion of chivalry towards the ladies, even when robbing them. To male victims, too, he extended the greatest courtesy, and it is recorded that he never demanded a traveller's purse without first raising his hat. The only times when his manners failed him were when he was dealing with regicides. For Captain Hind was an uncompromising Royalist.

The remarkable thing about this paragon of chivalry and old-world courtesy is that he was not of noble, not even of genteel, birth. (Anyone who still believes that gentlemen are born and not made had better skip this chapter. Hind just doesn't fit in with all that stuff about breeding.) Our hero was the son of a saddler of Chipping Norton, Oxfordshire, and his first job was at a butcher's. He might have had a better start in life if he hadn't shown as a boy some of the characteristics that were later to make him renowned all over the country; for his father, we are told, "put him to school, intending to make him a scholar, but he minded his wagish pastimes more than his book." He was just as "wagish" when it came to cutting up the meat, and after a brief apprenticeship he, "having a running pate, soon grew weary of that also, and in conclusion ran away from his master." Mr Hind Senior was not pleased to see him back. He wasn't going to have the boy hanging around the house doing nothing when he ought to be out earning his living. He said as much. Young James replied that the butcher had treated him harshly, and he softened his mother's heart sufficiently to wheedle £3 out of her. Then he set off for London.

Hind became an apprentice to other trades, and was soon in the company of a band of prigs (who were anything but self-righteous folk in those days). He tried his hand at several minor branches of crime, and for a small slip he was sent to the Poultry Compter. This was not a very desirable place of residence, and it is interesting to see what sort of environment helped to mould the character of this genteel highwayman. We have no authentic information about the state of the compter at that time, but here is an extract from a description of it written some sixty years later, after conditions had been improved:

"When we first entered this apartment, under the title of the King's Ward, the mixture of scents that arose from *mundungus* tobacco, foul sweaty toes, dirty shirts, the shit-tub, stinking breaths, and uncleanly carcases, poisoned our nostrils far worse than a Southwark ditch, a tanner's yard, or a tallow-chandler's melting-room. The ill-looking vermin, with long, rusty beards, swaddled up in rags, and their heads some covered with thrum caps, and others thrust into the tops of old stockings; some quitted their play they were before engaged in, and came hovering round us like so many cannibals, with such devouring countenances, as if a man had been but a morsel with 'em."

The above is a quotation from a very reliable book entitled *The London Spy*, by Edward Ward, published in 1696.

In such surroundings as these, or worse, young James met one Thomas Allen, highly placed in the ranks of prigs and leader of a gang of highwaymen. James was invited to apply for admission to the company, and when he and Allen were both released he was given his first horse. His apprenticeship was the stiffest he had yet had to undertake. Allen and his party took the new recruit to Shooter's Hill, and ordered him to hold up the first traveller who came along. They would stand by in case of emergencies, but James was told bluntly that they did not expect to have to interfere.

The youngster passed the test all right. Fortunately his victim was not disposed to put up a fight, and he handed over his money—fifteen guineas—with scarcely a murmur. Hind took it, and then, on an impulse, returned one guinea. " For handsel sake," he explained to the astonished traveller.

Some of the watching gang were severely critical of this unorthodox behaviour on the part of the novice. It wasn't done, they argued; it was against all the rules of the road. But Allen himself, less conservative than the others, had nothing but praise for young James, and prophesied a great future for him. He was accepted into the gang without any further probation.

The single gesture of Hind's was the forerunner of many acts of courtesy, and his influence on his colleagues was considerable. Highwaymen, it was said, were getting quite polite. Even the most hard-bitten of those who came in contact with Hind were infected with some of his quiet courtesy. Of course, highwaymen could afford to be polite in the later years of King Charles I's reign, when ostentatious display of wealth was the fashion. But these days were numbered. . . .

Hind was twenty-six when the Civil War broke out, and, like most of Allen's gang, he joined up at once. He quickly distinguished himself in the ranks, and his daring and powers of leadership were recognized. He was commissioned by Sir William Compton, and fought for Charles to the bitter end. He was in the siege of Colchester, and when the town was finally taken he escaped in the disguise of a woman. Five months later Charles was executed—and Captain Hind declared a private war on the regicides.

On leaving His Majesty's Forces the highwayman had gone back to Allen's gang, which was now mainly composed of ex-servicemen. Allen himself was as staunch a Royalist as any of them, and it was he who organized and led one of the most daring exploits in highway history: the waylaying of Oliver Cromwell.

The hold-up took place on the road from Huntingdon. Cromwell's carriage was strongly guarded, but Allen boldly led his men into battle. They fought as valiantly as they had for their late King, but with the same tragic results. Allen himself was among those taken prisoner, and he ended his life at Tyburn shortly after. Hind got away, but only just.

Cromwell's men gave pursuit, and he had to ride his horse literally to death to get clear of them.

The loss of Allen split up the gang, and Hind was in a bad way. The death of his horse meant the temporary abandonment of his profession—for the gallant Captain could not stoop to the trade of footpad. He could not resume gainful employment until he had another horse—and until he got some money he couldn't buy one. It was a vicious circle, which Hind broke when he came upon a horse already saddled and tethered to a hedge. He mounted, and was preparing to make off when the owner of the animal appeared.

"This is my horse," said Hind, with a disarming smile.

"The horse is mine!" shouted the owner, hurrying up.

Captain Hind allowed the man to approach. Then he explained the position.

"Sir," he said, "you may think yourself well off that I have left you all your money in your pockets to buy another, which you had best lay out before I meet you again, lest you should be worse used."

Then he rode off.

In the saddle once more, the highwayman was ready to resume operations against the Puritan leaders. He made no further attempts on the Protector, but his list of victims contains some imposing names. The first of these was Hugh Peters, uncrowned archbishop of Commonwealth England, whom he held up at Enfield.

Peters was no coward. He had no arms to meet the highwayman's pistols, but he "began to lay about him with texts of Scripture, and to cudgel our bold robber with the eighth commandment." But Hind had briefed himself for this encounter by mugging up the Bible himself, and he had his reply ready.

"Verily," he began, imitating Peters' best pulpit manner, "if thou hadst regarded the divine precepts as thou oughtest to have done, thou wouldst not have wrested them to such an abominable and wicked sense as thou didst the words of the Prophet, when he saith, 'Bind their Kings with chains, and their nobles with fetters of iron.' Didst thou not then, detestable hypocrite, endeavour from these words to aggravate the misfortunes of thy Royal master, whom thy cursed Republican party unjustly murdered before the gate of his own palace?"

This should have been enough for Peters, but the clergyman rashly attempted not only to defend his own conduct, but to rebuke Hind for his. In fact, he had some hard things to say about highwaymen in general, which stung Captain Hind's pride.

"Pray, sir, make no reflection on my profession," he said loftily, "for Solomon plainly says, 'Do not despise a thief.' But it is to little purpose for us to dispute," he went on, tiring of the wrangling. "The substance of what I have to say is this: deliver thy money presently, or else I shall send thee out of the world to thy master in an instant."

Hugh Peters could question his opponent's interpretation of the Scriptures, but the authority of his pistols was beyond challenge. He handed over his wealth, which amounted to thirty broad-pieces of gold. Then, with the highwayman's permission, he rode on.

For all his defiant show Peters was badly shaken by the encounter. Not till he had put some distance between his tormentor and himself did he slow down his horse's speed to a trot. Then he mopped his brow and sighed with relief. Then—then he heard a horse coming after him, and within a few minutes the highwayman was abreast of him again, smiling and doffing his hat.

"Sir, now I think of it," said Hind, "I am convinced this misfortune has happened to you because you did not obey the words of the Scripture, which say expressly, 'Provide neither gold nor silver nor brass in your purses for your journey,' whereas it is evident that you had provided a deal of gold. However," he went on, "as it is now in my power to make you fulfil another commandment, I would by no means slip the opportunity; therefore, pray, give me your cloak."

With a sinking feeling in his stomach Peters asked Hind to explain. The highwayman affected to be surprised that the clergyman did not understand his allusion.

"You know, sir," he said severely, "our Saviour has commanded that if any man take away thy cloak, thou must not refuse thy coat also."

Hugh Peters was in no mood for further theological disputes. The highwayman's reading of the Scriptures was a gross perversion—but those confounded pistols. . . . He handed over his cloak.

The story has an amusing sequel. The following Sunday Peters opened his usually lengthy sermon with the text " I have put off my coat, how shall I put it on? " It was an unfortunate choice, for the story of the parson's discomfiture had already spread. Barely had Peters uttered the text when a member of the congregation stood up and said seriously, " Upon my word, sir, I believe there is nobody can tell you, unless Captain Hind were here." There was much laughter in church, and the congregation were spared Peter's usual weekly harangue.

The next regicide on Captain Hind's list was Sergeant Bradshaw, whom he held up near Shaftesbury. Bradshaw did not know his man. He pompously announced his identity, expecting the highwayman to be suitably awed and take to his heels.

Hind laughed. As if he didn't know!

Then, forgetting his usual courtesy for a moment, he gave Bradshaw a piece of his mind.

" I fear neither you nor any king-killing son of a whore alive," he said. (Strong language for Captain Hind.) " I have now as much power over you as you lately had over the King, and I should do God and my country good service if I made the same use of it; but live, villain, to suffer the pangs of thine own conscience, till Justice shall lay her iron hand upon thee, and require an answer for thy crimes in a way more proper for such a monster, who are unworthy to die by any hands but those of the common hangman, or at any other place than Tyburn." After this lengthy sentence Hind paused for breath. Then he came to the point. " Though I spare thy life as a regicide," he told the speechless Bradshaw, " be assured that, unless thou deliverest thy money immediately, then thou shalt die for thy obstinacy."

Bradshaw delivered his money—a purse of silver amounting to about forty shillings. Hind flung it back at him. Gold was what he wanted, he said—the stuff that " makes fools wise men, and wise men fools, and both of them knaves." And if Bradshaw wanted to live to hang at Tyburn he had better look slippy about handing it over.

Bradshaw handed over.

After Bradshaw, Colonel Harrison. Hind got seventy guineas from him, and came the nearest to being captured since he had taken to the road.

By now the name of Captain Hind was known all over England. Almost every highway robbery of any size was attributed to him or his associates. Here is a typical newspaper report of the period:

" Last night was brought into this gaol [Bedford] two prisoners taken up upon pursuit by the county, for robbing some soldiers of about £300 upon the way, in the day-time; there were five in the fact, and are very handsome gentlemen; they will not confess their names, and therefore are supposed to be gentlemen of quality, and it is conceived they are of the knot of Captain Hind, that grand thief of England, that hath his associates upon all roads. They strewed at least £100 upon the way, to keep the pursuers doing, that they might not follow them."

The last sentence bears the stamp of the Hind tradition. Nothing could have pleased " that grand thief " more than the idea of his pursuers grubbing about in the road for stray guineas. And when it came to money Captain Hind thought big, and told his companions to do the same. " Disgrace not yourselves for small sums, but aim high, and for great ones; the least will bring you to the gallows "—that was his philosophy.

No robber—saving Robin Hood, of course—was more generous than Captain Hind. Not only did he give to the poor what he had taken from the rich, but sometimes he even changed the order of the process. A case of this occurred when he was riding through Warwick, and chanced upon an innkeeper being arrested for failing to pay a debt of £20 to the local money-lender. Without hesitating Hind paid the sum himself. It was handed over to Shylock, and the innkeeper was freed. His gratitude was profuse. It was a clear case for one on the house, of course—but Captain Hind begged to be excused. Another time he would be delighted—but at the moment he had some particularly pressing business to attend to. His business, of course, took him along the same road that the money-lender had taken. As soon as a lonely stretch of the highway was reached Captain Hind rode up to him.

"My good friend," he said, charming as ever, "I lent you of late a sum of twenty pounds." The money-lender was indignation at once, and Hind's tone changed. "Repay at once, or I take your miserable life," he snapped.

The money-lender repaid the money, and Hind was all square. But he had to show a profit if he was to earn his living, so he demanded another twenty—"for interest," he explained. It was an even higher rate than the money-lender himself had ever charged, which was saying a good deal, but it had to be paid.

Mention has been made of Hind's chivalry towards the ladies, and we have room for one story illustrating this feature of his character. The incident took place on the road between Petersfield and Portsmouth. Unable to find any regicides to rob, and being particularly hard up for cash, Hind rode up to a coach full of gentlewomen. There was no stand-and-deliver stuff about his approach. He politely asked the coachman if he would stop for a moment while he communicated with the occupants, and he saluted the ladies in his most charming manner. He was, he declared, an ardent admirer of all their sex. Indeed, it was because of this weakness of his, he explained, that he was making so bold as to ask for their assistance. He was deeply in love with the most charming girl in the world—present company excepted, of course—but, alas! his courtship was being impeded by a lack of that sordid stuff money.

"I am at this time reduced to the necessity of asking relief," he concluded apologetically, "having nothing to carry me on my intended prosecution of adventures."

By the time he had finished Captain Hind had the ladies almost in tears. Deeply moved, they declared that they could think of no cause more deserving of assistance than his, and nothing would delight them more than to help him; but, alas! they all found themselves in a similar condition to his.

All except one of them, they added incautiously. She had a
lot of money with her—giggles—but it wasn't hers. She was
going to be married, and was taking her dowry to her future
husband.

Captain Hind had a special smile for the blushing bride-to-
be. The dowry, he learned, amounted to £3,000. His smile
became still wider. Wasn't it ironical, said the ladies, that
they were all starving in the midst of plenty, as it were—all
hard-up for a bit of pin-money, while there was all that gold
in the coach? Very ironical, agreed Captain Hind, laughing
merrily. They all laughed together. It was a good joke.
And they liked this charming stranger. He was down on his
luck, but he hadn't lost his sense of humour. Who was he,
by the way?

Captain Hind introduced himself. The ladies' smiles began
to fade. Not—not *the* Captain Hind? The same. Not the—
not the——? Yes, ladies, at your service. Ooooooh!

Captain Hind excelled himself for courtesy. He would not
dream of taking all the dowry, and thus ruining that charming
girl's chances of a happy marriage, he said. But surely there
was enough for both of them? A mere thousand would see
him through with his affair, he said—and this must be regarded
only as a loan. While he was carrying out the transfer of the
sum he begged the ladies to make his excuses to the bridegroom,
and to explain to him how, " out of mere necessity, I have
made bold to borrow part of what, for his sake, I wish were
twice as much."

Then, giving the bride-to-be his blessing and wishing her
every happiness, Captain Hind saluted again and rode off.

The story has a sad sequel. In spite of Captain Hind's
fulsome apology the girl's fiancé adopted a very mercenary
attitude, and demanded that her father should make the
sum up to the £3,000 originally agreed upon. Indeed, he
positively refused to marry her for a paltry £2,000. The upshot
was that Papa declined, the engagement was broken off, and
the poor girl died of " grief and indignation "—but not, we
trust, against the gallant Captain Hind.

Meanwhile, news of Captain Hind's exploits against Roundhead leaders had reached the ears of the Royalist hierarchy, and

he was invited to The Hague to attend Council meetings. From there he went to Ireland, and fought at Youghal in the Marquis of Ormonde's Life Guards, being wounded in action. He escaped to Scilly, where he remained for eight weeks. Then he went to the Isle of Man, where he resumed his profession on the road.

But Captain Hind's career as a highwayman was drawing to an end. His ambition was to see Charles II back at Westminster, and in 1650 he went to Scotland. He was granted an audience with His Majesty, who commended him to the Duke of Buccleuch. In the following year the gallant Captain was in the thick of the fighting at Worcester. He got away after the rout, and went to London. There he remained in hiding, under the prosaic name of James Brown, in the house of a barber in Fleet Street. But his identity was discovered, and finally—on November 9, 1651—he was arrested.

As an important political prisoner Hind was brought before the Speaker of the House of Commons, who examined him " in regard to his late engagement with Charles Stewart, and whether he was the man that accompanied the Scots King for the furtherance of his escape." This was the first Hind heard of the King's escape, and he impudently told the Speaker that he was delighted at the news, but unfortunately could not claim any of the credit himself. He proudly admitted having fought at Worcester, but had not seen Charles since then. He was so obviously speaking the truth that the Speaker wound up the examination and sent the prisoner to Newgate.

Now the authorities were in a quandary over Hind. His popularity was enormous, and his arrest had created a sensation all over England. The Roundheads had no wish to make any more Cavalier martyrs than they could help. Accordingly no political charge was preferred.

So when Captain Hind came up for trial at the Old Bailey in December he was charged only with highway robbery. According to a report of the trial " he deported himself with undaunted courage, yet with a civill behaviour and smiling countenance." He had good reason to smile. The prosecution was unable to bring any reliable witnesses against him, and the case fell through for lack of evidence!

This seems astonishing in view of his recorded exploits, but the accounts of the trial are beyond disproof. That Royalist sympathizers who had been held up by him should refuse to give evidence is understandable enough; but what of Hugh Peters, Sergeant Bradshaw, Colonel Harrison, and the rest? It almost makes us wonder if the pro-Royalist biographers didn't invent—but we mustn't wonder things like that.

Hind remained in Newgate for another three months. He had scores of visitors, and was always in high spirits. Reporters hung round his cell to jot down his witticisms, which were numerous if not always witty. "There's no haste to hang true folkes," was one of his favourite aphorisms. Of his fetters he said, "These are filthy gingling spurs, but I hope to have them exchang'd ere long."

On March 1, 1652, the prisoner was removed to Reading. A new charge was brought up against him—the manslaughter of a friend whom he had killed in a quarrel. For this he was convicted, and sentence of death was passed. It seemed that the authorities were to get rid of this troublesome prisoner at last. But by a stroke of irony Hind was pardoned under Cromwell's recently passed Act of Oblivion, which granted an amnesty for almost all offences except one: high treason.

There was no help for it. There was only one way to bring Captain Hind to the gallows, and the Roundheads were forced to take it. He was transferred from Reading to Worcester, and there faced the charge of high treason.

"Well, God's will be done," was his comment when he heard the charge. "I value it not threepence to lose my life in so good a cause; and if it were to do again, I protest, I would do the like."

And so, on September 24, 1652, James Hind was hanged, drawn, and quartered as a traitor to his country.

The death of our hero was the signal for the publication of an amazing number of chapbook biographies, almost all of them highly eulogistic. They had such titles as *The English Gusman; or, the History of that Unparallel'd Thief James Hind*: and *Wit for Money, being a Full Relation of the Life, Actions, Merry Conceits and Pretty Pranks of Captain James Hind*. But his greatest distinction was the publication in his lifetime of a play entitled *The Prince of Prigs*, " repleat with various Conceits, and Tarltonian Mirth," and written by one " J.S." There is no record of this self-styled " Excellent Comedy " having been performed, but certainly it was actually printed and on sale even before Captain Hind's arrest.

CHAPTER SEVEN
Wicked Ladies

THE knights of the road were never short of girl friends. The glamour attributed to their profession was not entirely a posthumous acquisition, as the debunkers would have us believe. Contemporary newspaper reports and accounts of their trials make it clear that they had plenty of female admirers.

Now highwaymen in general were a pretty amorous crowd, and in their short and merry lives a faithful doxy ranked in importance second only to a faithful horse. The part of the doxy was no more a sinecure than that of the horse, either. She was expected to do a good deal more than provide her man with diversion in his leisure hours—though that came into it, of course. She was a good deal more than a kept mistress. She had to be ready to tip off the highwayman when he was in danger—and she had to keep her ears and eyes open for potential clients on the road. But only rarely was she required to assist at an actual robbery.

Highway robbery was a man's job. It called for just those physical qualities to which the adjective "manly" is usually given—strength, courage, cruelty, sure marksmanship, surer horsemanship. Yet, in spite of the physical disadvantages, there were some highwaywomen as well. Sometimes they worked as partners with men—but they were no more doxies than a lady doctor is a nurse. They carried pistols and wore masks and bade travellers stand and deliver in the traditional way. They also wore men's clothes, and took great care to conceal their sex—for obvious reasons. The highwayman's success depended more on his ability to scare his victims than to shoot straight. So highwaywomen, like the lady novelists, had to practise their professions under a masculine *nom de guerre* if they wanted to be taken seriously. And apart from that, they had their reputations to think of. Highway robbery was not considered respectable as a career for women.

Without any doubt the Mother of Highwaywomen was Mary Frith, better known as Moll Cutpurse. In her lifetime she achieved even greater notoriety than Captain Hind himself. While still a young woman she had a play not only written round her, but actually being performed to packed houses. This was Middleton and Dekker's *The Roaring Girle* (1611), a witty comedy which shows Moll in a highly favourable light.

The date of the birth of Miss Frith is obscure. According to some accounts it was in 1592, but that seems incredible. The chapbook *Life and Death of Mary Frith* gives it as 1589. However, the same work states that she died in 1659 in her " threescore and fifteenth year," which makes us hope that the author was more accurate in his facts than his figures. The year of her death is confirmed from several other sources, however, and it is certain that she lived to a bad old age. 1584 is generally accepted as her probable date of birth.

Mary was the daughter of a shoemaker in the Barbican, and it is said that she made her first appearance in the world with tightly clenched fists. She kept her fists clenched during most of her childhood, and used them on companions of both sexes. " A very tomrig or rumpscuttle she was, and delighted and sported only in boys' play and practice, not minding or companying with the girls." This did not presage any sexual promiscuity, however. Far from it. She grew up a " lusty and sturdy child," but scarcely beautiful.

Her parents put her into domestic service, which did not suit her at all. She hated housework, and " had a natural abhorrence to the tending of children." She wanted a man's job. So her father offered to get her apprenticed to a saddler—but that did not suit either. It seemed that she did not want a job at all, but just to be with the lads. She became such a troublesome young woman that her uncle, who was a minister, was called in, and he advised her parents to send her to the New England plantations, which seems a bit harsh. She was actually put on board a ship—but she was off again long before it sailed. From that time on she looked after herself.

According to Middleton and Dekker, Moll had " the spirit of

four great parishes, and a voice that will drown all the city."
She looked like a man, dressed like a man, and talked and swore
like a man. She sought male company in the same spirit as
she had in her childhood, asking no concessions and giving
none. She wanted to be treated on her merits, which were
sufficient to gain her admission to the exclusive " Society of
Divers, otherwise called file-clyers, cutpurses or pickpockets."
It was by her skill in this closed-shop union that Moll got her
nickname.

But she was not content to remain a pickpocket for long.
Setting up shop in Fleet Street, with the original object of
disposing of her gains at higher prices than the ordinary fences
would give, she soon became the unofficial receiver of the
society. It was not long before her function was extended to
receiver-general for other branches of crime. The fence in
those days had a privileged position in the underworld. The
Law did not regard him on the same plane as a thief, and it was
common for people to advertise rewards for the return of
stolen property " with no questions asked."

As Moll's reputation spread her business became more
profitable. Not only did criminals take their goods to the
back door of her shop, but the people who had been robbed
came in at the front in the hope of redeeming their property.
They were often prepared to pay more than the intrinsic
value for articles for which they had a sentimental affection,
and Moll could not have wished for better customers. She
made it a general principle to let the original owner have first
choice of her wares before offering them to the public. As the
profits from her sales increased, she was able to give better
prices for stolen articles; the older fences could not compete,
and were driven out of business; their customers followed the
rest of the crowd to Moll, until she was catering for the best
part of the large criminal population of the capital. Even
the upper strata of this fraternity—the highwaymen—brought
their pickings to Moll, and her regular clients included many
of the leading knights of the road, among them the gallant
Captain Hind.

Whatever was stolen, and by whatever means, it stood a very
good chance of ending up in Moll Cutpurse's shop. That was

the general opinion of most of London. Realizing the value of publicity, Moll encouraged the spread of such reports, and her sales went up more than ever. People stopped advertising for their property; they just went round to Moll's. And they could always rely on a square deal. Moll was scrupulously honest in all her transactions, and was trusted by robbers and robbed alike.

Moll Cutpurse was not a spendthrift, but a dry tongue and a warm heart accounted for a good part of her profits. She was always willing to help anyone down on his luck; and in the tavern after business hours she could hold her own with the hardest tipplers of the town. She had one very unfeminine habit which her biographer relates with evident disapproval. " In her time tobacco, being grown a great mode," he says, " she was mightily took with the pastime of smoking, because of its singularity, and that no woman ever smoked before her —though," the writer adds, more disapproving than ever, " many of the sex since have followed her example."

By all accounts Moll was an unrepentant sinner if ever there was one, but we have a record of her having done penance on one occasion. John Chamberlain, whose gossiping letters have gained him the title of the Horace Walpole of his age, tells us about it:

" Last Sunday, Mall Cutpurse, a notorious baggage, that used to go about in man's apparel, and challenged the field of diverse gallants, was brought to St Paul's Cross, where she wept bitterly, and seemed very penitent."

A touching scene—and what a pity Chamberlain has to spoil it. He goes on:

" But it is since doubted she was maudlin drunk, being discovered to have tippeled of three quarts of sack before she came to her penance."

Such was Moll Cutpurse, pickpocket and fence, known to every highwayman of note in the London area. But what of Moll Cutpurse, highwaywoman? All her biographers agree that she practised extensively on the roads, but they are very reticent about details. In fact there is only one story of any length about this part of her career—but fortunately it is a good one.

The incident occurred during the Commonwealth period—Moll was, of course, a stout Royalist—so our heroine must have been getting on in years at the time. The story runs that certain of her male associates had arranged to rob Lady Fairfax on her way to church, and while they were away she saddled her horse and rode off to Hounslow Heath to hold up the General himself. Single-handed she did it, in broad daylight, against the General and two servants. She had to use her pistol before Fairfax would yield, and wounded him in the arm. She collected 250 jacobuses from the Roundhead, and then, after shooting the servants' horses under them, rode off.

Unfortunately, at Turnham Green Moll's horse failed her, and in spite of desperate attempts to get away she was finally surrounded and taken prisoner. For the first time in her long career she found herself in Newgate Prison. But not for long. Money talks—and Moll had plenty of that. All the same, it needed a lot of money to out-talk General Fairfax, and getting her liberty cost Moll no less than £2,000.

Moll's takings in the shop dropped sharply under the Commonwealth, and like her highwaymen friends she was marking time and waiting for the Restoration. But time beat her in the end. She died in the year before Charles II returned, of the unromantic disease of dropsy. But when the great day came she was there in spirit. In her will she had left £20 for the celebration of the return of the King, and in those days this was quite enough to enable the boys to make a night of it.

In addition to the play by Middleton and Dekker contemporary literature contained a number of allusions to the " Roaring Girle." She appeared as a character in Nathaniel Field's *Amends for Ladies*, first published in 1618 but certainly written and performed at least eight years previously. The Stationers' Register for 1610 includes an entry reading " A book called *The Madde Prancks of Merry Moll of the Bankside, with her walks in Man's Apparel and to What Purpose*, written by John Day," but there is no record of this having been published.

Most Shakespeare glossaries credit her with having been the subject of a remark by Sir Toby Belch about taking the dust " like Mistress Mall's picture "; but the allusion is admitted to be obscure, and it is scarcely credible that Moll Cutpurse should have been such a household name as early as 1600. Besides, the name Moll, or Mall, as a shorter form of Mary, has a much longer history than Miss Cutpurse. As a proper noun it was certainly in use in the middle of the sixteenth century; and later it became a highly improper noun, almost synonymous with "doxy," and is coyly defined in the *Oxford English Dictionary* as "the unmarried female companion of a professional thief or vagrant." There was nothing like that about our Moll. One look in the mirror was enough to make her realize that "she was not meant for the pleasure or delight of man." (One look at her picture is enough to tell us that she was right.) A possible clue to the whorish meaning of the name is its use as a diminutive in that "learned clarke" Lewis Wager's *Marie Magdalene* (1566).

A very different type of highwaywoman was Joan Bracey. Born Joan Philips, the daughter of a well-to-do farmer of Northamptonshire, she was courted and conquered by a highwayman named Edward Bracey. When her father heard of the affair he threatened to turn her out of the house, so she went of her own accord, adopting her lover's name without going through the formality of the marriage ceremony. A doxy? Not by any means. She was Joan Bracey to her friends—but plain Mr Bracey when on business. She worked as a partner to Edward, dressing in his spare suit of clothes.

However, there was nothing of the "tomrig or rumpscuttle" about Joan. By all accounts she was a real beauty, and when in woman's dress she used her charms to attract new customers to the firm of Bracey & Bracey Limited.

The Braceys practised in the latter part of the reign of Charles II, and they did very well. After a time they had enough money to buy an inn near Bristol, which served as a convenient base for their further operations on the road. They were not above taking a bit on the side, however, and here again Joan's physical charms proved a great asset. She was popular in the taproom, and many a prosperous gentleman offered to improve her station in life. But she remained faithful to Edward, although she didn't mind a bit of fun with the boys.

One of Joan's most ardent admirers was a certain Mr Dacey,

said to be a man of some means. Several times he had made improper suggestions to her over his glass of ale, and at last Joan seemed to surrender. She arranged a tryst with him at the inn after closing time one night when, she said, her husband would be out of the house. The eager Mr Dacey was there at the appointed hour, dressed in his best suit of clothes. He was let in by the maid and escorted upstairs. The girl told him that her mistress was impatiently awaiting him in her bedroom, but for the sake of prudence she had asked if he would mind undressing in a spare room, just in case her husband came back suddenly. This seemed very reasonable to Mr Dacey, and he allowed himself to be shown into a room, where the maid, "with a frolicsome humour," assisted him in the removal of his clothes. When he was reduced to a shirt the maid, "putting out the candle on account of mere modesty," led him along the passage and opened the door of another room. It was in pitch darkness—more modesty, thought Mr Dacey—and as he was groping about in search of the bed he heard a key turn in the lock behind him. Realizing he was alone in the room, he banged on the door; whereupon the sweet tones of Joan Bracey informed him that there was another door opposite which led to the back entrance to the inn, and he could go as soon as he liked. But what about his clothes? he wanted to know. Well, it was dark outside, so what was he worrying about? Of course, if he wanted to wait till Edward came back. . . .

Mr Dacey was glad he had kept his shirt on.

Joan Bracey reached Tyburn in 1685, at the age of twenty-nine. The events leading up to her arrest are not recorded.

Yet another type of highwaywoman was Mary Blacket, of whom we hear nothing until she was arrested " for assaulting William Whittle in the highway and taking from him a watch value £4, and sixpence in money, on the 6th of August, 1726." Mary was the daughter of " very mean parents," who yet gave her education enough to enable her to read and write, and a thorough training in the fundamentals of domestic service—" which was the best station they ever expected she would arrive at." Mary went into service, and was well thought of. She left to marry a sailor, who gave her a baby and then went to sea again. He was still away when she was arrested for the robbery of Mr Whittle.

There was no record of any previous highway activities by Mary, and the case was treated as an isolated instance. It was sufficient for the death sentence, of course, and Mary was duly convicted and sent to Tyburn. At her trial she pleaded not guilty, her defence being that Mr Whittle must have got her mixed up with someone else. As a defence this was perfectly normal; but the remarkable thing was that she continued to declare herself innocent after she had been convicted, persisting in her denial of the charge even at the gallows. This made a deep impression on her contemporary biographer, who prefaces his account of her life with some general remarks about people who " have suffered though innocent of the crime for which they died." Certainly for a condemned criminal without a hope of a reprieve to conceal his guilt was a rare occurrence. There was a very real belief in a physical Heaven and Hell in those days, and the condemned highway robber had nothing to lose in this world and everything to gain in the next. Mary's behaviour at the end was admirably restrained; she blamed no one, declaring that her unhappy plight was caused by a mistake, " and not upon wilful design to do her prejudice." She went to chapel before she died, and asserted her absolute forgiveness of those responsible, " as freely as she hoped forgiveness from her Creator."

There seems to be good reason to doubt that Mary Blacket was a highwaywoman at all.

CHAPTER EIGHT

The Broad Highways

THE history of highwaywomen has taken us ahead of the main part of our chronicle. To pick up the story of the highwaymen again we must go back to the middle of the seventeenth century; in particular, the year 1660. Before we go on to the adventures of highwaymen after the Restoration, however, something must be said about the highways themselves.

Some idea of conditions on the roads during the reign of Charles II may be gathered from a passage in the chapter in Macaulay's *History of England* on the state of the country in 1685:

"Whatever might be the way in which a journey was performed, the travellers, unless they were numerous and well armed, ran considerable risk of being stopped and plundered. The mounted highwayman, a marauder known to our generation only from books, was to be found on every main road."

That is the sober judgment of a historian. Other writers put the matter much more strongly. The roads were infested with highwaymen. Some worked alone, others in small groups, yet others in larger bands. All were well mounted and well armed. They robbed by day as well as by night, with a bold impudence that made travellers cry out in exasperation: What is the Government doing about it?

The Government was doing nothing. The Law designed for the protection of travellers against highwaymen had scarcely been changed since the Statute of Winchester of 1285. The latter, a typical Act of a weak central Government, had thrown the entire responsibility on to the local authorities. The inhabitants of each township or "hundred" were answerable for all offences committed in daylight within their respective borders. Unless they could produce the body of the offender within forty days of a robbery, they were subjected to a collective fine to make good the loss sustained.

The main provisions of the Statute of Winchester were repeated in a further Act in 1354. Nearly two centuries later a new Act was passed under which the collective indemnity was cut to fifty per cent of the traveller's loss. This was simply a confession of weakness, and was brought in following the protests of the hundreds against ever-increasing demands made on them. In the sixteenth century the Sunday Trading Act exempted the hundreds from financial liability on Sunday offences, on the grounds that Sunday travelling was unnecessary and perhaps a little wicked.

All this was simply evasion of the issue, and did nothing to curb the activity of the highwaymen. The Statute of Winchester had been aimed against footpads rather than highwaymen. Circumstances were entirely changed by the emergence of mounted robbers and especially the invention of firearms. But the Law did not change. The hundreds could not pay in full, so the travellers suffered.

As it was, the only thing that saved the hundreds from being completely impoverished was the daylight clause. Their responsibility began at sunrise and ended at sunset, and so long as the highwaymen slept during the day and robbed at night the only sufferers were the individual travellers. If you journeyed by day you were protected by a free State insurance; if you went at night you had to hope for the best. So, of course, the majority of travellers kept off the roads after dark; and, of course, as the numbers of highwaymen increased faster than the numbers of travellers, there was a corresponding increase in the incidence of daylight robbery. And the hundreds had to pay.

The protection of travellers in London was somewhat different, and in the reign of Charles II a system of night watches was instituted. As this forms part of a separate subject, it will be dealt with later in conjunction with the establishment of the Bow Street Patrol.

Macaulay concludes his description of the state of the roads by observing that none were so bad for travelling as those leading to London. There were four main highways radiating from the capital, and each had its special black spots. Some of these have already come into our story, and all will certainly have a place in succeeding pages. In this chapter the reader will be formally introduced to the high spots—they were mostly hills—on each of the four main roads.

Without doubt the most famous highwayman's "beat" was on Hounslow Heath, on the Great Western Road. Its name keeps cropping up throughout the highwayman era, and it was favoured by the earliest exponents of the profession. Machyn's *Diary* contains the following entry for 1552:

"The xxj day of Desember rod to Tyborne to be hanged for a robery done on Honsley heath, iij talmen and a lake"— that is, three tall men and a lacquey.

An amusing story is told of an encounter between a highwayman and a tailor on the Heath. The latter, on being asked to hand over his wealth, addressed the highwayman thus:

"I'll do that with pleasure, but suppose you do me a favour in return? My friends would laugh at me were I to go home and tell them I was robbed with as much patience as a lamb; suppose you fire your two bull-dogs through the crown of my hat, it will then look like a show of resistance."

The request seemed reasonable enough, and the highwayman, pleased at the implied compliment to his marksmanship, fired both his pistols at the hat of the self-appointed William Tell. Whereupon the tailor promptly produced a pistol of his own, and the highwayman rode off without making any further demands.

One other story about the Heath must be mentioned. Although the highwayman was again anonymous, at least one of the characters in the incident was a very important little personage. The highwayman held up the first of two carriages, and found it occupied by a nursemaid and three children. He asked who they were.

"The grandchildren of your King," was the severe reply. And, indeed, one of them was Prince George, aged five, later to become King George III. Apart from the rather apocryphal story of Sir Gosselin Denville's robbery of King Edward II, this may be the only case of an English King having been held up on the highway.

But the highwayman was loyal to the Crown.

"God bless them," he said, and bade the coachman drive

on. Then he held up and robbed the occupants of the second carriage, who were just ordinary members of the Royal Household.

Another of the main highways, the Dover Road, was famous for two appropriately named eminences: Shooter's Hill, and Gad's Hill (gad = vagabond). As we know from Shakespeare, the latter was already famed for its highwaymen before the beginning of the seventeenth century. Shooter's Hill is not quite so well known, and we have a pretty little anecdote about this spot. There was no shooting on this occasion, but plenty of blood. It happened one dark night at the beginning of the eighteenth century, when three bold bad highwaymen—Will Ogden, Tom Reynolds, and Jack Bradshaw—were lying in wait for travellers. They were out of luck, however, and after an hour's waiting they were rewarded only by the appearance of a solitary pedestrian—a servant-girl. Normally they would have let her pass as not being worth robbing. But they observed that she was carrying a box. That might contain something, they thought; and business was too slack for them to be able to afford to pick and choose. Besides, it was an easy job. Bradshaw—said to have been a grandson of the great Sergeant Bradshaw—being the youngest, was detailed for the work.

It was, as they said, a straightforward job. Bradshaw just walked up to the girl, snatched away the box, and forced it open then and there. The contents were disappointing. Ignoring the girl, he pulled out some feminine garments, fifteen shillings in silver, and various oddments. There was also a hammer, which Bradshaw tossed on to the road with other articles which were not worth taking. Why the girl was carrying a hammer is not known, unless it was for biffing chance highwaymen on the head. Anyway, while Bradshaw was still pulling stuff out of the box the girl picked up the hammer and dealt him a shrewd blow on the temple. Before he could recover she turned the hammer round in her hand and used the claw to tear his throat open. Thereupon, not unnaturally, Bradshaw fell down on the road and died.

While the girl was packing up her belongings again a gentleman rode up and asked if he could be of any help. The girl explained what had happened, for all the world as if killing highwaymen with a hammer was an everyday occurrence. The gentleman then went through Bradshaw's pockets, and found some loose silver and a whistle. What he did with the money is not recorded; but he put the whistle to his lips and blew.

Now Ogden and Reynolds were still waiting in a near-by coppice for their companion to return. He should have been back long ago, of course; but as the victim was a girl, they realized there might be special reasons for Bradshaw's delay which he would not want investigated. Not wishing to embarrass him, therefore, they remained out of sight of the road all the time. But when they heard his whistle, which was the signal for danger, they rushed out at once.

When they saw the gentleman, the girl, and above all the prostrate body of Bradshaw, they rushed back a good deal faster.

The third main highway to London was the Great North Road, whose especial distinction was Finchley Common, made famous by Harrison Ainsworth's stories of Dick Turpin and Jack Sheppard. One highwayman, Peter Curtis by name, declared after his arrest that he had buried £1,400 there, but it hasn't been found yet. Another of the brethren, John Wigley, was suspected of having committed a murder in a barn, but the charge was never proven; the man he was supposed to have murdered was the husband of an old woman who sold brandy on the Common, and with whom Wigley admitted having what his biographer delicately calls "an unlawful correspondence." According to Wigley, "though the old man's death was sudden, yet it was natural." It was caused, he said, by an overdose of brandy, and in this explanation the woman supported him. Well, she ought to have known.

Surely the most unhappy of the numerous robbers who practised on Finchley Common was Joseph Picken, whom we shall call the "Henpecked Highwayman." The brief biography we have of him begins with the truism, "There cannot, perhaps, be a greater misfortune to a man than his having a woman of ill-principles about him, whether as a wife or otherwise." In Picken's case it was his wife. He met her

when working behind the bar in a Billingsgate pub, and fell for
her at once. After the marriage he "took the tap" at a
tavern in Windsor, and was soon doing quite well for himself.
But Mrs Picken was extravagant, and her mother, who went
to live with them, cost a bit as well. Before long Picken was
£30 in debt; and the next we hear of him is that he is out of a
job and living in a single room with his wife and mother-in-
law. The ladies occupied the only bed, by the side of which
"poor Picken used to slumber upon the boards, heavily dis-
consolate with the weight of his misfortune." Finally he
could stand it no longer.

"I am now quite at my wits' end," he told his wife. "I
have no way left to get anything to support us. What shall I
do?"

"Do?" she replied. "Why, what should a man do that
wants money and has any courage, but go upon the highway?"

Picken wanted money, but he hadn't much courage. However, it needed even more courage to defy Mrs P. than to go on
the road—and that was why Picken became a highwayman.
As may be expected, he didn't last long. He was caught less
than a week after he had taken up his new profession, and after
a brief trial was sentenced to death. Mrs Picken's conduct after
his conviction was deplorable. Just "as she had brought him
into all the miseries he now felt," says his biographer indignantly,
"so she left him to bear the weight of them alone, without
either ever coming near him or affording him any assistance."
However, the story ends more happily. The Henpecked
Highwayman confessed all his sins, forgave his wife everything,
and "behaved himself with amazing circumstances of quietness
and resignation" all the way to Tyburn.

The last of the four great highways was the Oxford Road,
of which the high spot was the aptly named Shotover Hill—
where John Cottington held up the Army pay-wagon. A
story is told of a certain barber who was held up on this hill,
but who could show nothing but an empty purse. And, of
course, the tools of his trade—but they wouldn't be much use
to a highwayman. The latter, however, was unwilling to let
his victim go for nothing, so he ordered him to dismount and
give him a shave.

He must have been pretty sure of himself to trust his neck to the barber's razor, but actually it never got as far as that. The unusual commission made the barber nervous, and while he was getting out his instruments he dropped his shaving-pot on a stone. It broke into pieces, which he hastily tried to gather up; but the highwayman's keen eyes caught the glitter of gold, and he became business-like at once. Twenty guineas the barber had hidden in the pot, and he had felt pretty safe from being robbed. But who could expect a highwayman to want a shave?

Each of the main roads leading out of London was infested by living highwaymen at all times—and by dead highwaymen all the time. That grim construction known as the gibbet was reserved for the very worst offenders, however; the general run of highwaymen got off with a mere hanging. The difference may not seem much to us nowadays, but criminals in the seventeenth and eighteenth centuries were very concerned about the future of their bodies. A decent burial was the aim of every respectable highwayman; and it must be conceded that gibbeting was a pretty indecent affair. "The chains rattled, the iron plates scarcely kept the gibbet together, and the rags of the highwaymen displayed their horrible skeletons," is one eye-witness description.

The popular feeling towards gibbeting was brilliantly recaptured by Tennyson in his ballad *Rizpah*, in which a woman laments her highwayman son:

They hang'd him in chains for a show—we had always borne a good name—
To be hang'd for a thief—and then put him away—isn't that enough shame?
Dust to dust—low down—let us hide! but they set him so high
That all the ships of the world could stare at him, passing by.
God 'ill pardon the hell-black raven and horrible fowls of the air,
But not the black heart of the lawyer who kill'd him and hang'd him there.

The fact that gibbeting was continued until 1834 excites no surprise. But what is remarkable is that it was not recognized by the law until as late as 1752. Of course it was a well-established practice long before Parliament gave it its blessing. Chambers's *Cyclopædia* of 1727 defines the gibbet as "a machine in manner of a gallows, whereon notorious criminals after execution are hung in irons, or chains, as spectacles, *in terrorem.*" Actually the antiquity of the gibbet has been traced to very early times. The first reference to it in English literature dates from the reign of Henry III, Matthew Paris reporting cases of gibbeting and also of gibbeting alive.

The avowed object of the gibbet was simply *in terrorem.* With a naïve faith in the force of example, otherwise respectable citizens approved of the gibbet as a deterrent to potential criminals. History reveals that it deterred no more highwaymen than capital punishment does murderers to-day. Instead, it became a place of pilgrimage for morbid sightseers. By those who had no personal connexions with the man on the gibbet it was regarded as something worth going out of one's way to see—the next best thing to attending the Tyburn Fair, in fact. In the *Annual Register* of 1799 we read that " eight gentlemen belonging to the Walton association formed a party to go to Hounslow to see Haines, the highwayman; on their way home they stopped at the Flower Pot, at Sunbury, till ten at night "— and got so drunk that three of them were drowned on the way back.

The authorities wanted to make the spectacles as permanent as possible, and sometimes the corpses were dipped in tar before being hung up; as in ancient Egypt, the dead had the benefit of antiseptic treatment long before it was extended to the living. However, the relatives and friends of the gibbeted malefactors made great efforts to rescue the bodies from their ignominious chains and give them a decent burial. The simplest way was to saw the gibbet-pole, but precautions were taken against this by an iron casing being put round it before erection. Then the only way to get the body down was to climb up the structure and try to unshackle the chains, which was as dangerous a task as it was gruesome. It had to be done at night, for, long before the gibbet had been legally recognized, it was an offence for anyone to try to remove a body once it had been hung up. As a further discouragement for would-be body-snatchers the supports of the gibbet were usually studded with a number of sharp nails. However, gibbets continued to be plundered. In an entry dated April 3, 1763, in the

Annual Register we read: "All the gibbets on the Edgware Road, on which many malefactors hung in chains, were cut down by persons unknown."

Before we leave the subject of the highways something must be said about one of the real plums of the profession: robbing the Royal Mail. This was not always so easy as our illustration suggests; indeed, it was regarded as one of the riskiest jobs on the road. But the rewards were good.

The particular story we are going to tell is a rare example of good detective work before the days of the Bow Street Runners. It was the Bristol Mail that was held up, on the road near Knightsbridge. The highwayman responsible was alone and masked, and did not answer to the description of any known malefactor. In actual fact it was his first adventure on the road. It was also his last.

His name was Hugh Houghton, and he had served in both the Navy and the Army. He was pressed into the former service as a youth, but rose to the rank of gunner's mate and left with a pension of £5 per annum. He enlisted in the Army—the Horse Guards—voluntarily, but was discharged with ignominy on a rather doubtful conviction of stealing clothes. "Whereby," states his biographer, "he fell into great difficulties for want of money."

In London Houghton took lodgings in the house of a Mr Marlow, and was soon heavily in arrears with his rent. He had no apparent means of subsistence, and Marlow was therefore very surprised when his tenant came one day and cleared his account. Marlow communicated his suspicions to the authorities, and the money was traced to a near-by brewer's, where Houghton had changed a twenty-pound note. The note was checked, and found to tally with one that had been stolen from the Bristol Mail.

Houghton's trial was interesting. The official from whom the mail-bag had been stolen stated that the robber was a man of Houghton's build, but that he could not positively identify him. The next witness for the prosecution was a fellow-lodger of the accused named Daniel Burton, who deposed that Houghton had more than once suggested to him that they should work together on the road, and that he had also made a proposal to rob their landlady, Mrs Marlow, but that her husband had got to hear of it. Marlow, in his evidence, declined to substantiate the latter story.

The only real evidence against Houghton was circumstantial, and this was very strong. Not only was he positively identified by the brewer as the man who had changed the twenty-pound note, but at the time of his apprehension other notes were found on him which also tallied with those stolen from the Bristol Mail. At the time of his arrest Houghton had made a statement in which he said that he had picked up the money in a pocket-book in Covent Garden.

Houghton stuck to this defence at his trial. On the day on which the mail was robbed, he said, he had found a bundle of papers, including the pocket-book, in Covent Garden. Discovering that they were part of the Bristol Mail, and " being at that time out of business and in great want," he had abstracted the pocket-book and sent the rest on to the P.M.G. Houghton denied Burton's evidence, saying that it was the latter who had offered him a partnership on the road, and declaring that he now believed that he had fallen into a deliberate trap set by Burton. His defence was supported by the evidence of two women who swore that he did not leave his lodgings all that night. (Unfortunately their evidence is not reported verbatim.) Finally, Houghton reminded the Court that he had served his country twelve years at sea and twelve on land, " and in all that time never had any reflection upon him until the unhappy accident in the Guards, which he said he was not guilty of, and had been since confessed by another man."

The accused was not shaken under cross-examination, and the jury took longer than usual to consider their verdict. But for the incontestable evidence of the banknotes Houghton would certainly have been cleared. There was clearly bad blood between him and Daniel Burton, and the latter's evidence was unreliable and probably malicious. But the story about finding the pocket-book in Covent Garden was too improbable. Was it likely, Houghton was asked, " that when a man had hazarded his life to rob the Bristol Mail, he should then throw away all the booty, and leave it in such a place as

Covent Garden, for any stranger to take up as he came by? " To which Houghton just shrugged his shoulders and persisted in his declaration of innocence. In the end he was found guilty and sentenced to death. Even after his conviction, however, he refused to admit his guilt, although he " made general confessions of his sins and pleased himself with high conceits of the Divine Mercy."

In Newgate his gaolers suspected him of planning to commit suicide, and special precautions were taken. All likely instruments were removed, the barber who shaved him was warned to be on his guard, and Houghton himself was kept under constant observation. But he made no attempts on his life, and on the morning of the day fixed for the execution he was observed " praying very devoutly in his cell." The gaolers gave him twenty minutes' privacy. When they came back they found him hanging by his belt from a grating, his handkerchief firmly knotted round his neck. He had cheated the gallows after all.

There was a good deal of conjecture at the time as to whether Houghton was really guilty. A strong argument in favour of his innocence was, of course, his refusal to confess before he died. The Ordinary, or prison chaplain, declared that " it is to be feared he was a hypocrite, and little of what he said can be believed." But Newgate Ordinaries, as we shall see in a later chapter, were themselves hypocrites, and, judging from their publications, little of what they said could be believed either. Houghton's biographer, whose account of the trial is a fine bit of impartial reporting, gives only a guarded opinion at the end:

" For my part, I am far from taking upon me either to enter into the breasts of men or to pretend to set bounds to the mercy of God, and therefore without any further remarks, shall conclude his life with informing my readers that at the time he put an end to his own being he was about forty-eight years of age, and a man in his person and behaviour very unlikely to have been such a one as it is to be feared (notwithstanding all his denials) he really was."

CHAPTER NINE

Restoration

THE first effect of the Restoration on the highway profession was a thinning out of the ranks as the gentlemen Cavaliers came into their own again. Many of them had their estates restored, and thus did not need to earn a living in this way; and, besides, it was no longer patriotic to rob officers of the State. The Captain Hind type of highwayman disappeared for ever.

However, there were exceptions. Not all the sequestrated property was returned to its original owners or their descendants, and some of the loyalest of the King's supporters found themselves little better off after the Restoration. Moreover, some of the gay young Cavaliers had acquired a taste for the adventurous life of the road, and were loath to go back to the unexciting social round. And, as in the reign of Charles I, there were some young gentlemen who were drawn to the road neither by financial necessity nor for political reasons, but simply because they could not live within their means.

Typical of the last-named category was Captain Dick Dudley. Born in 1635, the son of a Northamptonshire gentleman, Dick was too young to take an active part in the Civil War. His father was hard hit by the victory of the Roundheads, but he managed to have Dick educated at St Paul's School, and after Charles II returned he got the young man a commission in the Army. Dick was posted to Tangier, and as an officer he distinguished himself more for his rigid discipline than anything else. He was a terror on the parade-ground. On one occasion, when the ranks were imperfectly dressed, he ordered a sergeant to knock down a man who was slightly out of position. The sergeant obeyed, but not vigorously enough for Captain Dudley. "When I command you to knock down a man," he told the sergeant, "knock him down thus." To demonstrate what he meant he borrowed the sergeant's halberd and brought it down on the unfortunate soldier's head, splitting his skull in two.

Such conduct as this was deemed prejudicial to good order, if not to military discipline, and Dick had to get out his civvies again. Back in England, he lived like a gentleman, according to his own interpretation. Debts rose, and creditors pressed; Dick had no qualifications for employment other than good horsemanship and ability to shoot straight. Outside the Army there was only one profession for which these would be much recommendation, and Dick did not hesitate very long.

Harrow-on-the-Hill and Hounslow Heath were his favourite operational areas. For robbing the Duke of Monmouth on the latter he was committed to the Poultry Compter, which was described in the chapter on Captain Hind. Deciding that this was no place for an ex-officer and gentleman, Dudley broke out, and was soon back on the road.

This rascal had some redeeming qualities. Like Captain Hind, he had a Robin Hood streak in him, and could not pass a beggar. On one occasion he held up the Earl of Rochester and helped himself to a hundred guineas. The Earl was accompanied by his chaplain at the time, who thought that to keep on the right side of his patron the least he could do was to preach the highwayman a sermon. He began to expatiate on the sinfulness of robbing, and especially of robbing Earls.

Captain Dudley cut him short.

"I don't think I commit any sin robbing a person of quality," he said, "because I keep pretty close to the text, 'Feed the hungry, and send the rich empty away.'"

His biographer backs up this point of view. "This was true in the main," he says, "for whenever he had got any considerable booty from great people, he would very generously extend his charity to such whom he really knew to be poor."

We are told that Captain Dudley knew the inside of Newgate as well as the Poultry Compter, although how he lived to see the outside world again is a mystery, unless he escaped from Newgate too. He knew the Governor, Captain Richardson, as well; and it gave him great pleasure to bid that worthy stand and deliver.

Captain Richardson knew Dudley, and warned him that his

treatment would not be too gentle next time he was in Newgate. Dudley laughed that one off with a pretty long speech: "I expect no favour from the hands of a gaoler, who comes of the race of those angels that fell with Lucifer from Heaven, whither you'll never return again. Of all your bunches of keys, not one hath wards to open that door, for a gaoler's soul stands not upon those two pillars that support Heaven: Justice and Mercy. It rather sits upon those two footstools of Hell: Wrong and Cruelty." Then he came to the point. "Make no more words about your purse, for have it I will—or else your life!"

It is suggested that Dudley sometimes robbed in company with a mysterious person known as Swift Nicks, about whom we shall have a good deal to say shortly. But this is not confirmed, and most of his recorded exploits were single-handed affairs. On one occasion, however, he had more than one associate. This was when he held up a clergyman, and repeated Sir Gosselin Denville's jest of making the parson preach a sermon. It was a good effort, and the priest was allowed to keep his purse, and was rewarded with a collection from among the highwaymen which realized four shillings.

True to his principles, Dick Dudley robbed only the rich, and Dukes and Earls were special favourites of his. The Duke of Albemarle (General Monck) was one of his victims. Among his colleagues he had a reputation for honesty, and he complained bitterly when anyone cheated him. Not all receivers had the same professional integrity as Moll Cutpurse, and Captain Dudley spoke pretty sharply to one of them. "It is a hard thing to find an honest man or a fair dealer," he said. "You cursed rogue, there was, among the plate you bought of me, a cup with a cover. You told me it was only silver-gilt, and bought it at the same price with the rest; but it plainly appears, by the advertisement in the *Gazette*, that it was a gold cup and cover. I see that you are a rogue, and that there is no trusting anybody."

Captain Dudley shared the traditional antipathy of the profession towards the agents of the Law, and some of these suffered from his peculiar sense of humour. One J.P., whom he held up between Midhurst and Horsham, put up a good fight, and actually shot the highwayman's horse before he was wounded in the arm by Dick. Captain Dudley collected his money and valuables, and turned him off his horse. But he had not finished yet.

"Since Your Worship has grievously broken the peace in committing a most horrid and barbarous murder on my prancer, which with my assistance was able to get his living in any ground in England, I must make bold to take your horse by way of reprisal." As he had already done so, the magistrate did not raise objections. "However," went on Dudley, "I'll not be so uncivil as to let a man of your character go home on foot, so, for once, I'll make one Justice of the Peace carry another."

Evidently the Law was an ass even in those days, for the other "J. P." turned out to be a donkey which was grazing in a near-by meadow. Dudley made the magistrate mount the animal, tied his feet together under its belly, and sent him off thus to the next town, to the great amusement of the people and the greater displeasure of the Bench.

Dudley had an unusually long career for a highwayman. He was forty-six when he was caught, after trying to rob the Duke of Lauderdale on Hounslow Heath. The prosecution raked up eighty separate charges against him, and the Governor of Newgate had his revenge when, one cold February morning, Dick Dudley stepped into the cart for the ride to Tyburn.

There were not many "quality highwaymen" like Dudley in this period. Under King Charles II the profession flourished, but recruits came largely from the poorer classes. The allegiance to the Royalist cause of the older highwaymen was quickly justified. Wealth and fashion appeared on the roads again, and fine pickings were to be had. One gang, operating near Newark, collected as much as £1,800 in a single night. During the latter half of the seventeenth century, as Macaulay said, all roads were infested with highwaymen. The Restoration marked the beginning of their Golden Age.

The chronicles of highway activity during this period are embarrassingly comprehensive, and the historian is faced with the difficult task of making an arbitrary selection. Some names—Claude Duval and Will Nevison, for example—stand out from the others, and these will have to be given individual chapters. In addition to these rather exceptional characters space has been allotted for brief sketches of three more typical highwaymen. The rest must be squeezed into what remains of this chapter.

Thomas Wilmot, who was executed in 1670, was not important enough for a complete biography, but in one respect he was representative of a regrettably numerous class of the new highwaymen. He was a brute, a spiritual descendant of Thomas Dun. One incident suffices to show this side of his character. Holding up a lady in her coach, he ordered her to hand over a diamond ring she was wearing. It was difficult for her to get it off, and Wilmot was impatient; so he whipped out a knife and simply cut off her finger.

There are a number of other atrocity stories about the highwaymen of this age, and ladies travelled in danger of losing more than their money and jewellery. Whether or not there was a shortage of doxies, the highwaymen of the time adopted pretty forceful measures to satisfy their passions. Sometimes ladies were given the choice of surrendering their jewels or their honour. (Sometimes they kept their jewels.) But often they had no choice at all, but lost both in a night.

Patrick O'Brien was a ravisher, but he did not try to get above his station. When he held up Nell Gwynne, for example, he asked for her money as a favour, and did not mention her honour. (Admittedly it was scarcely a drawing-room topic.) His language was perhaps a little stronger than the gallant Captain Hind would have used, but no doubt Nell had heard worse when she hawked the oranges round.

"Madam," said Patrick, "I am a gentleman, and, as you see, a very able one. I have done a great many signal services to the fair sex, and have, in return, been all my life maintained by them. Now, as I know you to be a charitable whore, I make bold to ask you for a little money; though I never have had the honour of serving you in particular. However, if any opportunity shall ever fall in my way, you may depend upon it I will exert myself to the uttermost, for I scorn to be ingrateful."

What could Nell say after a pretty little speech like that?

She gave him ten guineas and a smile. Apparently whores didn't mind being called whores in those days.

During the reign of Charles II royal harlots were robbed almost as regularly as regicides had been during the Commonwealth, although the motives were not of the same political nature. After Nell Gwynne came the Duchess of Mazarin, one of the most beautiful of all the Court whores. The highwayman who held her up was James Collet, who seems to have been a bit of a card. Having once robbed a bishop of his robes, he adopted this costume as his working clothes, and employed four or five associates to masquerade as his servants. He was thus attired and equipped when he asked the Duchess for her money.

"I have about a hundred guineas in my pocket," she admitted, "which I am very loath to part with for nothing. But if your lordship—who is the first prelate whom I ever knew to go upon the highway—is pleased to throw a main for it, if it is my ill-luck to lose you are welcome to the gold with all my luck."

"Why, truly, madam, it does not become one in my coat to game," bantered Collet, "but being naturally amorous of your sex, I will oblige you so far as to throw a main with you for a hundred guineas."

Our Right Reverend Highwayman thereupon produced a pair of dice from somewhere in his episcopal robes, and by the side of the road he and the Duchess threw a main. They threw several mains. And not only did the Duchess retain her hundred guineas, but she won all Collet's ready cash into the bargain. Finally he was left with nothing but his horse and the clothes he stood up in. Last things last; he put his shirt on it. The Duchess won again; but, not wanting to deprive him of articles so essential for his livelihood—and perhaps because she was unlikely to find much use for a Bishop's robes—she offered to forego the prize.

But James Collet was a man of honour.

"Since, madam, it is your good fortune to break me," he said, "you are very welcome to keep what you have won. But truly, the next bishop that comes in my way shall pay for all."

Sure enough, three or four days later the Bishop of Winchester came in Collet's way, and got out of it minus fifty guineas and all his clothes. In his new suit Collet continued to exact collections throughout his widespread See for eight years, before he was caught, tried, and hanged.

There is one point about the story that remains obscure: what was Collet wearing when he said good-bye to the Duchess of Mazarin?

Another fellow with a sense of humour was Jack Bird. Though of humble birth and education, he shared Captain Dudley's taste for Dukes and Earls, and he too held up an Earl accompanied by his chaplain. But both the peer and the parson were of sterner stuff than the pair Dudley had had to contend with.

When Bird explained his business the Earl asked him, in language which caused the chaplain to turn his attention to the scenery and shook even Bird a bit, who he was. The highwayman declined to offer his card, but described himself as " an honest collector of taxes."

"So that is the way of it," said the Earl grimly. " I am very little anxious about the small sum I have about me—but intend you shall fight for it."

Bird motioned with his pistols, to show that he had the whip hand if it came to a scrap. But his lordship explained that by fighting he meant fisticuffs, and offered to lay all the money he had with him against nothing.

Bird was nothing if not a sportsman.

" That is an honourable challenge, my lord, provided none of your servants be near us," he said.

The Earl was a sportsman, too. He waved his servants away, and began to take off his coat. But here the chaplain intervened. It was not the thing for a belted Earl to fight with a highwayman, he pointed out; besides, if there was to be any boxing he would like a bout himself. The Earl was not easily convinced, and Jack had to wait patiently while the pair settled the matter. In the end the chaplain prevailed, and he removed his cloak and faced the highwayman.

By all accounts it was a first-rate fight. No ring, no gloves, no rounds, no seconds. The Earl was referee, but both contestants played fair. Jack was physically the stronger, but the chaplain was no novice at the game. They hammered away at each other for a full fifteen minutes before the parson finally confessed himself exhausted.

Jack was more than a sportsman.

"Now, my lord," he panted, "if it please your lordship, I will take a turn with you."

But his lordship would not take advantage of Jack's weakened condition. At the same time he did not want to hurt his feelings.

"If you beat my chaplain you will beat me," he explained, "for he and I have tried our manhood before."

And, handing the highwayman the twenty guineas he had in his purse, he and the chaplain bade Jack a good day and drove on.

Happily there were more Jack Birds than Thomas Wilmots in the reign of Charles II. But they represented the two extremes of the scale, and most of the highwaymen lay somewhere between them. Captain Dudley, as was said, was typical of a small minority. The majority were of poor families, with little education, and no pretensions to being gentlemen. They were just trying to earn a dishonest living, and were characterized by neither excessive courtesy nor unnecessary brutality. Their greatest redeeming feature was a sense of humour, and in private life they were usually both generous and extravagant. Beyond that it is impossible to generalize.

CHAPTER TEN

Confessions of a Highwayman

BEFORE we go on to the life-stories of the four leading highwaymen of the post-Restoration period a chapter must be devoted to an examination of one of the most valuable documents in highway history. To give it its full title, it is called *Jackson's Recantation; or, the Life & Death of the Notorious High-way-man now Hanging in Chains at Hampstead, delivered to a Friend, a little before the Execution.* The sub-title, or rather blurb, goes on: " wherein is truly discovered the whole Mystery of that Wicked and Fatal Profession of Padding on the Road." This document was published in 1674, the year of Jackson's execution.

The author's Christian name is not given, but the well-informed British Museum catalogue puts the work down to " Francis Jackson, alias Dixie "; which leads us straight away to another curious publication entitled *The Confession of the Four High-way-men, as it was Written by One of them, and Allowed by the Rest the 14th of this Instant April (being the Day before their Appointed Execution).* The names of the " high-way-men " are given as John Williams, alias " The Matchet," Francis Jackson, alias " Dixie," John White, alias " Fowler," and Walter Parkhurst, who seems to have practised under his own name. The sub-title of this document is also worth repeating— " This being desired to be made Publick by the Persons themselves, to prevent false reports of them when they are Dead."

Such, then, is the bibliography of this chapter.

From the title alone, *Jackson's Recantation* invites comparison with the work of John Clavel, published nearly fifty years earlier, which was described in an earlier chapter. The two have some common features, notably in their professed aims. Like the *Recantations of an Ill-led Life,* Jackson's work also purported to be a " Discovery of the Highway Law," and contained both " vehement dissuasions to all offenders " and "cautious admonitions and full instructions" to honest travellers in case the dissuasions were unheeded. There was also a special section for the guidance of innkeepers.

There were, however, a number of important differences between the two books, the least of which is that Clavel wrote in verse and Jackson in prose. Jackson prefaces his dissuasions and admonitions with a very interesting autobiography; and his information about the *modi operandi* of highwaymen is much more detailed than Clavel's. But the main reason that Jackson's is the more valuable of the two is because he could afford to write more objectively. Clavel dedicated his book to the King and all sorts of other people, and wrote for the express purpose of getting a Royal Pardon. Jackson, on the other hand, had no such hopes.

We must set against this the fact that the poem of John Clavel, Esquire, was doubtless entirely his own work, whereas Jackson's book was almost certainly drastically edited, if not actually ghosted. According to his own story he was the son of wealthy parents, but he says nothing about his education. Apart from a few stray vulgarities, which look as though they were left in on purpose, the style of the book is scarcely what one would expect from a highwayman. For example, the opening sentence:

"How vain are the thoughts of such who, whilst youth and strength accompany them, never consider they are a mere statue of dust, kneaded with tears and moved by the hid engines of restless passions; a clod of earth, which the shortest fever can burn to ashes, and the least shower of rheums wash away to nothing; instead thereof they bounce so high, and make so great a noise in the world, as if both the globes (those glorious twins) had been unwomb'd from the formless clouds by the midwifery of their brain."

The second sentence is better:

"Such was my disordered fancy."

Scarcely the language of the road, is it? All those mixed metaphors sound more like that of the pulpit—indeed, more like the publications of the seventeenth-century Newgate Ordinaries, or chaplains, who specialized in turning out moralizing biographies of condemned highwaymen. . . .

But we are assured that it is Jackson's own work, every word of it. At the end of the little book we find the following "Postscript":

"Reader, let me assure thee this is no fiction, but a true relation of Mr Jackson's life and conversation, penned by his own hand, and delivered unto mine to be made public for his countrymen's good, in compensation of the many injuries he hath done them. The introduction he writ whilst in Newgate, after sentence of condemnation, and desired me to apologize for it, fearing he had neither writ large enough of his true penitence nor had laid down sufficient dehortations from the commission of the like offences; the disorder he was in, lying under the horror of a speedy and more than common execution, may plead his excuse: the plainness of his style may admit of this plea, that he aimed at (as he confessed to me) nothing but the good of his countrymen, and that as he had picked their pockets, he thought it needless to tickle their ears with the gilded straws of rhetorical expressions. God, I hope, hath forgiven him his sins, and may we all amend by his errors, for which he now hangs in chains at Hamstead, a sad and dreadful spectacle to all beholders, and hoping you will pass by the faults of his writing and the press, I subscribe myself a well-willer to all."

(If the first sentence of the *Recantation* is a fair sample of the plainness of Jackson's style, perhaps it is as well that we were spared from having our ears tickled "with the gilded straws of rhetorical expressions.")

But obviously that first sentence, and much else besides, was written by the same hand as the "Postscript." The latter is signed "Samuel Swiftnicks," or in some editions simply "S. S." The name Swiftnicks crops up several times in highway history, usually in obscure contexts; but here, clearly, it was just a pseudonym. So for the moment we are no nearer to discovering Jackson's collaborator.

Let us read on. After this grandiloquent peroration we get a discourse in the same lofty style on the horrors of Newgate; not the physical inconveniences, however, but the spiritual sufferings of a man tormented by his own conscience. It is a gloomy picture. But just as we are beginning to despair, a great change comes over Jackson. Into his cell walks a minister—" or rather a charitable physician for my sin-sick soul." Immediately the whole picture is transformed—not from misery to joy, but rather to a calm, sober peace of mind that follows free confession and genuine repentance. Jackson tells us that for this metamorphosis he owed everything to the minister. He does not name him, but every reference is couched in glowing terms. And, as we have seen, Jackson certainly knew how to make his terms glow.

But we can guess who it was who wrought this magical conversion. What minister would visit a condemned highwayman in Newgate but the prison chaplain? Who, then, was the Ordinary in 1676? A gentleman named Samuel Smith.

Samuel Smith—" S. S."—Samuel Swiftnicks—more like the language of the pulpit. . . . At last we have the truth about the authorship of *Jackson's Recantation*.

But the Ordinary did not write the whole thing. The really important parts of the book were unmistakably the work of the highwayman himself. The contrast between these and the parson's interpolations is striking. Here is another bit of Smith:

" I say little of my parents more than that they were too indulgent to me, supplying my youthful extravagancies with money continually, in such superfluities, that my invention was frequently puzzled to find out ways for quick dispatch."

Now for Jackson, toned down by a bit of Smith in parenthesis:

" My breeches were so jag'd and tatter'd (that I may say without offence to the reader, though jocosely) they looked somewhat like those that are now call'd *à la mode*, and seem'd as if my arse, according to the proverb, was hung with points."

The above is Jackson's description of his plight after his invention had finally succeeded in finding ways of quick dispatch of the whole of his parents' fortune. Now the Devil tempted him, taking the shape of " a long purse " and lying in wait on the pavement in a deserted street. Jackson picked up the purse, and found it contained £60. At once he bought himself a decent suit of clothes and took rooms as the son of a country gentleman who had come to town about a lawsuit.

Then he bought such appurtenances as befitted a young man-about-town, including a silver-hilted sword, and, thus " gallantly equipt," set out to live by his wits. He soon got in with a crowd of card-sharpers and confidence tricksters, and with one of these he took to frequenting playhouses, cockpits, bowling-greens, skittle-alleys, and other places where good pickings were to be had. From these pursuits it was an easy graduation to the road.

Once, after robbing a coach near Barnet, Jackson was caught and put in gaol. But his companion got away with the loot, and before his trial Jackson managed to get in touch with the man he had robbed, and offered to restore to him the value of his property on condition that he would not give evidence against him. The man agreed, and Jackson was acquitted. Jackson's own comment on this is interesting, especially as it is the only case we have on record of an acquittal being bought in this manner. " There grew a kind of proverbial saying among the scout-masters of the road," he tells us, " that he can't be hanged without treason or murder who hath five hundred pounds at his command."

Soon after this his companion died, leaving nothing but his doxy, whom he bequeathed to Jackson. " I accepted of his legacy," Jackson tells us, and the Reverend Samuel Smith allows him to add, " and took possession immediately, without a forcible entry; for she made presently a willing surrender."

That girl was the ruin of Jackson. Her beauty, he said, was " scarc'ly paralleled "—but nor was her extravagance either. He did his best to pay her bills, but it was an uphill task; and when finally he had to tell her he was without means, she rewarded his kindness by walking out on him.

Meanwhile, notwithstanding his remarks about the ease with which one could purchase acquittals, Jackson had temporarily forsaken the road, and was back at his old card-sharping and confidence tricks. Shortly after his doxy had left him, however, he met some old acquaintances of his highwayman days. They had a drink and a chat about old times, and over a glass of ale Jackson told them his story. They rated him soundly for making such a fool of himself—not for keeping a mistress, of course, but for not keeping her in her place. " The thing is laudable to have a miss, though he have a handsome wife of his own," philosophized one of the crew, " and is agreeable to the custom and honour of the times; and," he added, doubtless with good reason, " should we throw any opprobrium on it, it would reflect upon ourselves."

At this point another of the company interrupted.

" Come, we trifle away time," he said. " Let us fall to business. It is a good while since we shared a booty; let us lie no longer idle, and if our brother will accompany us, instead of picking up here and there crowns and angels (which is a thing beneath us) let us resolve to ' Have at all.' A five hours' adventure may make us possessors of five hundred pounds."

Their brother protested that he hadn't a horse, but they said they would soon fix that. They did, too. Before very long Jackson and three others were on the road to Maidenhead. They stopped for lunch there, made a brief reconnaissance of the Thicket, and then went on to Reading. Here they split up into two pairs. Two went to one inn and two to another, with the intention of picking up information about travellers for the morrow.

The first two had business connexions with the landlord of their inn, and he tipped them off that he had a gentleman staying there who was going to Marlborough the next day, and whom he believed to be carrying a fair amount of ready cash. This intelligence was communicated to Jackson and his companion, who had so far not had any luck. After supper, however, they got into conversation with an attorney bound for London. Their talk naturally drifted from the weather to the other topical subject of the day, highwaymen. Jackson and his companion affected to be very worried about the prospects of being robbed, but the lawyer—a blustering type of fellow—laughed scornfully at their fears. There was no need to be robbed if you used your wits, he told them. After another drink he produced a bag containing a hundred and fifty guineas.

" These I will so conceal in the saddle I ride upon," he boasted, " that I will defy all the damned highwaymen in England to find them out. I have passed them several times in this manner, with good sums about me, and, for your further belief, I will show you in what manner."

Then he led them to where his horse was stabled, and revealed a cunningly contrived hiding-place in his saddle. Jackson and his companion thanked him for the tip, and the three went back to the inn.

Shortly afterwards they got a note from their colleagues at the other inn, naming a rendezvous, and, excusing themselves, the pair went out. A conference was held, and it was decided that the best strategy would be for Jackson and his companion to go after the traveller to Marlborough, while the other pair tackled the lawyer.

The results of the two engagements were a fine tribute to this staff-work. The attorney was actually speechless when the highwaymen went straight to his hiding-place; and the gentleman bound for Marlborough was found to be carrying no less than a hundred and twenty guineas—although he did not deliver them before wounding Jackson with a shot in the arm.

But after that Jackson stuck to the road. He tells us one or two more of his adventures, and then breaks off suddenly. The Reverend Samuel Smith continues his story for him, starting off with one of his usual lengthy sentences:

"Should I enumerate all the rogueries and robberies I committed, either singly or with others, relating in what manner they were done, I should waste too much time, and miss of that design which I purposed to myself, which is the general good of my countrymen; whereof I shall pass them all by, not so much as mentioning the last robbery I was guilty of, near Colebrook, when pursued by the country, opposed and apprehended by them, to the loss of our own, and the blood of some of them, the manner whereof is too generally known to be again repeated."

Fortunately for us, a full account of Jackson's last robbery is contained in the afore-mentioned *Confession of the Four Highway-men*. Substitute " Colnbrook " for Jackson's " Colebrook," and the story fits perfectly.

The actual robbery took place on the road between Staines and Hounslow, and it was a commonplace affair. But the sequel was amazing. It seems that Jackson and his companions—there were four of them, Williams, White, Parkhurst, and Slader, the last-named being unable to subscribe to the *Confession* for reasons that will become apparent—Jackson and his companions, then, had for some time been active in the Hounslow region, and the people of the county were up in arms against them. Literally in arms, too, equipped with a variety of weapons ranging from muskets to pitchforks. After the robbery in question the highwaymen received intelligence that a fair-sized force of volunteers were after them, and they retreated to Acton, and then to Harrow-on-the-Hill. Here they found a party of forty or fifty armed men waiting for them. To avoid a pitched battle they changed their course, and rode off via Paddington and Kilburn to Hampstead Heath. They were closely pursued all the way, and were engaged at several points along the road.

It was evening when the highwaymen reached the Heath, and they were in a bad way. Their ammunition had nearly run out, some of their swords were broken, and all were suffering from wounds or injuries and fatigue. Their horses were almost exhausted. Their only chance was to escape in the darkness of the Heath.

Had they known it, it was never a chance at all. News of them had gone in advance, and a body of two hundred irregulars was waiting for them.

Yet they fought to the end. Slader used his last shot to kill one of the attackers, and then was wounded himself. Jackson, too, committed his first murder, with a sword-thrust—hence, perhaps, his reluctance to go into details about the affair in his *Recantation*. Finally the five were taken prisoner and brought to Newgate Gaol. Slader died of wounds; but Jackson and the other three stood their trial, and were executed within four weeks of the battle on the Heath. For his murder Jackson was given the additional punishment of the gibbet.

The veracity of the account given by the four highwaymen—who wrote their confession " to prevent false reports of them when they are Dead "—cannot be rightly assessed, as there is a dearth of contemporary literature on the affair, however " generally known " it might have been. The main facts seem to be correct, but it is probable that many of the details were exaggerated. The highwaymen claimed that they held two hundred at bay on the Heath for an hour, which is scarcely credible; and besides, one just did not get two hundred ordinary citizens to band together and fight a gang of desperate highwaymen.

The autobiographical part of his book completed, Jackson goes on to that section designed "for the general good of my countrymen." This is of extraordinary interest to the student of the highway, and we make no apology for quoting from it at length. There is nothing like it in the history of the road.

Jackson begins by outlining his plan.

"I shall discover, first, what a highwayman is; how bound by oath; what order is prescribed; in what manner they assault; and how they behave themselves, in and after the action. In the next place my best endeavour shall be to dissuade these desperadoes to desist [sic] robbing on the highway, by showing them the certainty of their apprehension one time or other; and though they may a long time prosper in that vile course of life, spending high and faring deliciously "— but this is the Reverend Samuel Smith chipping in again, so we shall skip the next few lines; —". . . Lastly, instructions, not only for the honest traveller that he may pass in safety, but for the innkeeper to distinguish highwaymen from guests that are honest; all these I shall with sincerity run over particularly."

Highwaymen, says Jackson (more probably it is Smith again), are "devouring caterpillars of a corrupt and polluted nation." They are recruited mainly from "such that were never acquainted with an honest trade, whom either want of money or employment prompts them to undertake these dangerous designs; and to gain respect, they dub one another 'Colonel,' 'Major,' or at least a 'Captain,' who never arrived to a greater height than a trooper disbanded, or at the utmost a life-guardman cashiered for misdemeanour."

Here it must be remembered that Jackson was writing sixteen years after the Restoration, by which time the Cavalier officer highwayman like Captain Hind had disappeared.

The next part is more like how-to-do-it than why-you-shouldn't-do-it.

"Having made up a party, ere they proceed to act their villainies, they make a solemn vow to each other that, if by misfortune anyone should be apprehended, he shall not discover his complices; and that if he be prest hard to particularize his companions, he must then devise names for men that never were, describing their persons, features, and discovering their habitations, but so remote one from another, that the danger of the trial may be over ere sufficient inquiry can be made.

"And, further, to procure mercy from the bench, there must be a plausible account given, how you fell into this course of life: fetching a deep sigh, saying that you were well born, but by reason of your family falling to decay you were exposed to great want, and rather than shamefully beg (for you knew not how to labour), you were constrained to take this course as a subsistence; that it is your first fault, which you are heartily sorry for, and will never attempt the like again.

"Having taken a solemn oath to be true one to another, their next business is to acquaint themselves, by tapsters, hostlers, chamberlains, or others, what booties are stirring, how contained, and whither bound. But before they attempt the seizure, if there be any novices in the company, then they are instructed by the more experienced, as I was at first, after this manner.

"In the first place, you must have a variety of periwigs in your lodgings, and the like you must carry about, if occasion require the necessity of changing the colour of the hair; neither must you be without your false beards of several colours. For want of them, you may only cross your locks athwart your mouth, which is a good disguise; patches contribute much thereto. And lest your voice should be known another time by him that is robbed, put into your mouth a pebble, or any suchlike thing, which will alter your tone advantageously to your purpose.

"Being thus provided, a watchword must be framed, wrapped up in some question, as 'What's the clock?' or 'Jack, what shall we have for supper?' to avoid putting the traveller into suspicion; which, as soon named, you must instantly fall to work, seizing with your left hand the bridle, and with your right presenting a pistol. This so terrifies that he delivers instantly, for who will trust a pistol at his breast loaded with a brace of bullets, and a mouth discharging at the same time volleys of oaths, that if he deliver not instantly he is a dead man? But herein you may choose to believe him, for he [the highwayman] will be very cautious of murder, for fear of provoking the law to an implacability, unless it be when he is beset, that rather than run the risk of being seized, he must endeavour his escape by the death of one or more of his assailants."

In his diagnosis of the highwayman's reluctance to kill Jackson seems to do his profession an injustice. Highway robbery was enough to hang him. The only further "implacability" to which the Law could be provoked was what Jackson himself got—hanging in chains, or the gibbet. Admittedly this was a dreaded punishment; but it was no more effective as an example than any other punitive deterrent. Certainly we cannot believe that fear of the gibbet accounted for the amazing restraint in the use of firearms shown by the vast majority of highwaymen.

To return to Jackson's recipe for a highway robbery:

"Having o'ermastered them you set upon, then do you carry them into some covert, where you search so severely that nothing can be hidden from you. If in the strict inquiry gold be found privately, quilted in a doublet, or waistband of his breeches, I can hardly forbear smiling when I think in what manner these rogues will slave the poor man with 'villain,' 'cheating rascal,' for endeavouring to preserve his own, whilst he hath nothing else to say but that he is 'undone,' which they regard with as little as the hangman will do them at the place of execution. Having changed your horses for theirs, if better than your own, the next thing you do is to make them swear neither to follow you, nor to raise the country with a hue-and-cry upon you. Thus, leaving the poor traveller forlorn, away you ride to some strange place, or else where you are known and winked at, and there you share what unlawfully you got, not without the cheating one another.

"Now here, by the way, give me leave to descant on their prodigality, after an attempt that proves successful. London, the more is the pity, is their best sanctuary, and therefore after any robbery, they commonly repair thither; having as many names as lodgings, and both as changeable as a whore's dalliance with variety of persons. Their next care is to buy variety of splendid apparel, and, having bought his wench a new gown, and furnished her pockets with guineas, they then prosecute to the height all manner of debaucheries which by a mistake they name the Chief of Pleasures. And as their whore, so must their host participate with them in their gain, else all the fat is in the fire; for the vintner, innkeeper, etc., knowing very well what they are, and how easily they get their money, will be sure to enlarge their reckoning and make it swell prodigiously; neither must this be complained of, lest they refuse to keep their own counsel any longer.

"All the time they can spare from robbing and undoing poor harmless men is spent in wine and women; so that the sunshine of their prosperity "—confound it, that man Smith has got in again. But this is the end of Jackson's so-you're-going-to-be-a-highwayman section. Suddenly recollecting that his object was to keep people off the road rather than show them the way on to it, he continues rather unconvincingly, "Having thus endeavoured to fright highwaymen, I shall here take another course to scare them, if possible, and therefore in the first place I shall lay down directions how to know them as they ride on the road, with rules how to shun them, or, if robbed, how to pursue and apprehend them when they think themselves most secure."

Jackson does not carry out these ambitious aims fully, but his advice to travellers is a good deal more practical than was John Clavel's, and part at least deserves to be quoted:

"In the first place, when at any time you intend to travel, and cannot avoid carrying a sum of money with you, let no person know what charge you have, or when you will set forward. It is a custom, I confess (but I can assure you it is dangerous), for men the day before they begin their journey to take leave of their relations and friends, drinking healths round to the happy return of the traveller, who suspects not the least harm in all this; whereas, it hath been known that a father this way hath been betrayed by his own son; a brother by a brother; nay, one pretendedly dear friend betray another, by discovering to highwaymen when and which way he rides, bidding them to prepare accordingly, either to meet or overtake, and for the plot so laid he goes his share.

"Another way of setting they have. The gang shall ride before, out of sight, leaving one lusty fellow of their company behind, who shall ride very softly, expecting some person or other who shall overtake him. If three or four, he will single out one he thinks hath the most money; and, pretending much kindness, whispers him in the ear, saying he likes not those other men, and ask if he knows them. If not, he adviseth him by all means to slacken his pace, for certainly they are dangerous fellows. This timorous piece of credulity thanks him for his present care, and takes his advice; and not long after, brings him to the place where the confederates lie in ambuscado, who upon sight of them draws, bidding the other to do the like, and now begins a dangerous fight, as the traveller imagines, who through fear of bloodshed delivers his money, and persuades his champion to do the like, who, with much ado, at length condescends thereto. Having given him a private item which way they intend to ride, they set spurs to their horses, and are out of sight in an instant.

"Hereupon, this pretender to honesty will straight persuade you to assist him in making a hue-and-cry, in the carrying on of which to the same he will be the foremost, as seemingly most zealous in the apprehension of these robbers, to no other end than to lead you quite another way, till his brethren be out of all danger. I knew one notorious rogue (but by his sly and crafty deportment was looked upon to be a very honest gentleman) suffered himself to be robbed with three more, by four of his own confederates. The robbery being committed between sun and sun, he, with those three honest men, sued the county, and recovered the money they had lost."

The special dangers of Sunday travelling—which were referred to in our chapter on the highways—are dealt with in a passage that looks like the joint work of Jackson and Smith.

"Whensoever the traveller designs his journey, let him

consider the Sabbath day is a time not only unlawful, but more dangerous for robbing than any other. I need not expatiate myself on the illegality of the act, since there is a special command forbidding the breach of that holy day of rest, the violation whereof hath been frequently punished by being robbed; for, to speak the truth, that day hath been, and is still, chosen by highwaymen for the best and fittest time to commit their robberies; first because they are sensible that few travel then, but such who ride about some eminent concern, and they suppose to that end carry a considerable sum about them. In the next place, on that day the roads are most quiet, being undisturbed with great quantities of people, and therefore rob with more ease and greater security. Lastly, they know the county will not be so forward to pursue them with a hue-and-cry, whereas they cannot but be sensible that a judge will hardly be induced to make the county pay the reparation of a loss sustained by him who ought to have stayed at home and perform those duties required from him, proper to the day; and not wander abroad and leave his Creator's business undone, that he may do his own. If you needs must travel, you have days enough in the week to follow your urgent and importance affairs, with more security, the roads being then full of good company, if you will make choice of a convenient time, and be cautious whom you entertain into your society."

After this homily Smith leaves Jackson's elbow, and we get some more general hints for travellers.

"Be shy of those who are over prone in pressing into your company. It is more safe to entertain such who are unwilling to associate themselves with you, or if they do it is with such indifference that there need be urgency of persuasion to effect it. Now to the intent that you may distinguish an honest man from a thief or robber, take these informations and directions: first, if you suspect your company, halt a little, and in your stay observe whether they still hold on their course, or slack their pace, or, it may be, alight and walk with their horses in their hands. If you observe any of these, you may conclude them the justly suspected marks of a highwayman."

The rest of this section is too long to be quoted in full, for by the time Jackson reaches the end he has warned the traveller to suspect almost everyone on the road except himself—from those who put on a " Cypress hood or a vizard mask on your approach " to those who simply don't look you straight in the face when you talk to them. He gives a special warning against men disguised as rustics, with straw in their ears and a bucolic song on their lips. He advises travellers to avoid going alone wherever possible, but if they travel in a group not to huddle together. The safest method, he says, is strung out in pairs some distance apart. Finally, he tells the travellers that they can expect no help from the authorities:

" And now, ere I proceed, let me take notice of a great folly and abuse of the countrymen. When report is brought to a Justice of a robbery done in such a place, presently a watch is ordered to stand at that place, at the charge of the county. Is anyone so senseless, to think the highwaymen will voluntarily ride into the mouths of those who are appointed to apprehend them?"

Without waiting for an answer, Jackson goes on to warn travellers against looking on the watch as a security. Knowing that the latter will be a magnet to timid travellers, the highwaymen lurk in bushes near by, in fact using him as an unconscious decoy. And when it comes to action the watch is useless:

" Those watch-men are silly old decreeped men, and though a dozen of them, I have seen stand with halberts in their hands, yet have we robbed before their very faces, and they stand still the while, not daring to oppose us in the least." Once, he says, he and his companions set upon the watch, disarmed and bound them, took their places, " and standing with our Brown bills, as with authority, we stopped whom we pleased."

Finally, Jackson says, " It is now high time to inform the innkeeper how he shall distinguish highwaymen from honest travellers. In the first place, observe their curiosity about their horses, in dressing and feeding them: next you will find them asking of questions as who owns that horse, and who the other; what their masters are; whither travelling; and when will they set out. These are infallible signs of a highwayman. Nor must I omit this remark: let the ostler poise their cloak-bags, and he shall find them empty; for they carry only for show, and not to burden their horses.

"Next, let the chamberlain take notice when he shows them to a room, that they will soon dismiss him, and after that, let him listen awhile and he shall hear the gingling of money; and if he can but get a peep-hole for his eyes, he shall see them sharing their booty.

"It will be very requisite to enquire severally each one's particular name, and let your servants do the like. By this means you find them tripping, for they may easily forget a name they borrowed that very day.

"At supper-time let some one knock furiously and hastily at the gate; then mark them well, and you shall see them start, their countenances change, and nothing but fear and amazement appearing in each face; by which you may positively conclude them what you before did but imagine and suspect.

"If in the day-time they come into your inn, you may guess what they are by their trifling away their time, and staying somewhat longer than is requisite for baiting. You shall observe them sometimes looking out of the window, sometimes standing at the gate, for no other end but to mark what passengers ride by. If they see any person of quality to ride that way, or the garb discovers anything of a booty, you shall have them presently in all haste, as alarmed to horse, mount presently, as if some dear friend or near relation was just rid by, whom they must endeavour to overtake.

"At night they will come dropping into an inn severally, in divided companies, thereby to cross the number in the hue-and-cry; and will, when met, subtilly take no notice of one another; nay, to blind the eyes of suspicion they will inquire of the host what 'country gentleman' their own companions are; whether he knows them or not, and if it be convenient to join in company with them. If you find they have no jealousy of them, they will, as strangers, compliment one another whilst any eyes are on them; but withdraw, and watch them well, and you shall find them fall into their usual familiarity, and will not only rejoice at the success of their designs, but laugh at the credulity of the landlord."

Good, sound, and often subtle advice, it must be admitted; but not to be taken too seriously. It is based on the assumption that innkeepers were on the look-out for highwaymen, which, as Jackson knew as well as anyone—he as good as admitted it earlier in his book—was the very reverse of the truth. The wise innkeeper served the drinks and asked no questions. Highwaymen were good customers and bad enemies.

There is an air of haste about the concluding paragraph to the book, as if the author found himself pressed for time:

"Much more might be written on this subject, but since it is impossible to discover the whole art and mystery of the highway trade, let this suffice; for according to the proverb, new lords, new laws; so all new gangs have new orders, plots, and designs, to rob and purloin from the honest traveller."

Jackson's Recantation has been dealt with at length because it is unique in highway literature. Shorn of the tedious interpolations of the Reverend Samuel Smith, it gives a picture of the seventeenth-century highwayman which is worth all the later histories put together. There is, therefore, no need for further generalizing on this period; and the remaining four chapters allotted to the reign of Charles II will take the form of simple biographies.

CHAPTER ELEVEN

A Very Gallant Gentleman

"CLAUDE DU VALL ranks among his brother highwaymen as high as Rembrandt or Raphael among artists. He was, indeed, no less an artist in his own profession than they," says Charles G. Harper in all seriousness. And that, coming from a critical historian like Harper, is very high praise. Nor is he alone in his estimate of Du Vall, or Duval. Leigh Hunt, in a eulogistic essay in *The Indicator*, describes him as " an eternal feather in the cap of highway gentility." Duval also has the distinction of being one of the two highwaymen selected for mention above the footnotes in Macaulay's *History of England*; and our own *Dictionary of National Biography* has issued the Frenchman with a blue passport and endorsed it with the words " his fame resting hardly less on his gallantry to ladies than on his daring robberies."

Dare we, then, question the unanimous opinion of this impressive array of authorities? Yes, we dare. For we have examined the total evidence on which they based these glowing tributes. Most of the writers quoted above were decent enough to give a bibliography. It didn't take up much space. Almost the only authentic account of this highwayman is one slim volume entitled *Memoirs of Du Vall : containing the History of his Life and Death*, which was published " immediately after his execution "(1670).

Do we doubt the veracity of this little book, then? On the contrary. For once we have a contemporary biography of a highwayman in which we can place some trust. This is not one of your broadsheets or chapbooks rushed out for the sensation-hungry Tyburn mob. It is a serious essay, and its style at once proclaims it to be the work of a man of letters.

The *Memoirs* were published anonymously, but it has since been established that they came from the pen of one William Pope, M.D. Now, Dr Pope was a scientist of some repute.

In addition to his medical degree he held a professorship in astronomy at Oxford (as successor to Sir Christopher Wren), and was one of the original members of the Royal Society. For his biography of Duval to be properly understood it must be added that he was also a violent francophobe and a complete snob.

The *Memoirs of Du Vall* has a sub-title, which states that the book is " intended as a severe reflexion on the too great fondness of English ladies towards French footmen; which at that time of day was a too common complaint." There was nothing unusual about this sort of thing on the title-page of a book of memoirs of a highwayman, and it has been passed over as just another example of the conventional hypocrisy of writers of that time. It was nothing of the kind. Dr Pope was in deadly earnest.

The book is a brilliant satire—too brilliant, and far and away too subtle, as it turned out. Dr Pope holds Duval up to ridicule in so gentle a way that the unwary can easily take it all literally and miss the point. They have done, with astonishing naïveté. They have mistaken this biting skit for a pæan of praise. They have even solemnly quoted great chunks of Pope to show what a fine fellow Duval was—and it must be admitted that many of these passages out of context look innocent enough. But there is nothing ambiguous about the essay when read as a whole.

Alexander Pope was so resolved to consign worthless poets to oblivion that he wrote the *Dunciad*—and thus made sure their names would live as long as his. Fifty years earlier this other Pope did an even greater service for Claude Duval. Thanks to him the Frenchman has gained a place in the very front rank of English highwaymen, for the very qualities that were the object of Pope's keen but delicate wit.

It is far too late to try to cast Duval back into oblivion, nor have we the slightest desire to do so. We are not iconoclasts. Besides, even a correct interpretation of this hostile biography entitles him to a chapter in this book. But we feel that some attempt should be made to right the wrong done to Dr Pope. The surest way would be to reprint his essay in its entirety, but it is a bit too long for that. Instead, therefore, we shall give a brief summary, with as many quotations from the original as possible.

"Claude Du Vall," the essay begins, "was born in Anno 1643 at Domfront, in Normandy, a place very famous for the excellency and healthfulness of the air, and for the production of mercurial wits. At the time of his birth there was a conjunction of Venus and Mercury, certain presages of very good fortune, but of short continuance."

Here it must be explained that Pope, like most astronomers, had very little opinion of the pseudo-science of astrology. The object of this introductory paragraph was simply to prepare his readers for a satire. He continues in a similar vein:

"His father was Pierre Du Vall, a miller, his mother Marguerite de la Roche, a tailor's daughter. They lived in as much reputation and honesty as their conditions and occupations would permit."

Their occupations, of course, were scarcely conducive to reputation and honesty, as any seventeenth-century reader would understand. Millers had not changed since Chaucer's time, while tailors—we-ell. . . .

Having got his readers in the right frame of mind, Pope now proceeds with the satire proper.

"There are some," he says, "that confidently aver he was born in Smock Alley, without Bishopsgate, that his father was a cook, and sold boiled beef and porridge; but their report is as false as it is defamatory and malicious"—and, no doubt, a pure invention on Pope's part, as an excuse for working in the next sentence: "And it is easy to disprove it several ways, but I will urge only one demonstrative argument against it: If he had been born there, he had been no Frenchman; but, if he had not been a Frenchman, it is absolutely impossible he should have been so much beloved in his life and lamented at his death by the English ladies."

Having had his first tilt at the ladies, Pope's satire becomes more general again.

"It will not, I hope, be expected that I shall, in a true history, play the romancer and describe his actions from his cradle to his saddle, telling what childish sports he was best at, and who were his play-fellows; that were enough to make the truth of the whole narration suspected." Very disarming, Doctor; now we are waiting for a whopper. We are not disappointed. An old friar, Pope tells us, " accounted very expert in Physiognomy and Judicial Astrology," calls at the Duval ménage and—his hand having been crossed with silver—says young Claude " will be in extraordinary favour with women of the highest condition. . . . Now, from this story, the certainty of Physiognomy and Judicial Astrology is entirely proved," ends up Pope with a grin.

Coming back to Claude, the biographer goes on to tell us that the lad grows up and learns to speak French fluently. It was not particularly good French, as he lived in the country, but—adds Pope quickly—" I speak not this to disgrace him, for, could he have spoken never so good French, it is not in such high esteem there as it is here; and it very rarely happens that, upon that account alone, any great man's daughter runs away with a lacquey."

No mistaking the meaning of that, is there?

At the age of thirteen or fourteen our hero sets out into the wide world, equipped with his first pair of shoes and stockings, a suit, twenty sous, and a paternal blessing. His parents throw a third shoe after him for luck. Claude makes for Paris, and at Rouen he has the good fortune to fall in with several young Englishmen with their tutors going in the same direction, " to learn the exercises, to fit them to go a-wooing at their return home." They are only too delighted to find someone who speaks French in Rouen, Pope tells us, and they engage the boy as a servant. He journeys with them to Paris, and " in this condition he lives unblameably, unless you esteem it a fault to be scabby, and a little given to filching, qualities very frequent in persons of his nation and condition."

In Paris Claude managed to ingratiate himself with the colony of English exiles, who were waiting for the Restoration. So was Duval. When Charles II landed at Dover, the English colony packed their bags. So did Duval. He landed in England as page to a " person of quality "—believed to have been the Duke of Richmond.

He soon found reason to change his employment.

Highwaymen, as we have seen, were reaping the reward for

their loyalty to the monarchy. The old Puritan spirit of repression vanished, and life was gay again—for those who could afford to be gay. Smart coaches were back on the roads, and jewels flashed in the moonlight. It was the highwayman's dream come true.

Duval was among them, and he speedily made a name for himself. Not only did he earn the distinction of heading a long list of highwaymen for whose apprehension rewards were offered in the *London Gazette*, but he was beginning to be spoken of very tenderly over afternoon cups of tea. Duval had a way with him, the ladies said wistfully. It was almost a pleasure to be robbed by him. So different from the English boors, my dear. . . .

All this is certainly true. Although Pope's *Memoirs* are the only authority for the facts of Duval's life, other contemporary publications had several allusions to what they euphemistically called the "gallantry" of this highwayman. And he was talked about a good deal more than written about. Some pretty spicy stories went round concerning his success with the ladies. But the ladies themselves said he was just chivalrous and not like that at all—and disarmed their husbands with the tale of how he danced the coranto on Hounslow Heath.

This was the most famous of all Duval's exploits, and Pope describes it in detail. His is the only account extant, and it is usually quoted verbatim—in all seriousness, of course. It runs as follows:

"He with his squadron overtakes a coach, which they had set over night, having intelligence of a booty of four hundred pounds in it. In the coach was a knight, his lady, and only one serving-maid, who, perceiving five horsemen making up to them, presently imagined that they were beset; and they were confirmed in this apprehension by seeing them whisper to one another, and ride backwards and forwards.

"The lady, to show that she was not afraid, takes a flageolet out of her pocket and plays. Du Vall takes the hint, plays also, and excellently well, upon a flageolet of his own, and in this posture he rides up to the coach-side.

"' Sir,' says he to the person in the coach, ' your lady plays excellently, and I doubt not but that she dances as well. Will you please to walk out of the coach and let me have the honour to dance one currant [coranto] with her upon the heath?'

"'Sir,' said the person in the coach, 'I dare not deny anything to one of your quality and good mind. You seem a gentleman, and your request is very reasonable.'

"Which said, the lacquey opens the boot, out comes the knight, Du Vall leaps lightly off his horse and hands the lady out of the coach. They danced, and here it was that Du Vall performed marvels; the best master in London, except those that are French, not being able to show such footing as he did in his great French riding boots.

"The dancing being over, he waits on the lady to her coach. As the knight was going in, says Du Vall to him, 'Sir, you have forgot to pay the musick.'

"'No, I have not,' replies the knight, and, putting his hand under the seat of the coach, pulls out a hundred pounds in a bag, and delivers it to him, which Du Vall took with a very good grace, and courteously answered, 'Sir, you are liberal, and shall have no cause to repent your being so; this liberality of yours shall excuse you the other three hundred pounds,' and giving the word, that if he met with any more of the crew, he might pass undisturbed, he civilly takes his leave of him."

Now what could be fairer than that? Wasn't he the perfect gentleman? Such courage and daring, such grace. . . .

Such courage and daring, says Pope, tightening his lips. There were only five of the highwaymen (all armed and mounted of course), and yet they had the temerity to hold up a coach containing an equal number (including two defenceless women, of course)—oh, very bold! And such grace! Pope enlarges upon it, to make sure his reader hasn't missed any significant details: "He manifested his agility of body by lightly dismounting off his horse, and with ease and freedom getting up again when he took his leave; his excellent deportment by his incomparable dancing and his graceful manner of taking the hundred pounds."

This last part is not usually quoted. Later writers doubtless smiled tolerantly at the kindly doctor's simple-minded comments. (They were very patronizing towards him.) This bit of satire was usually summarized in some such sentence as "Pope went on to praise Duval for the many fine qualities he displayed on this memorable occasion." Such praise!

The next of Duval's adventures recounted by Pope is never quoted in its original form. The précis usually runs something like this. Duval and his companions held up a coach full of ladies at Blackheath. With the ladies was a child who had a silver feeding-bottle. This caught the eye of one of the highwaymen, who promptly snatched the bottle out of the child's mouth. The infant screamed, and so did the ladies. But they needn't have worried. Duval was there—what he had been doing while all this happened is not said—and he at once ordered the man to return the bottle to the child. "Sirrah," he is reported to have said, "cannot you behave like a gentleman and raise a contribution without stripping people? But perhaps you yourself have some occasion for the sucking-bottle, for by your actions one would imagine you were hardly weaned!"

There is again only one authority for this story, and that is Dr Pope. The popular version is very nearly based on Pope— but there is just one detail that has been altered. For according to Pope it was Duval himself who seized the feeding-bottle, and our gallant hero was forced to return it by one of his companions "whose name," says the doctor, "I wish I could put down here, that he may find friends when he shall stand in need of them." This is the only story in the *Memoirs* which openly shows Duval in a bad light, and so as not to damage his satire the writer affects to regret that his knight *sans peur et sans reproche* should have done such a thing. The last bit of dialogue in the later version was the invention of a famous eighteenth-century copyist; other writers, not content with the shameless distortion of Pope's account, have had the cheek to give it out as actually coming from the *Memoirs*!

With tears in his eyes Dr Pope comes to the last stage in Duval's glorious career. It is a sad one. The highwayman is captured—for shame!—while in a drunken stupor in a Chandos Street inn named the Hole in the Wall. But the fact that he was drunk, as Pope is quick to point out, must not be held against him. The very reverse, in fact. "Well it was for the bailiff and his men that he was drunk, otherwise they had tasted of his prowess; for he had in his pocket three pistols, one whereof could shoot twice, and by his side an excellent sword, which, managed by such a hand and heart, must, without doubt, have done wonders. Nay," he goes on, warming to it, " I have heard it attested by those that knew how good a marksman he was, and his excellent way of fencing, that, had he been sober, it was impossible he could have killed less than ten." And " he would have been cut as small as herbs for the pot before he would have yielded to the bailiff of Westminster."

But Duval was caught at last. He was tried, convicted, and sentenced to death. His last hours were in keeping with the rest of his career. " There was a great company of ladies, and these not of the meanest degree, that visited him in prison, interceded for his pardon, and accompanied him to the gallows." There is no doubt about the truth of this. Many wires were pulled, and it is on record that the King would have pardoned him had not Judge Morton threatened to resign in protest.

Claude Duval, only twenty-seven years old, was hanged at Tyburn on January 21, 1670, and many a husband sighed with relief. His admirers later gave him a fine funeral in St Paul's Church, Covent Garden, and his gravestone bore the following epitaph:

> Here lies Du Vall: Reader, if Male thou art,
> Look to thy purse; if Female, to thy heart.
> Much havoc has he made of both; for all
> Men he made stand, and women he made fall.
> The second Conqueror of the Norman race,
> Knights to his arms did yield, and Ladies to his face.
> Old Tyburn's glory; England's illustrious thief,
> Du Vall, the Ladies' Joy; Du Vall, the Ladies' grief.

Now we come to the climax of the satire. As we have seen, and as the author made clear in his sub-title, his bitter wit was directed against Duval's mistresses rather than the highwayman himself. (The aristocratic doctor would not have lowered himself to spill ink on a mere French footman.) Now, with brilliant irony, he puts his final exposure of the ladies' follies into the mouth of their hero. This is how he does it. After the execution, we are told, Duval's body was borne to the Tangier Tavern, St Giles's, for a "lying in state." It was carried with reverence to a room draped in black. Eight wax tapers were lighted, and the same number of tall gentlemen in long black cloaks kept vigil. Many were the mourners who went to pay their last respects—all ladies, of course, and most of a high station in life. They were masked, but Pope says he could publish a list of their names if he wanted to. Meanwhile, one of the attendants has suddenly found something of extraordinary value in Duval's pocket. It is a document which, when unfolded, turns out to be the "dying confession" which the highwayman forgot to deliver at Tyburn.

I think we have given enough quotations from Pope for the reader to guess the true authorship of this document from the style alone. And this must be reprinted in full. Here it is:

"I should be very ungrateful (which, among persons of honour, is a greater crime than that for which I die) should I not acknowledge my obligation to you, fair English ladies. I could not have hoped that a person of my nation, birth, education, and condition could have found so many and powerful charms to captivate you all, and to tie you so firmly to my interest, that you have not abandoned me in distress, or in prison; that you have accompanied me to this place of death, of ignominious death.

"From the experience of your true loves I speak it, nay, I know I speak your hearts; you could be content to die with me now, and even here, could you be assured of enjoying your beloved Du Vall in the other world.

"How mightily, and how generously, have you rewarded my little services! Should I ever forget that universal consternation amongst you when I was taken? Your frequent, your chargeable visits to me at Newgate? Your shrieks, your swoonings, when I was condemned? Your zealous intercession and importuning for my pardon?

"You could not have erected fairer pillars of honour and respect to me had I been a Hercules, and could have got fifty sons in a night.

"It has been the misfortune of several English gentlemen, in the times of the late Usurpation, to die at this place, upon the honourable occasion that ever presented itself, the endeavouring to restore their exiled sovereign: gentlemen, indeed, who had ventured their lives, and lost their estates, in the service of their prince; but they are died unlamented, and uninterceded for, because they were English. How much greater, therefore, is my obligation, whom you love better than your own countrymen; better than your own dear husbands? Nevertheless, ladies, it does not grieve me that your intercession for my life proved ineffectual. Had you gained me my life I must, in gratitude, have devoted it wholly to you; which yet would have been too short; for, had you been sound, I should have soon died of a consumption; if otherwise, of the pox."

Incredible as it may seem, this " confession " which Pope put into Duval's mouth after his death has been solemnly accepted by reputable historians as the highwayman's own unaided effort. Some, indeed—not so reputable, these—have gone so far as to make it appear that the speech was actually delivered by Duval at Tyburn!

Such, then, is the famous *Memoirs of Du Vall*, still quoted and misquoted as evidence of the noble character of the highwayman. What makes the historians' howler even more glaring is that Pope's own contemporaries saw the point all right. In the year following the publication of the *Memoirs*, Samuel (" Hudibras ") Butler wrote a mock-heroic " Pindarick Ode " entitled *To the Memory of the Most Renowned Du-Vall*. In this the poet describes how Duval

> Taught the wild Arabs on the road
> To act in a more gentle mode;
> Take prizes more obligingly than those
> Who never had been bred *Filous*
> And how to hang in a more graceful fashion
> Than e'er was known before to the dull English nation.

While the highwayman was in his cell in Newgate—

> Thither came ladies from all parts
> To offer up close prisoners hearts
> Which he received as tribute due,
> And made them yield up love and honour too

—but not literally, we take it, as he was kept in pretty heavy chains.

Some twenty years later Titus Oates, in a book with the intriguing title Εἰκων βασιλική, spoke strongly against " divers great personages of the feminine sex that on their knees made supplication for that insipid highwayman." He too poked a bit of fun at Duval, saying " it is true he was a man of singular parts and learning, only he could neither read nor write "—which would have given the historians a bit of a headache if it had come from anyone except Titus Oates.

It has been said that the only reliable source of information about Duval is Pope's pamphlet, and even the usually exhaustive *D.N.B.* bibliography gives little further help. That, of course, did not stop later writers from adding a good deal. One of Duval's eighteenth-century admirers heaped fresh laurels on his hero's brow by inventing a charming little anecdote of how the chivalrous highwayman seduced a girl of thirteen for a wager. The same chronicler added a racy tale about an adventure at an inn which is, alas, just another pirated edition of the greatest masterpiece in pornographic literature—Chaucer's " Reeve's Tale."

As we remarked at the beginning of this chapter, it is far from our aim to try to debunk Claude Duval. Though he may not have been quite so chivalrous as he has been painted, there is no disputing his success as a gallant. Let his fame go on for ever, then, let the legends about him flourish—let the ladies sigh for the good old Age of Chivalry. Believe what you like about him—but don't blame it on old Dr Pope.

CHAPTER TWELVE

The Golden Farmer

WILLIAM DAVIS is probably unique in highway history in having had an inn named after him. The inn was called the Golden Farmer, after the name by which he was generally known during the forty-odd years—possibly another record for the road—in which he practised the profession. But it was not a business name. The most remarkable thing about Davies is that not even his wife and children—of whom there were eighteen—ever suspected his highway activities.

Davis was born in Wrexham, Denbighshire, in 1627. Migrating to Gloucestershire, he married the daughter of a prosperous innkeeper. Then he leased a farm on the borders of Bagshot Heath, one of the most popular of the highwaymen's playgrounds outside the London area, as John Gay suggested in his *Journey to Exeter* (1715):

> Prepared for war, now Bagshot Heath we cross,
> Where broken gamesters oft repair their loss.

It was here that Davis got his nickname. He always paid in gold. No one seems to have thought this suspicious, though it should have occurred to some people that his own revenue could not all have been paid in the same coin. Instead, he was honoured for the practice. Indeed, he was a very respected man. He was a hard-working farmer, a good master to his men, an equally good father to his numerous children, and a pillar of the Church and generous contributor to all good causes. He was the sort of man who deserved to prosper.

Yet all the time he was leading a double life. Working single-handed, he made regular sorties on the Exeter road. Nor did he confine his criminal activities to the hours of darkness. He was a brilliant master of disguise, and made a speciality of daylight swoops on cattle-drovers returning from market, many of whom were personal acquaintances. But perhaps his most daring exploit was when he robbed his own landlord.

The landlord had called on Davis to collect the annual rent, and went away with seventy golden guineas. As soon as he was off the premises David did a quick-change act, donned his wig and stuffed his mask in his pocket, and then took a short cut across country to get on to the road ahead of the landlord. When the latter saw him Davis was already masked and had his pistols drawn.

"Come, Mr Gravity from Head to Foot, but neither Head nor Foot to the Heart, deliver what you have in a trice," he commanded in the special voice he reserved for the road.

The landlord pleaded poverty.

"All I have is two shillings," he said. "You would not take that from a poor man."

Davis told him he wasn't going to get away with that yarn.

"You seem by your manner and habit to be a man of better circumstances than you pretend," he observed. "Therefore, open your budget, or else I shall fall foul about your house."

The landlord shifted his ground.

"Dear sir," he said respectfully, "you can't be so barbarous as to rob an old man. What, have you no pity, religion, or compassion in you? Have you no conscience? You can have no respect for your own body and soul, which must certainly be in a miserable case, if you follow these unlawful courses."

Plucky, but scarcely tactful. Davis did not mince matters after that.

"Damn you, don't talk of age or barbarity to me," he snapped. "I show neither pity nor compassion to any. What, talk of conscience to me? I have no more of that dull commodity than you have, nor do I allow my soul and body to be governed by religion, but by interest. Therefore, deliver what you have, before this pistol makes you repent your obstinacy."

And so Davis got his rent back, and when the landlord later told him his tale of woe he was a very sympathetic listener.

This story does not show the Golden Farmer in a very

favourable light. The best that could be said of him is that he was not a hypocrite. But perhaps he was put out of temper by the landlord's attempt to cheat him with his story of the two shillings, and the rather nasty crack about his conscience.

Other tales of William Davis are in a lighter vein. For example, there was the inevitable lawyer story common to all famous highwaymen.

The lawyer's name was Squire Broughton, and he was a barrister of the Middle Temple. Davis met him far from his normal beat, so disguise was unnecessary. Broughton was travelling on the Oxford Road, bound for London, and the pair jogged along together. Chatting of this and that, Broughton mentioned that he was a lawyer; and the Golden Farmer at once asked if he would advise him on a point of law. He was a farmer, he said. A neighbour of his was letting his cattle stray over the boundary between their farms, and the animals were doing considerable damage. Was the case actionable?

" It is very actionable," the lawyer assured him, " being Damage Feasant."

" Damage Feasant? " said Davis. " What's that, pray, sir? "

The lawyer explained. He enjoyed hearing the sound of his own voice, and Davis was a good listener. He went into the matter in great detail, quoting Coke on Littleton and other authorities. By the time they reached Hillingdon, where they had both decided to stop for the night, he had gone deeply into the Law of Trespass. Davis, who had understood a good deal less than half, was very grateful. The following day the pair set out together, and as soon as they were in open country Davis raised another legal question.

" If I may be so bold as to ask you, sir," he said, " what is that you call Trover and Conversion? "

" That is easily explained," replied Squire Broughton, preparing himself for another lengthy dissertation. " It is ah action against one who has found any property, and, refusing to deliver on demand, converts it to his own use."

" And if I should find any money about you," put in Davis before the lawyer could go on, " and converted it to my own use, why, then, that is also actionable, I find."

"That's a highway robbery," replied the lawyer, smiling at his companion's choice of example, "which requires no less satisfaction than a man's life."

"A robbery!" repeated Davis, aghast. Then he changed his tone suddenly. "Why, then, I must e'en commit one for once, and not use it; therefore deliver your money, or else behold this pistol will prevent you reading Coke upon Littleton any more."

The lawyer expostulated. Davis must be joking. But the pistol told him he wasn't. It was no good remonstrating about the Law, because they had just been over that; so Broughton tried to scare him by talking of Heaven and Hell.

The Golden Farmer laughed.

"Why, you son of a whore," he said pleasantly, "thy impudence is very great to talk of Heaven and Hell to me, when you think there's no way to Heaven but through Westminster Hall. Come, come, down with your rhino this minute, for I have other gess customers to mind than to wait on you all day!"

The lawyer's rhino amounted to some fifty pounds, which Davis promptly "converted" to his own use.

Another time in his career William Davis robbed Sir Thomas Day, a Bristol magistrate—again in broad daylight and without wearing a mask. Indeed, when he met the magistrate on the road he told him a story about his having been robbed by highwaymen of £40 earlier that day. Sir Thomas tried to cheer him up by reminding him of the Law relating to daylight robberies.

"Truly, that would have been very hard," he said, "but as you had been robbed betwixt sun and sun, the county, upon suing it, must have been obliged to make your loss good again."

So being robbed during the day was nothing to worry about, said Davis. Nothing at all, Sir Thomas assured him. And he would get the £40 back? Certainly he would—the county would pay—but what was he doing with that pistol . . . ?

But the county would pay, Sir Thomas—there was nothing to be worried about. He would get the money back—he said so himself. . . . And the price of his horse, too, Davis hoped, as he shot the beast to prevent pursuit. Then, collecting the magistrate's money, he rode away.

A pretty story, but there was just one flaw in it. Under the Act of 1585 liability of the county had been reduced to fifty per cent of the loss sustained.

From these stories it will be seen that the Golden Farmer had a sense of humour of sorts, but precious little courtesy. Typical of his lack of manners is the tale of his approach to a traveller on Finchley Common. He had spent a few days in this district without any luck, and had had about enough of the Common when he espied a solitary traveller. He rode up boldly and gave the man a hearty thwack on the back with the flat of his sword.

"A plague on you, how slow you are!" he shouted. "To make a man wait on you all this morning—come, deliver what you have, and be poxed to you, and go to Hell for orders!"

Funny? Well, not for the traveller. And then there was the case of the poor tinker—there was no Robin Hood streak in the Golden Farmer—who was trudging wearily across Blackheath when Davis rode up.

"Well overtook, honest tinker," Davis greeted him. "Methinks you seem very devout, for your life is a continual pilgrimage, and in humility you go about almost barefoot, thereby making necessity a virtue."

"Ay, master," answered the tinker, on whom all this wit was wasted, "needs must when the Devil drives, and had you no more than I, you too might go without boots and shoes."

"That may be," conceded the Golden Farmer. "And I suppose you march all over England with your bag and baggage?"

"Yes, I go a great deal of ground, but not so much as you ride," replied the tinker stolidly. "And I'll have you to know that I make a great deal of pains for a livelihood."

"Yes, I know thou art such a strong enemy to idleness that, in mending one hole, you make three rather than want work."

"That's as you say," replied the tinker, who was getting a bit tired of Davis. "However, sir, I wish that you and I were farther asunder, for i'faith I don't like your company. Indeed," he added bluntly, "I have a great suspicion of you."

"Have you so?" said Davis cheerfully. "Then great it shall not be without a cause. Come, open your wallet, and deliver that parcel that's in it."

The tinker told Davis that he was a hundred miles away from home, and if he took all his money he would have to beg to get back.

"I don't care if you have to beg your way two hundred miles," replied the Golden Farmer, "for if a tinker escapes Tyburn and Banbury, it is his fate to die a beggar."

Witty? The tinker didn't think so. Yet stories like this are told with glee by the Golden Farmer's admiring biographers. They are repeated here, because William Davis was probably the nearest to the average highwayman of the period that could be found. He was not physically cruel, but he had no courtesy. He was equally lacking in chivalry. In his dealings with the ladies he behaved himself to the extent of keeping in his saddle, but his language was something horrible. So horrible, in fact, that we shall have to be content with a couple of the milder specimens.

At Salisbury—the Golden Farmer travelled around—Davis stopped a coach full of gentlewomen, all of whom surrendered their wealth except one. Davis's original biographer tells us that she was a Quaker, but that may well have been a bit of personal prejudice. This is what Davis is reported to have said to her:

"You canting bitch! If you dally with me at this rate, you'll certainly provoke my spirit to be damnable rude to you! You see these good women here who were so tender-hearted as to be charitable to me, and you, you whining whore, are so covetous as to lose your life for the sake of mammon." Davis couldn't stand meanness. "Come, come, you hollow-hearted bitch, unpin your purse-strings quickly, or else I shall send you out of the land of the living."

Equally strong language was served out on the occasion of his meeting the Duchess of Albemarle, and on this occasion the Golden Farmer is said to have used physical violence as well. But it was only her jewels he was after. The Duchess was attended by two footmen as well as the coachman and postilion, and they put up a stiff fight before the highwayman had all their hands above their heads. The Duchess was rather slow in parting with her treasures, and Davis treated her to a bit of plain speaking.

"You bitch incarnate," he began, "you had rather read over your face in the glass every morning, and blot out pale to put in red, than give an honest man, as I am, a small matter to support him in his lawful occasions on the road."

It must be said in mitigation that this was just the sort of language the Duchess understood. Before General Monck married her she was plain Nan Clarges, blacksmith's daughter and washerwoman, whom Pepys called "Dirty Besse." In the safety of his diary Pepys described a dinner he had at the Albemarles' with the words "dirty dishes, a nasty wife, and bad meat."

By the time Davis had finished his little speech the Duchess was still fumbling with the diamond rings she was wearing. Hearing sounds of other travellers on the road behind, the highwayman thereupon grasped her hand and tore the rings off her fingers, snatching her watch in the same movement. He got away just in time.

Accounts of the final capture of the Golden Farmer vary considerably. The matter is not of very special interest, so we shall merely take the most likely version. According to this his career came to an abrupt end because of an act of carelessness that ill befitted such a seasoned veteran. Robbing a coach on the Exeter road one night, he omitted to make a search for firearms, and turned round to ride off. Instantly one of the occupants of the coach shot him in the back, and he toppled off his horse and was easily captured.

When the identity of the highwayman was discovered it caused a sensation. The Golden Farmer—a respected and respectable citizen—he must have gone mad. . . . Then Davis confessed, and the whole story came out. After that there could be no more doubting. Even Mrs Davis, stricken with grief, had to believe it. Their sons, most of whom had become respectable farmers themselves by this time, hung their heads in shame; and their daughters, understanding only too well where their fat dowries had come from, tried to forget that they had ever borne the name of Davis.

Accounts of the place and date of Davis's execution are divergent, but the authority of the Portledge Papers seems as reliable as any. The entry is dated 1690, and reads:

"The notorious offender the Golden Farmer was executed according to warrant in Fleet Street, and his body hangs in chaynes on Bagshot Heath."

CHAPTER THIRTEEN

Old Mob

WHY he was called " Old Mob " is a mystery. He was baptized as Thomas Sympson, in Romsey, Hampshire. The date of his birth is also unknown, though it must have been in the first part of the seventeenth century. He was a contemporary of the Golden Farmer, with whom he had occasional business relations. He lived in Romsey all his life—which was an exceptionally long one for a highwayman—but his affairs frequently took him far afield.

Old Mob always aimed high. His " official " biography is packed with names of the famous, and he had more than a nodding acquaintance with many of the notables of his period. His first adventure of which we have any record was with one Sir Bartholomew Shower, knight, whom he met one day on the road between Honiton and Exeter. Daylight robbery was pretty common in those parts, and the knight was travelling light. When called upon to part up he obeyed quite cheerfully, for he had only a little small change on him. But that did not satisfy Old Mob.

" My demands, sir, are very large and pressing," he explained. " You must instantly draw a bill for one hundred and fifty pounds and remain in the next field for security till I have received the money."

This struck Sir Bartholomew as a bit of a tall order, and he said so. He assured the highwayman that he would never get such a bill honoured. But Old Mob knew better. Sir Bartholomew was well known in Exeter. All he had to do, said Old Mob, was to draw up a bill, payable on sight, on one of the city's leading goldsmiths, and he would do the rest himself. He became somewhat insistent, and Sir Bartholomew soon found himself in the next field writing out the bill. To make sure of his security Old Mob tied the knight to a tree and turned his horse loose; then he rode off to Exeter.

It was a lonely spot, and the knight's feelings must have been mixed when he saw Old Mob return some time later. The highwayman was pleased to inform him that his mission had been successful.

"Sir," he said gaily, "I am come with a habeus corpus to remove you out of your present captivity." And he released Sir Bartholomew, leaving him to return home on foot.

The next man of note to fall foul of this enterprising highwayman was John Gadbury, a famous astrologer. He was carrying only nine sovereigns at the time, but he made desperate efforts to retain them. He pleaded poverty and appealed to Old Mob for compassion. But again Old Mob knew his man.

"Are you not a lying son of a whore," he asked—rhetorically, we suppose—" to pretend you want money, when you hold twelve large houses of the planets by lease parole, which you let out regularly to the Stationers' Company at so much per ann.?"

To this John Gadbury had no suitable reply, and he had to thank his stars it was only nine pounds.

Old Mob loved catching a fraud. After the astrologer he waylaid a notorious quack who went under the name of Cornelius-à-Tieburgh. This unlicensed practitioner was rash enough to try to preach to Old Mob on the iniquity of going about ruining honest folk. Old Mob let him have it for that.

"This is the Devil correcting sin with a witness," he began. (The comp. must have slipped up there. Surely he meant "with a vengeance.") "Can I ruin more people than you, Mr Theophrastus Bombastus?" Amazing that an uneducated fellow like Old Mob should know all about Paracelsus, isn't it? "You are a scrupulous and conscientious son of a whore"—either Old Mob or his biographer was a bit shaky on adjectives—" to tell me of ruining people. You have put out more eyes than the smallpox, made more deaf than the cataracts of the Nile, lamed more than the gout, shrunk more sinews than one that makes bow-strings, and killed more than the pestilence!"

After that the quack parted up without a word.

Old Mob's next victim was a lady of very high or very low standing, according to which way you look at it. She had been christened Louise de Kéroualle, and for services rendered (unspecified) had been created Duchess of Portsmouth by a grateful monarch. Old Mob picked her up on the London–Newmarket road, and she thought he must have made a mistake.

" Do you know who I am? " she demanded.

Old Mob knew all right.

" Yes, madam," he replied. " I know you to be the greatest whore in the kingdom, and that you are maintained at the public charge. I know that all the courtiers depend upon your smiles, and that even the King is your slave. But a gentleman-collector upon the road is a greater man, and more absolute, than His Majesty is at Court. You may now say, madam, that a single highwayman has exercised his authority where Charles the Second of England has often begged a favour."

The Duchess of Portsmouth had no wish to say any such thing. But, according to his zealous biographer, Old Mob was off again before she could open her pretty mouth.

" I am King here, madam," he told her, " and I too have a whore to keep on public contributions. Therefore I must presume to take what you have, without asking any more questions."

Nobody had had the chance to ask any questions so far. But at last the Duchess managed to get a word in.

" You dare not! " she said.

" I durst if I die for't," said Old Mob grimly. He was losing his patience. " Therefore, you outlandish whore, deliver! "

The Duchess delivered. As a result of that encounter Old Mob was the richer by a necklace, a gold watch, two diamond rings, and two hundred pounds in hard cash.

If we are to believe his biographer—which isn't easy—Old Mob was a very talkative highwayman. He treated most of his victims to similar homilies, and on one occasion treated a lady to a recital of a lengthy poem before coming to the inevitable point. But we must not inquire too closely. And certainly we can well believe that he had something to say to his next victim, even if it wasn't quite what his biographer said it was.

The victim in question was none other than Judge Jeffreys, and he asked the same question as the Duchess of Portsmouth. Old Mob knew him all right. They had met before, in rather different circumstances. His Honour had delivered a sermon on that occasion, and now Old Mob was returning the compliment.

"I don't doubt that when justice has overtaken us both," he said, "I shall stand at least as good a chance as your lordship, who have already written your name in indelible characters of blood by putting to death so many hundred innocent men, for only standing up in defence of our common liberties, that you might secure the favour of your prince. 'Tis enough for you to preach morality upon the Bench, when nobody dares to contradict you; but your lessons can have no effect upon me at this time."

This was pretty good stuff, and it is a pity that the biographer rather spoils the effect by adding that Old Mob followed this up with "fifty oaths and imprecations," which unfortunately aren't repeated verbatim. The end of the story was that Old Mob relieved His Honour of fifty-six guineas.

One last tale of Old Mob. His victim this time was a peer of the realm, but, for reasons that will become obvious, the biographer suppressed his name. Old Mob happened to be in Bath at the same time as his lordship, and he learned that the other was going to London on horseback. Old Mob decided to go the same way, and with a view to making it easier to strike up an acquaintance he dressed himself as a woman. Although the account does not say as much, we may be reasonably sure, in the light of what happened later, that he was prompted to adopt this ruse by some knowledge of his lordship's character.

The peer was not so rash as to make the journey alone, and he left with six attendants riding with him. The highwayman had expected this. He set off soon after, and caught up with the convoy when they were passing through open country. Old Mob couldn't have been very old at this stage of his career, for his lordship at once invited the highwayman to ride with him. If Old Mob had designs on him, so had he on "her," and he was anything but slow. They hadn't been talking for long before, Old Mob's biographer tells us, "his lordship being amorously inclined, he was for fulfilling the primary command, Increase and multiply." It seems that he made his desires known in pretty blunt language, while they were jogging along the road. Old Mob fluttered his eyelashes, looked as coy as any highwayman could be expected to, and said that he really didn't think it was quite the thing. His suitor pressed the point, and at last, feeling that the demands of modesty had been satisfied, the object of his desire " told his lordship that was there any place of privacy she would be very proud of gratifying his request; but to expose herself before half a dozen attendants that were with his honour, she would not for the world."

His lordship had to admit that this was reasonable. Happily they were approaching a wood that struck him as the very thing they wanted. He told his attendants—who were too used to this sort of thing to show any surprise—to wait for him on the road, and then he and his "dear bit of a groat" rode into the wood.

His lordship was not the kind of man to waste time on useless preliminaries. "Alighting with an intention of enjoyment in the folds of love," we are told, "his lordship, for an introduction to the fount of pleasure, was for taking up the petticoats." Tut, tut, my lord!

At this point we feel we owe our readers an apology. Not for what we have quoted, but for what we aren't going to quote. Decency forbids us to go as far as his lordship did. Writers had more licence two or three centuries ago. We must be old-fashioned. We shall have to rely on our reader's imagination to fill in the gap, and pick up the story at the final bit of quick-fire cross-talk:

HIS LORDSHIP. What a plague's the meaning of your wearing breeches, madam?

OLD MOB (producing a pistol). Nothing, but to put your money in!

After a long and varied career Old Mob was caught in the end. At his trial he faced no fewer than thirty-six indictments, and was convicted on thirty-two. He was hanged on September 12, 1691. In his "dying confession," which might have been written by anyone, he affirmed that "while he continued to rob on the highway, he prayed at the same time that God would forgive it, and that eased his mind something."

This old ruffian had one special claim to fame. As far as we know he was the only highwayman ever to have attained the distinction of becoming a grandfather.

CHAPTER FOURTEEN

The Yorkshire Robber

TWO highwaymen achieved undying—if posthumous—fame by getting a mention in Macaulay's *History of England*. Claude Duval was one. The other was—no, not Dick Turpin; he doesn't even get into the footnotes. It was a man named William Nevison, whose career Macaulay summarized as follows:

" He levied a quarterly tribute on all the northern drovers, and, in return, not only spared them himself, but protected them against all other thieves; he demanded purses in the most courteous manner; he gave largely to the poor what he had taken from the rich; his life was once spared by royal clemency, but he again tempted his fate, and at length died, in 1685, on the gallows of York."

From which he seems to have been, as highwaymen go, quite a good type. The popular ballad was still more complimentary, but it is such bad verse that we can quote only a couple of stanzas:

> Did you ever hear tell of that hero,
> Bold Nevison, that was his name?
> He rode about like a hero,
> And with that he gained great fame.
>
> He maintained himself like a gentleman,
> Besides he was good to the poor;
> He rode about like a bold hero,
> And he gained himself favour therefor.

Nothing about levying tribute here. And " maintained himself like a gentleman "—what have we here? Another Duval? No, not exactly. We are told that " in all his pranks he was very favourable to the female sex, who generally gave him the character of a civil, obliging robber." But no corantos, no lovelorn matrons, no jealous husbands. Nevison kept his sex life to himself. Which is the best definition of a gentleman, anyway.

There are plenty of records about this highwayman, and all are confused and contradictory. If we are to believe them all, he was born simultaneously in Wortley, Agnes Burton, Pontefract, and Upsal, near Thirsk. We shall call him a Yorkshireman and leave it at that. The year of his birth has been narrowed down to either 1639 or 1640. He was baptized either William or John, and he spelt his name either Nevison or Nevinson. He went under the alias of John Brace, or Bracy, or perhaps Johnson. According to one account he was of " honest, well reputed and reasonably estated parents "; by another testimony he was " brought up profanely." In some versions there were two separate Nevisons, William and John; it has been suggested that the confusion arose because he was never in the same place for very long.

From the mass of conflicting evidence we have ferreted out some sort of life of this famous highwayman. It seems that he began his career of crime when still at school, where he was noted for being " the ringleader of all his young companions in rudeness and debauchery." (The latter word had a less particularized meaning when this was written.) He stole apples and poultry and, finally, a silver spoon from his father. The latter reported this misdeed to the village dominie, and young William got a thrashing. He had a double revenge by getting up in the middle of the night, helping himself to £10 out of his father's cash-box, and a saddle and bridle from the stable; then he stole the schoolmaster's horse, and rode off to London. Fearing that he might be traced by means of the horse, he did not sell it but slit its throat.

William was about fourteen by this time, and " a lusty, well-looking lad." He invested part of his new wealth in a suit of clothes, and looked round for somewhere to make his fortune. A brewer gave him a job, and he worked steadily for three years, during which time his slate was clean. Then, deciding that there was no future in it, he had another look round. He was rewarded by the sight of £200 belonging to his master. He took this opportunity with both hands—it was in specie—and left the country.

Reaching Holland, William met a burgher's daughter, and eloped with her. They took the burgher's money and jewels as a wedding present, and as a result they spent their honeymoon in prison. Nevison escaped. What happened to the burgher's daughter we do not know, and here she disappears from the story. The Yorkshireman got to Flanders, where he enlisted in one of the English regiments in the Spanish service, under the command of the Duke of York (later James II). He fought at Dunkirk, and it is recorded that he displayed conspicuous bravery, although the *London Gazette* is silent on this point.

Soon after this Will deserted and returned to England. Here, we are told, he decided to live " a pleasant life at the hazard of his neck, rather than toil out a long remainder of unhappy days in want and poverty, which he was always averse to " (*i.e.*, he became a highwayman).

One evening, fairly early in his new vocation, Nevison met a couple of farmers coming towards him on the road. They warned him not to go forward, because they had just been robbed of £40 by three highwaymen less than half a mile away.

Nevison thanked them for their warning, but announced that he was going on.

" Turn back with me," he said, " and show me the way they took, and my life to a farthing, I'll make them return your money."

The farmers had nothing more to lose, so they agreed. Soon they spotted the three highwaymen in the distance, and Nevison went forward alone. When he reached the three he halted.

" Sir," he said to the nearest one, " by your garb and the colour of your horse you should be one of those I look after; and, if so, my business is to tell you that you borrowed of two friends of mine forty pounds, which they desired me to demand of you, and which, before we part, you must restore."

" How? " said the highwayman, taken aback. " Forty pounds? Damn you, sir! What, is the fellow mad? "

" So mad as that your life shall answer me if you do not give me better satisfaction," replied Nevison, pressing his pistol against the man's chest. With his other hand he got hold of the reins of the man's horse.

" My life is at your mercy," said the highwayman.

" No, 'tis not that I seek for, but the money you have robbed those two men of who are riding up to me," was the reply. " You must refund it."

The farmers joined Nevison, and the highwayman handed over what he had got. It did not amount to £40, and he explained that his companions had the rest. They had disappeared as soon as they saw Nevison meant business.

Dog eats dog? It looks like it—but remember that Nevison was new to the profession, and doubtless had still to learn the finer points of the gentlemen's rules of etiquette.

He now committed his prisoner to the charge of the two farmers, and announced his intention of going after the other two. And that, you will say, was the last the farmers saw of their £40. But that is where you're wrong.

Nevison took his prisoner's horse, and eventually came up with the other two men. They naturally thought it was their companion, and asked him about the upshot of the affair.

"Gentlemen, you are mistaken in your man," Nevison told them. "Though, by tokens of his horse and arms he hath sent me to you for the ransom of his life, which comes at no less than the prize of the day, which if you presently surrender, you may go about your business. If not, I must have a little dispute with you at sword and pistol."

Later in his career Nevison learned not to talk so much. He wouldn't have had a later career if one of his adversaries on this occasion had not been a bad shot—for the little dispute began while Nevison was still making his speech. But he didn't give them a chance for a second shot. He fired back, and wounded one in the shoulder. After that they both surrendered, and Nevison relieved them of their night's earnings. The farmers were not the only ones to have been held up, and out of the three highwaymen together Nevison got the sum of one hundred and fifty guineas.

What did he do then? Make off with the lot? Certainly not! He had told the farmers he would get their money back for them—and he rode back and handed it over. Forty pounds, that is; the rest he kept as payment for the service.

Will Nevison had plenty of variety in his life on the road. On one occasion he fell in with a whole " canting crew," as they frankly called themselves. (Canting wasn't hypocrisy in those days.) They were not highwaymen, but a motley collection of beggars and thieves banded together in a society with special rites. This merry crowd invited Nevison to have a drink with them, and after a few mugs of " Rum-booz " he applied for admission to the society—probably out of curiosity more than anything else. He said nothing about his former essays in crime, but passed himself off as an apprentice who had run away from his master, which wasn't exactly untrue.

The leader of the band, who seems to have been a bit of a card, made a little speech in which he described the life of the society. " Do we not come into the world like arrant beggars, without a rag upon us? " he said. " And do we not all go out of the world like beggars, without anything saving only an old sheet over us? Shall we be ashamed to walk up and down in the world like beggars, with old blankets pinned about us? No, no; that would be a shame to us indeed. Have we not the whole kingdom to walk at our pleasure? Are we afraid of the approach of quarter-day? Do we walk in fear of sheriffs, sergeants, and catchpoles? Who ever knew an arrant beggar arrested for debt? Is not our meat dressed in every man's kitchen? Does not every man's cellar afford us beer?—and the best men's purses keep a penny for us to spend! "

The next question was not rhetorical. The leader asked Nevison if he had any " loure " in his " bung." That was Greek to the Yorkshireman, and it had to be translated. The leader explained that he was inquiring about the contents of Nevison's pockets.

" Eighteenpence," said Nevison, producing it, " and you're welcome to it."

The money was accepted with thanks, and set aside for payment for " bowze " for the initiation ceremony. The ceremony itself was simple. The leader of the band poured a quart of beer over the head of the novice, saying the while:

" I do, by virtue of this sovereign liquor, install thee in the Roage, and make thee a free denizen of our ragged regiment, so that henceforth it shall be lawful for thee to cant, and to carry a doxy, or mort, along with thee, only observing these rules: first, that thou art not to wander up and down all countries, but to keep to that quarter which is allotted to thee; and, secondly, thou art to give way to any of us that have borne all the offices of the wallet before; and, upon holding up a finger, to avoid any town or country village where thou seest we are foraging for victuals for our army that march along with us. Observing these two rules, we take thee into our protection, and adopt thee a brother of our numerous society."

After this beer was used for better purposes than washing Nevison's hair, and there was a good deal of dancing and singing and general jollification. Then the leader spoke again.

"Now that thou art entered into our fraternity," he told Nevison solemnly, " thou must not scruple to act any villainies which thou shalt be able to perform, whether it be to nip a bung, bite the Peter Clay, the lurries crash, either a bleating cheat, cackling cheat, grunting cheat, Tib-oth-buttery, Margery Prater, or to clay a mish from the crackman's." More Greek, and Nevison wondered what he had let himself in for. But the leader soon explained. " That is," he went on, " to cut a purse, steal a cloak-bag or portmanteau, convey all manner of things, whether a chicken, sucking-pig, duck, goose, or hen, or steal a shirt from the hedge; for he that will be *quier cove* (not my italics), a professed rogue, must observe this rule set down by an ancient patrico in these words:

> " Wilt thou a-begging go,
> O per se-o, O per se-o,
> Then must thou God forsake,
> And to the devil thee betake,
> O per se-o, O per se-o."

Nevison accepted this condition, and promised to do all the things outlined, even to steal a shirt from the hedge if he saw one there. All the same, when the leader held up his hand for silence again the new " quier cove " began to feel a bit uneasy. Fortunately it was much better stuff this time.

" Because thou art but a novice in begging, and understandest not the mysteries of the canting language," he said, " thou shalt have a doxy to be thy companion, by whom thou mayest receive instructions."

The lady selected for this responsible position turned out to be about fourteen years old—which, says Nevison's biographer with vicarious relish, " tickled his fancy very much, that he had gotten a young wanton to dally withal." But if Nevison thought there was anything improper about the canting crew he was mistaken. The leader of the band called for the patrico, or high priest, to officiate at the wedding ceremony. A hen was killed, its head cut off, and the body laid on the ground. Nevison was placed on one side, and the girl on the other, and without asking any questions about willingness or otherwise to either party the patrico pronounced them man and wife.

After more jollification the band repaired to a neighbouring barn for the night. Nevison remained there just long enough to consummate the marriage; then he slipped out quietly and went on his way. It had been good fun while it lasted—especially the last part—but his ambitions were a cut above those of the canting crew. They were a decent crowd, and very hospitable, but hardly on the same social plane as a highwayman. In such company Nevison could scarcely hope to maintain himself like a gentleman.

Before we leave the subject of the canting crew, here is a set of " laws " laid down by the leader of a band named William Holliday (hanged in 1695):

Art. I directs—That none of his company should presume to wear shirts, upon pain of being cashiered.

II.—That none should lie in any other places than stables, empty houses, or other bulks.

III.—That they should eat nothing but what they begged, and that they should give away all the money they got by cleaning boots among one another, for the good of the fraternity.

IV.—That they should neither learn to read nor write, that he may have them better under command.

V.—That they should appear every morning by nine, on the parade, to receive necessary orders.

VI.—That none should presume to follow the scent but such as he ordered on that party.

VII.—That if anyone gave them shoes or stockings he should convert them into money to play.

VIII.—That they should steal nothing that they could not come at, for fear of bringing a scandal upon the company.

IX.—That they should not endeavour to clear themselves of vermin, by killing or eating them.

X.—That they should cant better than the Newgate birds, pick pockets without bungling, outlie a Quaker, outswear a lord at a gaming-table, and brazen out all their villanies beyond an Irishman.

The fourth commandment shows that Holliday knew a thing or two about leadership.

To return to Nevison. By all accounts he was a successful highwayman, and within a few years he had saved quite a lot of money. After one very good haul (£450 in cash) from a grazier returning from market he decided to retire.

He was now twenty-one.

Will Nevison returned home. He had made his modest fortune in London, he explained. Whether his father believed this tale is doubtful, but he asked no questions. When he saw the amount of his son's fortune he forgave him everything, including the little matter of £20. The fatted calf was killed, Will was welcomed back into the bosom of the family—and his father retired as well. And they lived happily ever after. That is, until the old man died. Then, already tired of the quiet country life, Will Nevison went back to the road.

It was during this second phase of his career that he became famous. He no longer played a lone hand, but went into partnership with one Thomas Tankard of Lincoln and Edward Bracy of Nottingham. The latter, whose surname Nevison borrowed on occasions, got into an earlier chapter in this book on the strength of his wide-awake "sleeping partner," Joan.

The three soon became famous for their exploits and especially for their generosity to the poor. But, as Macaulay suggested, they were not so popular with drovers and graziers, who had to pay their protection money every quarter. According to a contemporary of Nevison's, who claims to have known the highwayman by sight, he "had the country in such awe that the carriers paid him rent, duety, to let them alone, others lent him money that he might let them passe quietly." Before long Nevison became the recognized leader of a sizable gang, and a pamphlet published in 1674, with the snappy title *Bloody News from Yorkshire,* tells how he and twenty of his men had a pitched battle with fifteen butchers riding to Northallerton Fair.

Nevison fell foul of the Law more than once. He spent a short time in Wakefield prison, but got out again. Then, in March 1676, he was arrested again and confined in York Castle. At the Assizes he, in company with one Jane Nelson (his doxy?), was charged and convicted of robbery and horse-stealing. He appealed, promising to turn King's evidence against his old companions if he was allowed to live. On this condition he was reprieved; but as he did not carry out his promise, he was kept in gaol indefinitely. Finally, together with other prisoners, he was drafted into " Captain Graham's company designed for Tangier."

Nevison did not go to Tangier. He had had some experience of deserting from the Army, and it stood him in good stead now. He was soon back on the road—back with the companions whom he had refused to betray. But now there was a price on his head, and some of his associates were not so loyal. Before long he was back in gaol again—this time in Leicester. The warders were taking no chances with this slippery customer, and he was securely fettered as soon as he got there, and a strong guard was mounted. Escape seemed impossible, and his friends came to pay what they thought would be their last respects. Among his callers was a man who professed to be a doctor; what credentials he produced and what pretext he made to see Nevison are not revealed in the account, nor are we going to worry about little details like that. The "doctor" got in, examined the prisoner, and made a swift diagnosis of plague.

The mere word was enough to scare the guards. They didn't care two hoots if Nevison was on the verge of death, but they knew enough about contagious diseases to realize their own danger. Prisons in the seventeenth century were favourite breeding-grounds for plague, and previous epidemics had taken a heavy toll of prison staffs. The doctor's report was speedily passed on to higher authority, with the result that Nevison found himself in a cell on his own. Contrary to his expectations, however, security measures were not relaxed, but enforced from a greater distance. The guard stopped outside.

The doctor called regularly two or three times a day, and on one occasion he brought a colleague. The latter was actually a painter by trade, and while in the cell he daubed parts of Nevison's body with blue spots ("as are forerunners of approaching death in plague"). The doctor then administered an anæsthetic ("prepared a dose whereby the spirits were confined"), and shortly afterwards informed the Keeper that his patient had died.

A jury was quickly summoned, and the inquest was held in the cell—or rather in the corridor outside it. The doctor's evidence was regarded as more than sufficient, and none of the jurors thought it necessary to examine the body. One look through the door was enough for them.

The doctor obligingly arranged for the body to be taken away, and the burial took place the same day.

Nevison the highwayman was dead at last: but Nevison's ghost lived on. At least, that was what travellers in Leicestershire said. The very night after he was buried a traveller was held up and robbed on one of his favourite haunts by the dead spit of the deceased. The same thing happened a few nights later, and again, and again.

It is not surprising that Nevison's ghost was an even more successful highwayman than Nevison himself had been. A brave man might challenge the authority of a couple of pistols—but not when they were in the hands of a man he knew to be dead and buried. The highwayman cashed in on this fear of the supernatural, and no doubt his physician received a handsome fee for his services.

In July 1681 Nevison was nearly caught again. An innkeeper of Hawley named Darcy Fletcher, who had given him asylum more than once, was tempted by the offer of a reward and arranged with his brother to hand the highwayman over. Accordingly the next time Nevison stayed at the inn they slipped some knock-out drops in his beer, and then sent word for the constable to come during the night. But the dose wasn't strong enough, and Nevison tumbled to the plot. He fought his way out, killing Darcy Fletcher with a pistol-shot. The spot where the affray took place is marked by a stone near Howley Farm, Morley.

We have the testimony of Sir John Reresby, Governor of York Prison, that by his efforts Nevison was apprehended in the same year and sent back to the Castle. But this veteran prison-breaker escaped again, without blue paint this time, and Sir John petitioned Charles II to issue a further proclamation, pointing out that not only was Nevison a terror to travellers, but he "had threatened the death of several justices of the peace wherever he met them." The proclamation duly appeared in the *London Gazette* of October 1681, with an offer of £20 for information leading to the arrest of *John* Nevison, who "hath lately murdered one Fletcher, who had a warrant from a justice of peace to apprehend him." Further information about him was gained from the confession of a lady member of his gang named Elizabeth Burton, who gave details of robberies of butchers, merchants, and other travellers. According to her account Nevison's headquarters was at the Talbot Inn, Newark, and his operational zone included York, Lincoln, Nottingham, and Derby.

Elizabeth Burton's statement did not lead to Nevison's arrest, but it was a woman who betrayed him in the end. She was landlady of the Plough Inn, Sandal, near Wakefield, where the highwayman often used to put up for the night. A Captain William Hardcastle, who lived within a stone's throw of the inn, got to know of this, and offered the landlady half the reward if she would tip him off next time Nevison came.

On March 6, 1684, Captain Hardcastle got the message "Sir, the bird is in the cage." He collected the Constable of Sandal and one of his assistants, and the three were let into the inn at midnight. Nevison was asleep in his room, and he didn't have a chance. He was securely bound and taken back to his old quarters in York Castle. According to the records of Wakefield Sessions the journey took three days. The entry runs as follows:

"9th Oct. 1684. Order for Constable of Sandal to pay John Ramsden 10s. 6d. for the Constable of Sandal and Will. Hardcastle, gentleman, three days conveying one Nevison, a highwayman, to the Castle of York, and 2s. 6d. for obtaining the order."

The trial did not last long. When Nevison was brought into Court, according to the old ballad—

> And when then he came to the Bench,
> " Guilty or not Guilty " they to him did cry.
> " Not Guilty," then Nevison said,
> " I'm clear e'er since the same Day
> That the King did my Pardon grant,
> I ne'er did rob anyone, nor kill
> But that Fletcher in all my life,
> 'Twas in my defence, I say still."

This reference to a Royal Pardon seems to bear out what Macaulay said about Nevison, although there is no official record of its having been granted. But it is a point which will come up again in the next chapter.

On March 15, 1684—not 1685, as Macaulay had it—Nevison was hanged on the appropriately named Knavesmire. A contemporary diarist, in a note on the execution, remarked that " he hath left much debt at severall alehouses in the country where he haunted." An enterprising London publisher rushed out a chapbook entitled *The Yorkshire Robber ; or, Capt. Hind Improv'd*, according to which he was " a person of quick understanding, tall in stature, every way proportionable, exceeding valiant, having also the air and carriage of a gentleman."

Nevison died almost at the close of the reign of Charles II. It would be untruthful—though temptingly convenient—to say that his death marked the end of an era; for highwaymen generally seem to have been little affected by the Revolution. But before we continue the story under the House of Orange we shall use this as a stopping place, and turn our attention to a rather knotty problem.

CHAPTER FIFTEEN

Who Rode to York?

"And when I am gone, boys, each huntsman shall say,
None rode like Turpin so far in a day."

AND thou, too, Brave Bess!—thy name shall be linked with mine, and we'll go down to posterity together."

So said Dick Turpin—in the pages of Harrison Ainsworth's novel *Rookwood*. The fact that the prophecy was fulfilled owes everything to Ainsworth's literary skill—and nothing to Turpin's horsemanship.

Ainsworth's description of the ride to York is too well known for anything but the briefest of summaries. It is stirring blood-and-thunder stuff, right from the moment when Turpin, a pistol in each hand and his bridle between his teeth, clears the spikes of the old Hornsey toll-bar. Closely pursued by the Chief Constable of Westminster and other agents of the Law, our hero " rattles on in superb style," Ainsworth tells us, singing lustily and soliloquizing as the moonlit countryside flits by. The end is dramatic. He reaches York just as the deep bell of the Minster clock tolls out the hour of six—and Bess, gallant Bess, drops dead of a literally broken heart, while Turpin, heartbroken in his turn, " weeping and swearing like a man beside himself," and " kissing her lips, covered with blood-flecked foam," delivers a touching funeral oration. It is a fine climax, although the bit about kissing is perhaps a little too sugary even for the horse-worshipping English. Turpin is with difficulty parted from his beloved by a gipsy friend, and then—this is important—repairs to the bowling-green.

It is a good story; but, in the unequivocal words of *Encyclopædia Britannica*, " pure fiction."

Thanks to Ainsworth—who claimed that he wrote the whole story of the ride to York, amounting to nearly 20,000 words, in a day and a night—Turpin's ride is now such a popular episode in our national history that one might question the wisdom of exposing its untruth. All the most valuable beliefs are based on fictions. Would it not be better, perhaps, to let people go on enjoying this harmless tale?

The answer is that they will anyway.

Ever since the publication of *Rookwood* in 1834 historians have been unanimous in denying the truth of the legend. Dick Turpin never rode to York, they said; there was a famous ride to York, but it was accomplished while Turpin was still a boy, or perhaps before he was born.

This was proved by a wealth of carefully documented evidence, all very convincing. Every reference to Turpin in chapbook literature was produced with a flourish—for none said anything about a ride to York. The *Genuine History of the Life of Turpin*, a chapbook published in the year of his execution, contained no mention of the ride. Equally reticent was the more reliable *Trial of the Notorious Highwayman Richard Turpin*, "taken down in Court by Mr Thomas Kyll, Professor of Shorthand ... to which is prefix'd a large and genuine history of the life of Turpin, from his birth to his death. ... The whole ground on well-attested facts, and communicated by Richard Bayes, at the Green Man on Epping Forest, and other persons of the county of Essex."

The Turpin legend thus disproved, our learned antiquaries went on to give the true facts about the ride to York—and at once their unanimity disappeared. The evidence against Turpin was irrefutable, but negative. The historians dug deeper in the archives, and fell to arguing among themselves as to who really did ride to York. Let us leave them there for a bit.

There was no Turpin controversy. No one got up and defended Ainsworth's version. No one even questioned the weighty evidence of the historians. It was just ignored. The encyclopædists made notes for amendments to future editions, but otherwise the antiquaries had been wasting their time. They had proved to the public that Turpin never rode to York; the public yawned—and went back to Ainsworth. Who cares if it's true or not? It's a good story, isn't it? Much better reading than old Professor Dryasdust's stuff.

And if you go to York to-day you might still find someone to point out the spot where Black Bess sank exhausted to the ground. And why not? If you go to Nazareth you can see five Carpenter's Shops, each one guaranteed authentic—if you're prepared to pay for the pleasure.

Ainsworth was convicted and vindicated. (I doubt if he cared either way. *Rookwood* was selling well enough.) He had become the target of some sharp criticism, most of which was unfair. He was a novelist, not a historian; he never suggested the story was true. He had heard the legend, and it seemed good copy—that was all.

Where the learned historians made their biggest mistake was in not realizing that they had dug up even better copy. They were too keen on getting the facts right down to the last detail to think of this. Actually, after all their labours they never got to the bottom of the matter, and the ride to York is likely to remain the biggest mystery in the history of highwaymen. But we can offer a version which, if not true, is nearer to the truth than Ainsworth's, and—much more important—contains the material for an even better story. It is too late now, of course. Dick Turpin has been in the saddle for over a century, and is unlikely to be displaced. Good luck to him! But here's the other story, as related by Daniel Defoe in his *Tour through the Whole Island of Great Britain*:

"From Gravesend we see nothing remarkable on the road but Gad's Hill, a noted place for robbing of seamen, after they have received their pay at Chatham. Here it is that a famous robbery was committed in or about 1676, which deserves to be mentioned. It was about four o'clock in the morning, when a gentleman was robbed by one Nicks on a bay mare, just on the declivity of the Hill, on the west side. Mr Nicks came away to Gravesend, and, as he said, was stopped by the difficulty of getting the boat near an hour, which was a great discouragement to him; but he made the best use of it, as a kind of 'bate to his horse; from thence he rode across the county of Essex, through Tilbury, Horndon and Bilerecay to Chelmsford. Here he stopped about half an hour to refresh his horse, and gave him some balls; from thence to Braintre, Bocking, Wethersfield; then over the Downs to Cambridge;

and from thence, keeping still the cross roads, he went by
Fenny Stanton to Godmanchester and Huntingdon, where he
and his mare 'bated about an hour. Then, holding on the
North Road, and keeping a full larger gallop most of the way,
he came to York the same afternoon; put off his boots and
riding cloaths, and went dressed as if he had been an inhabitant
of the place to the Bowling Green, where among other gentlemen was the Lord Mayor of the City. He singled out his
Lordship, studied to do something particular that the Mayor
might remember him by, and accordingly lays some odd bets
with him concerning the bowls then running, which should
cause the Mayor to remember it the more particularly, and
takes occasion to ask his Lordship what o'clock it was; who,
pulling out his watch, told him the hour, which was a quarter
before or a quarter after eight at night. Some other circum-
stance, it seems, he carefully brought into their discourse
which should make the Lord Mayor remember the day of the
month exactly, as well as the hour of the day.

"Upon a prosecution which happened afterwards for this
robbery, the whole merit of the case turned upon this single
point. The person robbed swore as above to the man, to the
place, and to the time, in which the fact was committed—
namely, that he was robbed on Gad's Hill in Kent, on such a
day, and at such a time of the day, and on such a part of the
hill, and that the prisoner at the bar was the man that robbed
him. Nicks, the prisoner, denied the facts, called several
persons to his reputation, alleged that he was as far off as
Yorkshire at that time, and that particularly, the day whereon
the prosecution swore he was robbed, he was at bowles on the
public green in the city of York; and to support this he produced the Lord Mayor of York to testify that he was so, and
that the Mayor acted so and so with him there as above. This
was so positive and so well attested that the jury acquitted him
on a bare supposition that it was impossible the man could be
at two places so remote on one and the same day."

Wot, no moonlight? No Black Bess? No Chief Constable
after him? No gold-braid coat and cocked hat and great
jack-boots? Just "Nicks"? Who was this Nicks, anyway?

Be fair, now. Of course it isn't as colourful as *Rookwood*.

Defoe was writing a chronicle, not *Robinson Crusoe*. There's no knowing what he might have done with the story if he'd used it for fiction. The moonlight and Black Bess and the Chief Constable and the gold-braid coat, cocked hat, and great jack-boots are just decorations. Take them away, and compare Ainsworth's version with Defoe's. Wasn't Turpin's mission rather pointless? In the story of Nicks, on the other hand, the motive is everything. He accomplished the feat of riding 190 miles in fifteen hours not just for bravado, or a wager, or even because he was chased; but for the very sensible purpose of establishing an alibi.

And Defoe hasn't finished yet. He's not so sure about the next part—but would the novelist care? Here it is:

"There are more particulars related of this story, such as I do not take upon me to affirm—namely, that King Charles II prevailed on him, on assurance of pardon and that he should not be brought into any further trouble about it, to confess the truth to him privately, and that he own'd to His Majesty that he committed the robbery, and how he rode the journey after it, and that upon this the King gave him the name or title of Swift Nicks instead of Nicks."

What Ainsworth missed!

Defoe's story is, of course, sufficient evidence by itself to disprove the whole Turpin legend. The *Tour* was first published in 1724, when Dick Turpin was still an apprentice to a Whitechapel butcher. Had Ainsworth not sent him to the bowling-green it is conceivable that there might have been two separate rides—though the learned antiquaries, with their wealth of knowledge about Turpin's life, would easily have made short work of that theory. So we must accept the fact that the story of Nicks was fathered on Turpin. Not by Ainsworth, though. He was told the Turpin legend as a child.

Defoe's was not the only pre-Ainsworth account of the ride to York. Another account gave the place of the robbery as Barnet, but the date still as 1676, and added the information that the amount stolen was 560 guineas. Later, that charming observer of the English Baron von Poellnitz told a story similar in substance to Defoe's.

Much later, and after the publication of *Rookwood*, Dickens, in a moment of rank plagiarism, repeated Defoe's story (without acknowledgment, and without bothering to rewrite it properly) in *All the Year Round*. To cover up the theft—and perhaps, too, because he thought the story needed brightening up a bit—he embellished Defoe's simple prose with some of the clichés which, when used by Dickens, are usually termed graphic or vivid. (When I use them they are just clichés.) Thus Nicks's horse became " a blood mare, a splendid bay "; the highwayman " dashed across Essex, full tilt to Chelmsford," and " flashed on " and " slipped past " until " whiz—he darted through York gate." Dickens judged he would be hungry, so his hero " snapped up some food, and tossed off some generous, life-giving wine " before he " strolled out, gay and calm, to the bowling-green," where he " sauntered up to the Mayor "—and so on.

This is Dickens the journalist at his worst. Moreover, like all bad journalists, he could not even get his facts right. At York he gave Nicks a suit of " green velvet and gold lace " (ready-made, or did he take his tailor with him?), and in copying Defoe he carelessly wrote Fenny Stratford for Fenny Stanton, which makes nonsense of the whole story.

If there is one thing worse than plagiarism it is inefficient plagiarism.

Let us get back to Defoe's account. Who was this mysterious Mr Nicks? And what about the Royal Pardon? Did Charles II really amend his name to " Swift Nicks "?

It is this last question that caused most of the trouble among the learned historians. One of their number found a copy of a Royal Proclamation offering £20 for the apprehension of a highwayman named " Swift Nicks " dated December 1668—eight years *before* the date Defoe gave for the ride to York! Heedless of the consequences, the antiquary triumphantly waved this document in the face of his colleagues. A little later another of their number got out the *London Gazette* of November 18, 1669, in which a similar reward was offered for the apprehension of " divers lewd and disorderly persons " whose names included " Swift Nix, alias Clerk."

Two conclusions could be drawn from these facts. Either Defoe got the date wrong (in which case he might have got the whole story wrong), or the particulars such as he did not take upon himself to affirm were fictitious. Take your choice—it's really of no importance. But there remains the most intriguing part of the whole business to settle: who was Mr Nicks?

If Shakespeare wasn't Shakespeare, he must have been Bacon. If Nicks wasn't Turpin, he must have been—why, our old friend William (or John) Nevison (or Nevinson)! So said some. Without going too deeply into the matter, let us look at the evidence.

First of all, it is pretty certain that at some time in his career Nevison received a Royal Pardon. Macaulay thought so, and the old ballad was emphatic about it. Further, the usually reliable *Records of York Castle* state that "Charles II christened him Swift Nick"—a very strong point indeed. Unfortunately the same *Records* give his Christian name as John, which is probably wrong. Then it is a fact that he was brought up for trial (with Jane Nelson) in 1676—the date Defoe ascribed to the ride; but here the opponents of the Nevison theory point out that he was not acquitted but actually condemned to death. Finally, he was renowned in his lifetime as an exceptionally fine horseman; "Nevison's Leap," near Ferrybridge, bears testimony to this.

Such is the evidence in favour of Nevison. Pretty slight, isn't it? Better than Turpin's claim—at least he was old enough—but hardly convincing. And who was the Lord Mayor of York at the time? Where are the records of the trial? No answer. And the evidence raked up against it is pretty damning. According to one seventeenth-century account Mr Nicks, after being acquitted, was given a commission in Lord Montcastle's regiment in Ireland, "and afterwards lived very honest." That wasn't our Nevison, was it? And the chapbook lives of Nevison, including the hot-from-the-press *Yorkshire Robber*, have no more to say about any ride to York than has the *Genuine History of the Life of Turpin*.

Well, if it wasn't Nevison, who was it? Did anyone ride to York? Was it possible, anyway? A hundred and ninety miles in a day seems good going.... But we can't dismiss it on that account. The ride was a physical possibility, all right. A greater distance has been covered in even shorter time by a number of horsemen. That the ride was accomplished on one horse is less likely, but that wouldn't have been necessary. The rider had to stop at several inns to " 'bate " the animal—and himself—and he must have been sufficiently well known in some of these to be able to change mounts.

A possible clue to the mystery is to be found in Fuller's *Worthies of England*. A certain John Lepton, Esquire, it is said, made a wager that he would ride between London and York six times on successive days—three times each way—completing each journey before sunset. He started out on May 20, 1606, and collected his money on May 25—" to the greater praise of his strength in acting, than to his discretion in undertaking it," is Fuller's dry comment.

Is it suggested, then, that the worthy John Lepton was Mr Nicks? Not at all. The point about the story is that a ride from London to York had for long been regarded as the acid test of horsemanship. Lepton's wager was typical. Now we know that the old chroniclers of the highwaymen were always emphasizing the equestrian prowess of their heroes; and we know too that they were not above grafting all sorts of stories into their " true and genuine " biographies. What could be more natural, then, than a story of a daring ride to York being attached to a highwayman?

Macaulay himself suggested as much at a dinner given by the Marquis of Lansdowne. According to the historian the legend of the ride was at least three hundred years old—that is, more than a century before the date given by Defoe—and had been fathered on to a succession of highwaymen.

The truth about the ride to York remains a mystery, but there is nothing mysterious about Black Bess. Bless her broken heart, she never even existed! It is true that it has been suggested that the Black Horse Inn in Broadway was named after her; but, alas, that famous old inn was doing a good trade while Turpin was still cutting up meat in Whitechapel.

Black Bess was not Ainsworth's invention, however. That indefatigable chronicler of the roads Charles G. Harper—one of Ainsworth's sternest critics, incidentally—has unearthed a ballad which found its way into print nine years before *Rookwood* was published. The first verse runs:

> Bold Turpin upon Hounslow Heath
>   His black mare Bess bestrode,
> When he saw a Bishop's coach and four
>   Sweeping along the road.

Vaguely familiar, isn't it? Perhaps this version is better known:

> Bold Turpin vunce, on Hounslow Heath
> His bold mare Bess bestrode-er;
> Ven there he see'd the Bishop's coach
> A-coming along the road-er.

Yes, Sam Weller, of course. And let us be fair to Dickens: he did not try to pass it off as his own this time. All the same, he omitted to mention where he got it from, so we shall have to do that for him. He read it in a story called "Harry Halter" included in Horace Smith's *Gaieties and Gravities*, published in 1825.

Harper draws our attention to the lower-case "b" in the word "black" in the second line of the original version, and drily remarks that "it was reserved for Ainsworth to discover the worth of alliteration and the demand it made for two capital B's."

There is an added interest about this ballad. It is too long to be given here in full—Sam Weller thought the same—but the substance is as follows. Turpin stopped the coach, killed the Bishop's chaplain, and relieved the Bishop himself of his valuables. Then he whispered to his mare ("who luckily wasn't fagged")—

> "You must gallop fast and far, my dear,
> Or I shall be surely scragg'd!"

Then, believe it or not—

> He never drew bit, nor stopp'd to bait,
>   Nor walk'd up hill or down,
> Until he came to Gloucester's gate,
>   Which is the Assizes town.
> Full eighty miles in one dark night,
>   He made his black mare fly,
> And walk'd into Court at nine o'clock
>   To swear an Alibi—

without even waiting to be arrested, apparently.

Is not this Defoe's Mr Nicks all over again, with Dick Turpin once more in the saddle? But why Gloucester? Harper's suggestion is as good as any: that the poet was stuck in the last stanza for a rhyme to " Sheriff Foster."

There is another story—but enough! If we start delving any deeper into the archives we shall find ourselves willy-nilly in the mournful company of the learned historians.

CHAPTER SIXTEEN
War Criminals

THE brief reign of James II, and the accession to the throne of William and Mary, meant nothing to the highwaymen. So long as the country didn't fall into the hands of those killjoy Republicans again, it didn't matter much who was king. More important in its effect on the profession, however, was the War in Europe.

Wars show up on graphs of the history of crime as clearly as on a date-chart. As always, there were many deserters; as always, deserters became criminals because they were already fugitives from the Law; as always, the Government had not the intelligence to grant an amnesty after the War was over.

In actual fact the crime statistics shot up more sharply than ever after the signing of the Treaty of Ryswick. This was because of the wholesale unemployment that followed the disbandment of the greater part of the Army. The deserters had got on the road first—but the more loyal of the ex-comrades were soon represented among the highwaymen.

This influx of ex-soldiers did not raise the tone of the profession, which had already dropped sadly since the Cavalier days. Yet there were some similarities between the two periods. The philosophy of many a disbanded and disillusioned soldier of 1697 was little different from that of the ex-Royalist of 1643, who wrote:

> To beg is base, as base as pick a purse;
> To cheat more base of all theft—that is worse.
> Nor beg nor cheat will I—I scorn the same—
> But while I live, maintain a soldier's name.
> I'll purse it, I—the highway is my hope;
> His heart's not great that fears a little rope.

Fairly typical of the deserter class of highwaymen was John Withers. Fighting in Flanders taught him to hold life cheap, and he thought nothing of killing a man for the sake of a few pounds. In the case which led to his arrest it was only a few shillings. This happened after Withers and a companion had unsuccessfully held up a gentleman and his servant near Beaconsfield. The latter resisted, and the highwayman only just got away. Withers's horse was shot under him, and he made his escape sharing the saddle of his accomplice. The gentleman and his man gave chase, and in these circumstances they naturally began to gain on the pair. Seeing that they had no chance of getting clear with only one horse for the two of them, Withers and his friend took to their heels across country. By this means they shook off the pursuit, and continued their way on foot in the direction of London.

Outside the capital, to get a little much-needed money the pair waylaid a postman, and robbed him of eight shillings. As the robbery was carried out in broad daylight, and neither Withers nor his friend was even masked, they took the simple precaution of eliminating the only actual witness of the affair. To be exact, Withers cut the postman's throat. As an added precaution they buried the body in a near-by stream, weighting it by cutting the corpse open and filling the stomach with stones.

Withers was, as has been said, typical of one class of highwaymen. Still, the deserters from the Army did not hold a monopoly in barbarism on the road. However hard some of the old chroniclers try to conceal it, when it came to sheer brutality some of the sons of what they called " good families " could put their less-favoured colleagues in the shade. For example, take the case of William Cady.

The qualifications for the highway profession did not include a University degree, but at least one graduate graced the road with his presence. William Cady, B.A. (Cantab.), the son of a famous surgeon, was born a gentleman, and continued to dress like one and look like one. Thus, when he came upon Viscount Dundee crossing Bagshot Heath on horseback, accompanied only by two footmen, Cady had no difficulty in persuading his lordship that he was a gentleman. A gentleman in distress, too; he explained to the peer that he had been robbed by highwaymen only a few minutes previously, and indicated the direction in which the men had gone. His lordship promptly despatched his two footmen to try to catch the scoundrels—and once the men were out of sight and earshot young Cady put a bullet through his lordship's horse and robbed him of a gold watch, a gold snuff-box, and sixty guineas in cash. As a result of this the *London Gazette* shortly afterwards published a proclamation offering £100 reward for Cady's apprehension.

But William Cady could be brutal as well as artful. One cannot help feeling that his University education was largely wasted when one reads of the treatment he meted out to a lady who tried to cheat him of her wedding-ring. She and her husband, a well-to-do hop-merchant, had been happily married for twenty years, and that ring was of great sentimental value to her. But Cady had no time for sentiment. He wanted the ring, and was deaf to her pleas. Then the lady had an inspiration. She took a chance on her appendix and swallowed the ring.

Cady's next act is described by his biographer with an admirable economy of words:

" He shot her through the head, ripped her open, and took the ring out of her body in the presence of her husband."

William Cady was finally executed in 1687. His behaviour in Court was very unseemly. At the Old Bailey he called the Lord Mayor and the Recorder " a couple of old almswomen."

Highwaymen generally were not noted for their originality. The ancient tradition of appearing on a horse, armed and masked, in a lonely stretch of road, was followed like a ritual. Even the words of the challenge did not vary. Full credit, therefore, to Jonathan Simpson (no relation to Old Mob), for bringing a little innovation to the profession. The son of a wealthy Cornish merchant, as a youth Simpson was apprenticed to a Bristol linen-draper and made a good marriage. But somehow he got on the road, and there he stayed until the Great Frost of 1689, which lasted for thirteen weeks. Ice on the roads made travelling dangerous, and there was a temporary lull in business. Instead of journeying in carriages and on horseback, people of means stayed in London and resorted to the frozen Thames, which became quite fashionable. Jonathan Simpson followed his clients. The price of skates rose sharply, but he bought a pair, and joined the well-to-do in their winter sports. Of course Simpson had to adapt his methods to the circumstances. The ice was no place for this stand-and-deliver business, but demanded a speedier method of approach. After a bit of practice he found that the simplest way was to sneak up from behind, and trip your victims up. Once down, they were easy to rob—and then you just skated away while they were struggling to get up.

Our skating highwayman has another claim to fame. After being caught, tried, and convicted, he was reprieved at the very last moment, while waiting for Jack Ketch to adjust his collar at Tyburn. This in itself was an unusual occurrence, and one which the Tyburn crowd took pretty badly. But some of Simpson's friends, doubtless with more than idle curiosity, asked him afterwards how he manged it. He said he knew nothing about it, and that the whole thing was still a mystery to him.

"But did you not think of a reprieve when you stood at Tyburn?" he was asked.

"No more than I thought of my dying day," he replied.

More in the tradition of the old school of highwaymen was "Captain" James Whitney. We have kept him till last because he was probably the most interesting highwayman of the period. He was bold and gallant and a bit of a gentleman, but his rank must remain within quotes. He was not an ex-officer, nor even an ex-soldier. He was one of those "Captains" to whom Francis Jackson referred in his *Recantation*, his only claim to the rank being that he led one of the most daring bands of highwaymen of the latter part of the seventeenth century. But he had many of the redeeming qualities of the old Cavalier Captains, and there is more humour and less brutality about his exploits than we find in most of the chronicles of the period.

There are a number of chapbook biographies of James Whitney, the best being a quaint tract called *The Jacobite Robber*. The significance of the title is not apparent from the contents. Whitney seemed to bear no special grudge against the House of Orange, nor do we read of his ever having done anything to further the cause of the Old Pretender. Indeed, not till the end of this little biography is there any mention of Jacobite plots—and then the reference is to an offer of Whitney's to expose such a plot in return for a pardon! Of that more later. If he was not a good Jacobite he was a very successful robber, and the chapbook has some lively tales of his adventures on the road.

Whitney was born of "mean, contemptible parentage" in the county of Hertfordshire. Like so many highwaymen, his first job was as a butcher's apprentice—although why this trade should have been so provident in recruits for the road is a complete mystery. Young James was not a very willing worker, and after a short while he got the sack. What he did then is another mystery; but it must have been something more lucrative than carving meat, for the next we hear of him is as a full-blown landlord of an inn.

Innkeepers in the seventeenth and eighteenth centuries had to keep on the right side of the outlaw as well as of the law. Not only were highwaymen good customers, but they were quick to take offence if it was indicated that their custom was not desired. And an offended highwayman could play the very devil with a small roadside business. It was all very well for the Government to warn innkeepers of the gravity of harbouring highwaymen, but no one was going to protect them if they didn't. James Whitney fell into line with most landlords.

For a time he did quite well for himself. The highwaymen were hard drinkers and good payers. It did not worry him where the money came from, so long as it landed up in his till. And he liked their company. They liked this landlord, too. He was their type—just the sort of man for the road, in fact. As his biographer put it, he was "notably stored with all those ingredients and qualifications that are requisite to fit a man for such a vocation." They told him as much, though doubtless in less polished language. But he just smiled and shook his head. He was doing all right—thanks to the highwaymen. "Whereas," the biographer sagely observes, "should he trade for himself, and scour the highways to the tune of 'Dammee, stand and deliver,' he must certainly at one time or another make a pilgrimage to Tyburn, and swinging in a rope he had a mortal aversion to, because his prophetical grandmother had formerly told him it was a dry sort of death."

A very wise grandmother, and a wiser grandson for following her advice. With such a practical way of looking at things there seemed no reason why Whitney should not live to a ripe old age behind his bar while the highwaymen went one by one to the gallows. And so he might have done if he hadn't been possessed with an imp of mischief and a desire for excitement and adventure. He fought against it, but it was a losing battle. They were a merry crowd, these highwaymen. He liked them in the inn—yet he was always conscious of a difference between him and them. He had their confidence, but he remained outside their profession. And they were only too ready to welcome him into their society. They pointed out " the meanness and servile condition of his present calling—how he was obliged to stand cap in hand to every pitiful rascal that came to spend sixpence in his house; that with all his care and diligence he only got a little poor contemptible pittance, scarce sufficient to pay his brewer and baker."

Now, this, of course, was not strictly accurate, but Whitney was too good a business man to contradict it. And there was certainly something in that cap-in-hand business. Moreover, on the practical advantages of changing his vocation the highwaymen were eloquent. " He would find money come flowing in like a spring tide upon him; he would live delicately, eat and drink of the best, and, in short, get more in an hour than now he did by nicking and frothing and wrong reckonings for a whole twelvemonth together." The landlord took this last in good humour, and it was not far from the truth. As for the gallows, his customers went on, " A man of courage and bravery ought never to be afraid of it, and, should the worst come to the worst, better gentlemen by far than himself had made a journey to the other world in their shoes and stockings."

At last Whitney was won over, though more by his own desires than by the allurements of the highwaymen. He sold the inn, bought a fine horse, and joined them on the road. Their judgment of his " ingredients and qualifications " was fully borne out. He quickly showed that he had inherited "all the courage, boldness, and dexterity of the famous Claude Du Vall and the Golden Farmer, and the rest of his other noble predecessors."

Whitney's first victim was "a jolly red-faced son of the Church, bravely mounted, with a large canonical rose in his ecclesiastical hat and his gown fluttering in the wind." Whitney met him about two miles from St Albans, and addressed him as follows:

"Reverend sir, the gentlemen of your coat having, in all conscience, enough preached the edifying doctrine of passive obedience and non-resistance, and now I am fully resolved to try the experiment, whether you believe your own doctrine, and whether you are able to practise it. Therefore, worthy sir, in the name of the above-mentioned passive obedience and non-resistance, make no opposition, I beseech you, but deliver up the filthy lucre you carry about you."

At least that is what the author of *The Jacobite Robber* says he said, but of course he was not present to take it down in shorthand.

The jolly son of the Church let Whitney down by showing no inclination to passive obedience, though he failed to put up any physical resistance. But of course Whitney's pistols might have been responsible for that. Anyway, the highwayman "soon eased him of his mammon," and also his new sacerdotal habit, and left him to his contemplations.

But "Captain" Whitney was not especially inimical to the clergy. It was the rich ones he was after. Scarcely had he left this prosperous cleric when he came across a humble village parson clad in a tattered gown and who looked as if he hadn't had a square meal for a month. Clearly there was nothing here for Whitney to take. So he gave instead—not only some money, but the "spick-and-span sacerdotal habit" he had acquired a short time previously.

There are many more instances of practical socialism in Whitney's career. It was Robin Hood all over again, with a dash of Captain Hind thrown in. On Hounslow Heath Whitney held up a usurer, who pleaded poverty and a large family, but to no avail. When forced to deliver, he ventured to say some unkind things about looking forward to seeing Whitney riding backward in a cart on the way to Tyburn.

Riding backward? The words gave Whitney an idea. It was not an original idea, as we have seen, but it always raised a good laugh. He just sat the money-lender on his horse the wrong way round, tied his hands and then his legs under him, and cracked his whip.

Whitney was a staunch upholder of the unwritten laws of his profession. Once, on Bagshot Heath, he accosted a prosperous-looking gentleman and demanded his purse.

" Sir, 'tis well you spoke first, for I was just going to say the same thing to you," said the man coolly.

" Why, are you a gentleman thief, then? " said Whitney.

The other replied that he was, and Whitney lowered his pistols. There was still some honour among thieves.

That evening Whitney went to a near-by inn to put up for the night. Among the other customers there he was surprised to see this same man. The latter did not recognize Whitney, for he had been disguised at the time of their encounter; and something—perhaps intuition—stopped him from introducing himself again. As a result of this he was able to overhear the man telling another customer how he had saved a hundred pounds that morning by posing as a highwayman. The third party was greatly impressed. He himself, he said, was carrying " a considerable sum of money," and was worried about the dangers of being robbed. Would the gentleman who had outwitted the highwayman so neatly mind if he travelled in his company on the following day? The gentleman was delighted with the compliment, and after arrangements were made the pair retired for the night. So did Whitney. But he was up early the next morning.

He gave them a quarter of an hour's start, and then went after them.

He wore a different disguise this time, and the other self-styled " gentleman thief " again failed to recognize him.

" We were going to say the same to you," was his glib reply when Whitney demanded their purses.

" Were you so? " he said pleasantly. " And are you of my profession, then? "

They assured him they were.

"If you are," he told them earnestly, "I suppose you remember the old proverb, 'Two of a trade can never agree'; so you must not expect any favour on that score. But to be plain, gentlemen, the trick will do no longer; I know you very well, and must have your hundred pounds, sir—and your 'considerable sum,' sir, let it be what it will, or I shall make bold to send a brace of bullets through each of your heads. You, Mr Highwayman, should have kept your secret a little longer, and not have boasted so soon of having outwitted a thief."

Although most of Whitney's recorded deeds were single-handed affairs, it is pretty well established that he was the captain of a fair-sized gang. There were rewards offered for most of them as well as for himself. Perhaps he realized that they could not get away with it for ever; perhaps he remembered again what his prophetic grandmother had said about hanging being "a dry sort of death." Anyway, once, after robbing a peer whom he recognized as one of the King's closest advisers, he suggested to his lordship that he would take thirty of his followers to fight for the King in Flanders if he would grant them a free pardon for all past offences. Before his lordship had time to reply Whitney whistled, and at once his troops appeared on the road. But the offer was rejected.

Whitney was twice in Newgate. The first time he escaped despite the handicap of a 4-lb. weight on each leg. But his freedom was short-lived. He was betrayed to the authorities by one Madam Cosens, the *patrona* of a bawdy-house in Milford Lane, off the Strand, where Whitney was wont to spend his leisure hours. The house was very disorderly that night, for he fought for an hour before he was finally overpowered.

Whitney was a showman to the end. While awaiting his trial he sent for his tailor, and had him make "a rich embroidered suit, with perug and hat, worth £100." Despite these preparations for his death, however, he made strenuous efforts to get a pardon. This was where the Jacobite part came in. In a petition to the King he offered to disclose a plot to murder him while hunting in Windsor Forest, which would surely be carried out otherwise. His Majesty was not so naïve as to accept this, and survived Whitney by several years. Whitney tried again. He offered to raise a troop of eighty cavalry to fight against the French. It was probably within his power to do this, but again the offer was refused.

Whitney was executed in February 1693. "He seem to dye very penitent," concluded his biographer, "and was an hour and a halfe in the cart before being turned off."

James Whitney was a gangster, and in this respect he was representative of his times. His followers included at least a proportion of deserters from the Forces; and the disbandment of the Armies of Flanders a few years after his death led to the formation of increasing bodies of armed highwaymen on the same pattern. This gang element in the profession persisted well into the following century.

But the eighteenth century deserves to start with a new chapter. And before we continue the biographical history of the highwaymen this seems a suitable point at which to pause for a little and consider some more general aspects of the profession.

CHAPTER SEVENTEEN

In Old Newgate

MOST of the stories told so far have had abrupt endings. Adventures on the road have been described with varying amounts of detail, but the climax has in most cases been dismissed in a single sentence: he was committed to Newgate and executed at Tyburn, or words to that effect.

Newgate was the highwayman's prison. It had a long history, and was waiting for our highwayman when he emerged at the beginning of the seventeenth century. We do not know exactly when it first began to take in guests, but the gate itself was built about the middle of the twelfth century. It was probably first used as a gaol during the reign of King John, and the historian Stow has dug up a record dated 1241 which tells us that " the Jews of Norwich were hanged for circumcising a Christian child; their house, called the Thor, was pulled down and destroyed; Aron, the son of Abraham, a Jew, at London, and the other Jews were constrained to pay twenty thousand marks at two terms in the year, or else be kept perpetual prisoners in *Newgate of London*, and in other prisons." Fourteen years later came the first reported escape from the gaol, for which Henry III imposed a fine on the city of London amounting to 3,000 marks, which was one way of raising money.

Newgate was a royal prison until 1400, when Henry IV made a present of it to the citizens of the capital. From that time on its history is fairly well documented. It was anything but exclusive. Almost anyone could get into Newgate, and during the next four centuries it housed a motley collection of murderers, thieves, forgers, debtors, and political and religious offenders. The latter class included both Roman Catholics and nonconformists, though rarely together; it depended upon which sect the Church of England happened to be persecuting at the time. During the period of the Commonwealth it provided temporary accommodation for many Royalists, who were succeeded after 1660 by similar numbers of Roundheads.

The prison was partially destroyed in the Great Fire of 1666, and it had already suffered many epidemics of infectious disease. Even by contemporary standards prisons were considered overcrowded, under-ventilated, dirty, verminous, and lacking in sanitation. Nobody did anything about it, of course, except after such incidents as the following:

"About this time (*i.e.*, 1577), when the Judges sate at the Assizes in Oxford, and one Rowland Jenks a Bookseller was question'd for speaking opprobrious Words against the Queen, suddenly they were surpriz'd with a pestilent Savour, whether rising from the noisome Smell of the Prisoners, or from the damp of the Ground, is uncertain; but all that were there present, almost every one, within Forty Hours died, except Women and Children; and the Contagion went no farther. There died Robert Bell, Lord Chief Baron, Robert d'Oyley, Sir William Babington D'Oyly, Sheriff of Oxfordshire, Harcourt, Weyman, Pettiplace, most of 'em Men in this Tract; Barham the famous Lawyer, almost all the Jurors, and Three Hundred other more or less."

That was in Oxford, but it was typical of all prisons of the time. When it was discovered that infectious disease was no respecter of persons some steps were taken to improve conditions. They could not have been very effective, for nearly two hundred years later, we are told:

"Newgate was rendered so infectious by an uncommon number of prisoners, confined together in close unwholesome apartments, that the very air they breathed acquired a pestilential degree of putrefaction. This contagion, brought by the foul cloaths and infected bodies of the criminals into the Court of the Old Bailey, at the Session in May, produced a pestilential fever amongst the audience." According to the *Gentleman's Magazine* fatal casualties included Sir Sam Pennant, Lord Mayor, Charles Clark, Esq., Baron of the Exchequer, Sir Thomas Abney, Justice of the Common Pleas, Sir Daniel Lambert, Alderman, and other notables, as well as two barristers and eight members of the jury.

One of the best descriptions of conditions in Newgate at this

In Old Newgate

time is contained in a poem published in 1705 entitled *A Glimpse of Hell; or, a Short Description of the Common Side of Newgate*, apparently written by an inmate. It is too long to be quoted in full, but here is a selection from it.

> Of which I will a prospect give,
> And tell you how the captives live,
> That on the Common Side are penn'd,
> Till debts are paid, or life doth end.
> They trouble not the upholsterer's trade,
> Their beds are by the joiner made,
> Of sturdy oak, that will not fail,
> Except a softer board of deal,
> That is reserv'd for quality,
> For softness, not formality.

At meal-times—

> Some hungry souls, with scarce a rag on,
> Cut, slash, and eat, like hungry dragon;
> And grease themselves from jaw to groyn,
> For napkins are as scarce as coin.

For those with some money there is beer and tobacco and choice of "ladies, pritty, yet not nice." Among these more fortunate members of the community—

> When pots on pots are multiply'd,
> Some merry, others stupifi'd,
> Some laugh, some cry, some fight, some play,
> Some curse, some swear, some preach, some pray,
> Till, having drank away their reason,
> Their wits begin to be in season;
> And every single word they spoke
> Stunk both of Logick and of Smoak.

Newgate had another fiery cleansing in 1762, in which two prisoners were burned alive. The damage to the buildings, however, was relatively slight. Shortly after this Parliament voted £50,000 for a new building, and in 1770 the Lord Mayor laid the foundation stone. In 1778 the architect told the Government that an additional £40,000 would be needed for the completion of the work. Two years later the gaol was burnt down in the Gordon Riots.

Rebuilding began immediately after, and nine years later the philanthropist John Howard paid a visit to the gaol. This is what he found:

"In three or four rooms there were near one hundred and fifty women crowded together, many young creatures with the old and hardened, some of whom had been confined upwards of two years: on the men's side, likewise, there were many boys of twelve or fourteen years of age, some almost naked. In the men's infirmary there were only seven iron bedsteads; and, at my last visit, there being twenty sick, some of them, naked with sores, in a miserable condition, lay on the floor with only a rug. There were four sick in the infirmary for women, which is only fifteen feet and a half by twelve; has but one window and no bedsteads; sewers offensive; prison not whitewashed."

The eventual reform of Newgate was accomplished almost entirely by the efforts of Elizabeth Fry. This period of its history, however, lies outside the highwayman era, and therefore must remain outside this book.

A curious ceremony of Old Newgate was the ringing of the "Execution Bell." This dated from 1612, when a Merchant Tailor named Robert Dowe died leaving an annuity of twenty-six shillings and eightpence to the Vicar and Churchwardens of St Sepulchre's Church, in return for which they were to ensure that two solemn exhortations were pronounced to condemned prisoners in Newgate on the night before each execution. (As executions seem to have come round pretty regularly, this was scarcely over-payment.) The proclamations were uttered by the sexton of the church, who went round with a handbell. One of these bells can be seen in the church. His detail was to "come down in the night-time, and likewise early in the morning, to the window of the prison where they lie, and there ringing certain tolls with a hand-bell appointed for the purpose, he doth afterwards (in most Christian manner) put them in mind of their present condition and ensuing execution, desiring them to be prepared therefor, as they ought to be. While they are in the cart, and brought before the walls of the Church, at the beginning of their journey to Tyburn, there he shall stand ready with the same bell, and, after certain tolls, rehearseth an appointed prayer, desiring all the people there present to pray for them. The beadle also of Merchant Taylors Hall hath an honest stipend allowed to see that this is duly done."

The first proclamation began as follows:

THE EXHORTATION TO BE PRONOUNCED TO THE CONDEMNED PRISONERS IN NEWGATE, THE NIGHT BEFORE THEIR EXECUTION

> You Prisoners that are within,
> Who for Wickedness and Sin,

after many mercies shewn you, are now appointed to dye tomorrow in the forenoon: give ear and understand, that tomorrow morning the greatest bell of St Sepulchre's shall toll for you, in form and manner of a passing bell, as used to be tolled for those that are at the point of death. To the end that all godly people hearing that bell, and knowing that it is for you, going to your deaths, may be stirred up heartily to pray to God to bestow His Grace and Mercy upon you while you live: I beseech you, for Jesus Christ, his sake, to keep this night in watching and prayer for the salvation of your own souls, while there is yet time and place for mercy . . .

The second proclamation was in a similar vein. It is also recorded that the Church presented each condemned man with a bunch of flowers as he passed on his way to Tyburn.

In 1783, when the place of execution was changed from Tyburn to the Old Bailey itself, the ceremonial had to be modified. The two proclamations were amalgamated and put in verse form, doubtless to help the bellman to remember the words. The new proclamation was delivered at midnight, and ran as follows:

> All you that in the condemned hole do lie,
> Prepare you, for to-morrow you shall die!
> Watch all, and pray, the hour is drawing near
> That you before the Almighty must appear:
> Examine well yourselves, in time repent,
> That you may not t' eternal flames be sent.
> And when St Sepulchre's bell to-morrow tolls,
> The Lord above have mercy on your souls.
> *Past twelve o'clock* !

Incidentally, the ringing of the great bell of St Sepulchre's on execution mornings was continued until 1890, when a resident of a near-by hotel made a successful complaint about the noise.

Accommodation in Old Newgate Prison was divided into three classes: the Press Yard, the Master's Side, and the

Common Side. The first of these, and the most exclusive, has a history of its own and will have a chapter of its own. Of the other two we have a vivid description in the *Memoirs of the Right Villanous Jack Hall*, highwayman, published in 1708.

"Now, as concerning the humours of the Master Side," he begins, "when a scholar in iniquity comes there by virtue of a *mittimus*, he is delivered up to the paws of the wolves, lurking continually in the lodge for a prey; where, as soon as he is adorned with a pair of iron boots, and from thence conducted (provided he has *gilt*) over the way, to Hell; for, really no place has a nearer resemblance of the eternal receptacle of punishment than the Master Side: for the cellar, where poor relentless sinners are guzzelling in the midst of debauchery, and new invented oaths, which rumble like thunder through their filthy throats, is a lamentable den of horror and darkness, there being no light but what they procure from the help of one of that greasie company, whose mystery is, by a subtle metamorphosis, to turn night into day with what they get from butcher and kitchen wenches' industrious savings."

Every night at nine o'clock, Hall goes on, "they are hurry'd up before their drivers, like so many Turkish slaves, to their kennels, which are join'd like so many huts, as tho' they took their order from martial discipline. In these several apartments both males and females are confin'd till they distil a little oil of *argentum* for the favour of going into the cellar, to spend their ill got coin with speed, to make the old proverb good, Lightly come, lightly go."

Now Hall comes to the Common Side. "Those scholars that come here," he says, "having nothing to depend on but the charity of the foundation, in which side very exact rules are observ'd; for, as soon as a prisoner comes into the turnkey's hand, three knocks are given at the stair foot, as a signal a collegian is coming up: which harmony makes those convicts that stand for the *garnish* as joyful as one knock, the signal of the baker's coming every morning, does those poor prisoners who, for want of friends, have nothing else to subsist on but bread and water."

Garnish, as it was called, was the admission fee to Newgate. In those days going to prison was an expensive business. First the newcomer had to pay sixpence to the "trunchion officers," who then handed him over to the old lags, "who hover about him like so many crows about a piece of carrion." The fee was six shillings and eightpence—and if the new arrival can't pay he forfeits his clothes. Barely has he been relieved of this sum when the cook comes along for threepence for dressing the "charity meat." He is quickly followed by the two "swabbers," who demand three halfpence apiece for cleaning the place out, which was a sinecure in any case. If the new "collegian" has anything left after all this he can, on payment of a shilling, gain admission to the Middle Ward, which, says Hall, "to give the devils their due, is kept very neat and clean." In the Middle Ward he has to pay a further one shilling and fourpence to his comrades, and "then he is free of the College and matriculated."

According to the *Gentleman's Magazine*, "garnish" was abolished in 1752, but we find references to this custom in the reports of Parliamentary Committees in 1814 and 1836.

If the newcomer could not afford the Middle Ward, Hall goes on, he must be content with the Lower Ward, "where the tight slovenly dogs lye upon ragged blankets, amidst unutterable filth, trampling on the floor, the lice crackling under their feet, make such a noise as walking on shells which are strew'd over garden walks. To this nasty place is adjoining the Stone Hold, where convicts lye till a free pardon grants 'em liberty from tribulation; but, not making good use of mercy, come tumbling headlong in again. This low dungeon is a real house of meagre looks and ill smells; for lice, drink, and tobacco is all the compound."

All seventeenth- and eighteenth-century accounts of Newgate make special reference to the way debtors and convicts waste what money they have left on drinking and especially gambling. Jack Hall, who was a bit of a philosopher as well as a highwayman, offers a very reasonable explanation for this improvidence. "They huddle up their life as a thing of no use, and wear it out like an old suit, the faster the better," he says; "and he that deceives the time at cards and dice, thinks he deceived it best, and best spends it."

Jack Hall takes us all round the prison, and even gives us a peep into "Jack Ketch, his kitchen, where, in pitch, tar, and oil, he boils the quarters of those traitors who deserve to suffer for the several sorts of High Treason." Finally we come to the women's quarters in the Common Side, "where there are a troop of hell cats lying head and tail together, in a dismal, nasty, dark room, having no place to divert themselves but at the grate, adjoining to the foot passage under Newgate, where passengers may, with admiration and pity, hear them swear extempore, being so shamefully vers'd in that most odious prophanation of Heaven that vollies of oaths are discharg'd through their detestable throats whilst asleep. And, if any of their acquaintance gives them money, then they jump into their cellar to melt it, which is scarce so large as Covent Garden cage, and the stock therein not much exceeding those peddling vituallers who fetch their drink in tubs every brewing day."

Such was Newgate at the beginning of the eighteenth century. Now for the Press Yard.

CHAPTER EIGHTEEN

"So You Won't Talk?"

WILLIAM SPIGGOT was a very ordinary highwayman. He was one of the motley crowd that infested Finchley Common at the beginning of the eighteenth century, and his career was undistinguished. Indeed, right up to the time of his arrest he had not done anything good or bad enough to earn him the barest mention in these exclusive pages. But when he stood in the dock and heard his indictment he did something—or, rather, he didn't do something—that earns him a high place in our Roll of Dishonour.

William Spiggot refused to plead.

Now when a prisoner "stood mute," as the Law termed it, there could be only two reasons: either he was dumb, or he didn't want to speak. Of course, the Law did not put it quite so simply as that. The point at issue was defined as being "whether his standing mute arises from his contempt of Court, or be really an infirmity under which he labours from the hands of God." The job of determining this was entrusted to "an inquest of officers, that is of twelve persons who happen to be by." If this "inquest" decided the affliction was indeed an Act of God, continued the Law, the Court should proceed as if the prisoner had pleaded not guilty. If, on the other hand, they came to the conclusion that God had had nothing to do with it, but the man was just plain cussed—then the prisoner should be despatched to a particularly grim place called the Press Yard.

For reasons that will shortly become apparent, the Press Yard would have been a pretty deserted spot if it had had to rely solely on wilful mutes for tenants. The Keeper of Newgate Prison thought the same. There were several rooms looking on to the Yard, and he let them off to the more affluent of the inmates of the prison. To make the offer more attractive he added to the advantages of superior accommodation a promise of very relaxed discipline. This was a big draw, and the Keeper never wanted for applicants. Indeed, one of his tenants—who later wrote an anonymous *History of the Press Yard*—complained bitterly that " Two, sometimes Three, lie in a Bed, and some Chambers have three or four Beds in them, contrary to several Acts of Parliament." But the Keeper held himself above the Law. The Press Yard, he said, was not part of the prison at all, but belonged to the Governor's house.

There was no Rent Restriction Act in Newgate, and the Keeper charged his tenants eleven shillings a week. In addition, each newcomer was required to pay twenty guineas' key money. Of course he never got the key; but in spite of the overcrowding, he was able to make himself pretty comfortable. The Press Yard became a sort of club. Beer could be had in plenty (at a price), diversions included a private skittle alley, and members could invite their girl friends (also, presumably, at a price).

Such, then, was the Press Yard at Newgate. Only occasionally was it used for the purpose for which it had been designed—and named. This was for the punishment legally known as the *peine forte et dure*—a comparatively mild description. Generally it was simply called " the Press." It was specially reserved for prisoners who refused to plead.

Now William Spiggot was indicted together with another highwayman, one Thomas Phillips. It created a bit of a stir in Court, therefore, when both these worthies " stood mute." The phrase is a legal one, and not to be taken too literally. It does not mean that the prisoners feigned dumbness. Spiggot, at least, was vociferous in his muteness. He declared to the Court that he would not plead unless his horse was restored to him.

Of course he was wasting his breath. Since the reign of William and Mary the Law had been uncommonly clear on this point. Whoever apprehended a highwayman, it said, was entitled to possession of " his horse and furniture." The only exception to this rule was when the horse was proved to have been stolen from someone else; in that case it had to be restored to its former owner, which was just bad luck on the apprehender. But however he had got it the highwayman forfeited all rights to the animal as soon as he was arrested.

Highwaymen were being apprehended pretty frequently in those days, and, as they usually obtained their horses the easy way, this question of ownership was constantly cropping up. There were plenty of disputes between the apprehender and the professed owner, who was required to prove his claim. The highwayman, who was usually too busy thinking about Tyburn to take much interest, generally let the pair fight it out between themselves. Anyway, he knew he couldn't get anything out of it. The Law on this point was well known.

And, of course, William Spiggot knew it as well as the next man.

It did not take the " inquest of officers " long to absolve God from all responsibility in the matter of Spiggot's eloquent muteness, and the Law took its course. The Judge told Spiggot in good eighteenth-century English that he had had it. Still Spiggot refused to plead without his horse. His Honour warned him of the consequences, but the highwayman was adamant. Tom Phillips, it seems, was taking a similar attitude, though the records tell us nothing about any horse in his case. But the upshot of it was very definite. Spiggot and Phillips were sentenced to the Press.

Here is one version of the form of the sentence:—

" You shall go to the place from whence you came, and there being stripped naked and laid flat upon your back on the floor, with a napkin about your middle to hide your privy members, and a cloth on your face, then the Press is to be laid upon you, with as much weight as, or rather more than, you can bear. You are to have three morsels of barley-bread in twenty-four hours; a draught of water from the next puddle near the gaol, but not running water. The second day two morsels and the same water, with an increase of weight, and so to the third day until you expire."

We said the Press wasn't used much.

There was only one Press at Newgate, and it was Phillips's honour. At the last moment, however, he suddenly found his tongue and pleaded not guilty. (He had a comparatively pleasant death at Tyburn.) Spiggot remained deaf—and dumb

—to all the Judge's warnings, and was led off to the Press Yard. Our picture shows what happened there. The Press was a simple instrument, consisting only of a board of wood with weights piled up on it. Spiggot started off with 350 lb. on his chest, and that was just about as much as he could bear. After half an hour another 50 lb. was put on, and that was more than he could bear. He gave in.

Like Phillips, Spiggot was given the chance to plead again—although there was no obligation on the Court to permit this. Once the sentence of the Press had been pronounced the prisoner could not demand to be released just because he felt like it. However, clemency was exercised in the case of Spiggot, and he was allowed to return to the dock. The story has a happy ending. He pleaded not guilty, was convicted, and accompanied Phillips to Tyburn.

It has already been emphasized that the Press at Newgate was not used very often. It is hoped that by now the reader will be wondering (unless he's read the same books as I have) why it was ever used at all, and what lunatic of a fellow this Spiggot was to put up with half an hour of it. And what was all this business about the horse, anyway?

Spiggot was not mad. He was just very brave—and very devoted to his family. The business about the horse was just a blind. He knew it wouldn't be taken seriously, nor did he want it to be. His aim—believe it or not—was to get himself under that Press and die there. For Spiggot, contrary to appearance, knew the Law very well.

The Law said that if he pleaded guilty and was found guilty all his property was liable to forfeiture to the Crown. If he pleaded not guilty and was found guilty, went on the Law, the same thing would happen. As far as Spiggot was concerned, that seemed to cover every possibility. (He hadn't a cat-in-hell's chance of being acquitted.) But there was another way. If, said the Law in 1720, the prisoner did not plead at all, his property could not be confiscated, but would pass to his dependants in the normal manner.

But for anyone to refuse to plead in 1720, you will say, blood would have to be a good deal thicker than water. In Spiggot's case it must have been very thick indeed.

It may be thought that callous ruffians such as highwaymen would be the last people to care what happened after they had gone. Strangely enough, many of them cared a good deal—though few quite as much as Will Spiggot. It must be remembered that the confiscation of a criminal's property usually meant that his dependants were left utterly destitute. The Law, or at least its agents, took it for granted that everything in his house must have been his own property, and the widow of a condemned highwayman got short shrift if she appealed for redress.

It was considerations such as these that led Spiggot to submit to the Press. All honour to him, then. And who will blame him for having jibbed at that extra 50 lb.?

As a point of interest it may be noted that, some sixty years before the Spiggot case, one Major Strangeways chose the same sentence and stuck it out to what must have been an exceptionally bitter end. Unfortunately for us the gallant gentleman was not a highwayman—he only murdered his brother-in-law—and his story will have to be left out.

Possibly inspired by Spiggot's fortitude, another highwayman followed him into the Press Yard only a few months afterwards. His name was Nathaniel Hawes, and he too was a Finchley Commoner. He was not much of a highwayman, for he allowed a man he was trying to rob to turn the tables and hand him over to the authorities. But his moment came when he went into the dock.

Like Spiggot, Hawes was surprisingly talkative for a mute. He wagged his tongue long and loud, informing the Court that he would die as he had lived: a gentleman. He would only plead, he said, if they restored the clothes that had been torn off his back at the time of his apprehension. "No one shall say I was hanged in a dirty shirt and a ragged coat," he declared.

Whether or not his clothes were included in the horse's furniture, they were treated by the Court in the same way as Spiggot's horse. Hawes was escorted to the Press Yard.

Compared with Spiggot, he was let down pretty lightly. He had to hold up a mere 250 lb.—but that was too much for him. He gave in after only seven minutes, and was allowed to plead and stand his trial. He was executed in his dirty shirt and ragged coat, and his next of kin didn't even get them back.

The reader will probably wonder why Spiggot and Hawes went to the trouble of bringing in all this stuff about their horses and clothes when they could have got what they wanted (?) just as well by saying nowt. The reader ought to wonder, because the author has been wondering about the same thing for a long time, and can still find no completely satisfactory answer. Three suggestions are offered, but with more diffidence than will be found in most of these pages. On this point your guess is as good as mine.

First, the prisoner might have felt a bit uneasy about the methods the " twelve persons who happen to be by " would use to satisfy themselves about the cause of his muteness. Second, he knew the Law was sometimes flexible, and he may have feared that if his true intentions were too obvious a way might yet be found to swindle his dependants out of his property. Third—and this is my own favourite—highwaymen were, as we have seen, invariably boastful and flamboyant to the last— especially at the last. Their trial and execution gave them the audience they had wanted all their lives, and they went out to get all the limelight they could. Would it be natural, therefore, for a man of this calibre to be content to pose as a mute on what he knew to be positively his last public appearance?

One more would-be martyr of the Press demands mention. His name was Edward Burnworth, and he reached Newgate five years after Nathaniel Hawes. Burnworth is noteworthy because, in the words of his contemporary biographer, he aimed at " bringing rapine into method " along the lines of *banditti* of the Continent. He was a gangster born before his time and in the wrong country.

Burnworth was the son of a painter, and began work as an apprentice to a Grub Street buckle-maker. Before long, however, he began to associate with " those loose incorrigible vagrants who frequent the Ring at Moorfields." He quickly distinguished himself in the art of cudgel-playing, the biographer goes on, and " such other Moorfields exercises as qualify a man first for the road and then for the gallows." The Ring at Moorfields was run at that time by a man named

Frazier, and Burnworth's performances won him the sobriquet of " Young Frazier." This pleased him, and he used the name for the rest of his short life. Out of respect for the dead we shall do the same.

Young Frazier began his career of crime as a pickpocket, and soon found himself in Bridewell. During his imprisonment, continues his biographer, " instead of reflecting on the sorrows which his evil course of life had brought upon him, he meditated only how to engage his companions in attempts of a higher nature than they had hitherto been concerned in." When he got out of gaol he at once put his plans into action, and soon had a number of his old cronies working under him. They started off as housebreakers, and under his leadership they did pretty well out of it. Other forms of robbery followed, and before long Young Frazier was performing such audacious deeds as holding up the Earl of Scarborough in Piccadilly. (The Earl was sober at the time, so the attempt was a failure.)

Meanwhile, Young Frazier had fallen foul of one Thomas Ball, who kept a gin-shop in the Mint. As a side-line Ball had recently taken up Jonathan Wild's old profession of thief-catching, and he very nearly trapped Young Frazier. That mistake cost him his life. It was Young Frazier's first recorded murder.

Now it so happened that Young Frazier was lodging at the time with the wife and sister of an old friend named Kit Leonard. Kit was away on holiday, in one of His Majesty's prisons, and his future was pretty black. So he told the authorities the identity of his wife's lodger. Mrs Leonard connived at this waiving of the rules of hospitality, and before long Young Frazier and some of his associates were on trial for their lives.

Young Frazier made no claims about his horse or his clothes. He just refused to say anything. Various attempts were made to induce him to plead. At the Judge's order his thumbs were tied and strained with pack-thread. But Young Frazier was deaf to such blandishments, and dumb to His Honour, and so off he went to the Press Yard.

Newgate had got in bigger and better weights since Spiggot's time, for Young Frazier found himself propping up no less than 424 lb. on his chest. He bore the weight manfully, striving to end his sufferings by bashing his brains out on the stone floor. The High Sheriff watched the performance, and every now and then put in a word or two about the advantage of pleading. Young Frazier stuck it for one hour and three minutes. Then he gave in. The trial was held on the following day, and at one o'clock in the afternoon he was condemned to the gallows.

In addition to courage Young Frazier had a sense of humour which not even the Press could destroy. After he was convicted he amused himself by drawing sketches of himself. (This was easy for him, explains his biographer, because he was the son of a painter.) He drew himself in a number of different attitudes, including several representations of his idea of what he had looked like under the Press. One of these, it is said, was later engraved in copper and used as the frontispiece to a sixpenny chapbook—which, unfortunately, has not survived.

By submitting to the Press Young Frazier tried to do his best for his family; and, although he failed, his family did their best for him. His mother went to see him in prison, taking a few small presents which she intended to give him when the warders weren't looking. But the warders were no more blind than Young Frazier was dumb, and Mrs Burnworth was soon relieved of a fine selection of files and similar instruments. For this she got a prison sentence herself.

After the execution Young Frazier's body was hung in chains—" to the joy of all honest people," remarks his biographer—over the sign of the Fighting Cock, in St George's Fields.

Here our history of the Press must end. The *peine forte et dure* lasted a good many years longer, not being legally abolished until 1772.

A few words may be added about the office of Keeper, or Governor, of Newgate.

When Henry IV gave the prison to the citizens of London in 1400, the new owners drew up a *Liber Albus*, which included, among other rules and regulations, a paragraph on the duties of that most important person the Keeper. It ran as follows:

"Item, the said Sheriffs shall not let the Gaol of Newgate to ferm, but shall put there a man, sufficient and of good repute, to keep the said gaol in due manner, without taking anything of him for such Keeping thereof, by covenant made in private, or openly. And the Gaoler, who by the said Sheriffs shall be deputed thereunto, shall make oath before the Mayor and Aldermen that neither he nor any other for him shall take fine or extortionate charge from any prisoner for putting on or taking off his irons, or shall receive monies extorted from any prisoner. But it shall be fully lawful for the said gaoler to take from each person, when set at liberty, four pence for his fee, as from ancient times hath been the usage; but he shall take from no person at his entrance there, nor shall he issue suddenly, by command of the Mayor and Aldermen, without other process. And if he shall be found to commit extortion upon anyone he shall be ousted from his office, and be punished at the discretion of the Mayor and Aldermen and Common Council of the City."

All these rules were broken at some time, and some were broken at all times. Keepers invariably had their share of garnish, and payment of rent by tenants of the Press Yard was regarded as a normal perquisite of the office. The value of the appointment may be judged from the following extract from a curious seventeenth-century publication entitled *England's Calamities discovered*, by James Whiston:

"The Keeper's place of Newgate was lately sold for £3,500. Now, upon such a prodigious sum paid only for the head tyrant's jurisdiction of those stone walls and iron grates; considering likewise the numerous turnkeys, sutlers, and all his subjanizaries, to be all fed and fattened also from the fees of their lower posts; what annual income must that gaol raise, and how raise, to answer such a saucy purchase?"

The question is unanswered, but Mr Whiston has no doubt as to the main source of the Keeper's income. It comes from payment by such as " would get unloaded of so many pounds of iron, or purchase a sleeping hole a little free from vermin, or with wholesome air enough to keep his lungs from being choked up."

This state of affairs was largely unchanged at the beginning of the nineteenth century, which is as far as our history goes. In 1813 the Government appointed a Committee to inquire into the condition of the gaols of the city of London, and the Committee's report contained the following revealing passage:

"The keeper of Newgate receives a salary of £450, in addition to which, all the fees and rents are paid to him, and, from this fund, he pays the servants of the prison; above which expense, an income remains to himself of from £600 to £1,000 a year, which is not, in the opinion of your Committee, too great for an office of such difficulties and responsibility; but they greatly object to the manner in which that salary is paid. No part of a gaoler's income ought to be exacted from his prisoners."

CHAPTER NINETEEN

Concerning the Ordinary

SEVERAL references have been made in previous chapters to the office of the Ordinary, or chaplain, of Newgate Prison. From all accounts—and especially those of the Ordinaries themselves—it was a thankless appointment. The holder had to spend most of his days in the dirt and squalor of Newgate, among the very dregs of humanity. He had to suffer innumerable insults and obscenities. He had no say in the management of the prison, and had to observe gambling, drunkenness, and even lechery going on all round him. (With regard to the last, some idea of the state of affairs in Newgate may be gained from the case of the female prisoner who brought an action against a male prisoner for rape within the precincts of the gaol. In Court the man admitted that intimacy had taken place, but pleaded that it had been with the consent of the other party—which was regarded by all as a perfectly legitimate and proper defence.)

It was a thankless job, then, that of the Ordinary. The only compensation was that it was pretty well paid. But what did that mean to the chaplains?

Well, it meant that there was never any difficulty in filling the appointment, and that once it was filled it did not become vacant again until the chaplain's death.

John Howard's report on Newgate in 1777 lists the Ordinary's perquisites as follows:

"The chaplain (or Ordinary), besides his salary, has a house in Newgate Street, clear of Land Tax: two Freedoms yearly, which commonly sell for twenty-five pounds each; Lady Barnardiston's legacy, six pounds a year; an old legacy paid by the Governors of St Bartholomew's Hospital, ten pounds a year; the City generally presents him once in six months with another Freedom. He engages, when chosen, to hold no other living."

Nor did he need to, indeed. For his appointment brought him yet another source of income. He received the condemned prisoners' last confessions—and retailed them to the sensation-hungry mob at a halfpenny each.

It was the Reverend Samuel Smith who started the racket. In spite of his interpolations, *Jackson's Recantation* sold well; and as the author was not there to receive his royalties, the chaplain looked after them for him. Smith held office for another twenty-four years after Jackson's execution, and plenty of broadsheets and chapbook biographies came from his ready pen. No detail of the prisoner's life was too lurid for Samuel Smith. Indeed, the spicier the better, as his publishers were quick to tell him. In the anonymous *History of the Press Yard*, from which we quoted in the last chapter, we have an amusing anecdote about Smith which we can take as a fair epitome of the Ordinary's attitude to his charges. When the prisoner came to make his confession, Smith opened the attack with the following words:

"Well, boy, now it's thy turn to unbosome thyself to me. Thou hast been a great Sabbath-breaker in thy time, I warrant thee. The neglect of going to Church regularly has brought thee under these unhappy circumstances."

"Not I, good sir," replied the prisoner innocently. "I have never neglected going to some Church or other, if I was in health, morning and evening, every Lord's day."

This was the wrong answer from the Ordinary's point of view, and he frowned with displeasure.

"How, no Sabbath-breaker?" he said, as if personally offended. But Sabbath-breaking was not such very good copy, he reminded himself. He went on more hopefully, "Then thou hast been an abominable drunkard, that is most certain."

But again the prisoner refused to take his cue.

"Nor that neither," he declared. "I was never given to that vice during the whole course of my life, having always had a mortal aversion to strong liquor from my cradle, as my friends tell me."

The Ordinary began to lose patience.

"Save the boy's mad," he said. "I never had one criminal

under my hands before that was neither a Sabbath-breaker
nor a drunkard." He decided to try threats. " Child, prithee
recollect thyself, it will be better for thy reputation after thou
art dead for the world to know that thou diest a penitent."

But the boy was obdurate; and when the Ordinary put the
third question in his repertoire he made it clear that he would
accept no denial. If the young man was neither a Sabbath-
breaker nor a drunkard, he said, with heavy emphasis on the
"if," then "no doubt he had been a flagrant whoremaster."
Before the lad could reply the Ordinary added that he could
see the signs on his countenance—" which told him that the
lust of the flesh had gain'd the predominance in him over his
other passions." In other words, he was prepared to excuse
the prisoner for having gone to church and remained
abstemious if he would supply him with an account of his
lechery.

Never was a condemned man slower to take a hint.

" You are under a mistake there, also, good Mr Ordinary,"
said the youth calmly. " I have not known what a woman is,
carnally, to this day, as I hope for salvation in the world to
come."

If salvation depended upon Mr Smith he would have had
a much better chance if he had confessed to a score of doxies.
Upon hearing this reply, says the chronicler of the affair,
" Sam began to be in a great pet." Raising his voice, he cried
out:

" Why, the Devil's in this young fellow, without all manner
of question. He will neither own himself a Sabbath-breaker,
a drunkard, nor a whoremaster—the only three topicks I can
always enlarge upon—and yet has the impudence to say he
hopes to be saved! " He made one last effort. " Sirrah, you
must be one of these three, that you must; therefore recollect
yourself; set all your faculties of remembrance at work, or I
shall be at a loss to say anything of you in my paper."

This blunt speaking upset the boy.

" Then it's nothing with you to be a thief ? " he said bitterly.
" I am sure I find it otherwise, for I am justly condemn'd for
so being."

" Get out you of my sight," shouted the Ordinary, exasperated. "Such case-hardened rogues as you would ruin the sale of my paper. I'll e'en write you down as obstinate!"

"And so," says the historian, "he did. But others afterwards came in, and made him amends by more ample confessions."

The dialogue, of course, was the historian's own composition. He was a prisoner in Newgate about twenty years after Samuel Smith's death, and he gives us the anecdote, which he was told by an old lag, without passing opinion on its veracity. However, judging from the publications of Mr Smith and his successors, we may accept it as giving an accurate picture of the attitude of the Ordinary to the condemned prisoners.

Smith died in 1698, and, as was usual, his coveted appointment was sold to the highest bidder. This was the Reverend Paul Lorrain, believed to have been of Huguenot extraction. He scorned the use of a pseudonym for his literary efforts, and turned out broadsheets by the score. A list of his publications takes up four columns in the British Museum catalogue.

It must be confessed that they do not make very interesting reading. Paul Lorrain was an extraordinary hypocrite—even for an Ordinary. All the prisoners, according to his account, came in unrepentant sinners; but after his ministrations—for which they were alleged to have expressed their deepest gratitude—they were magically converted in much the same way as Jackson had been by Samuel Smith. The following is typical:

"He seem'd all along, from the time of his trial to that of his death, to be very willing to learn and practice those religious duties which (by his own confession) he had too much neglected before. He desired both my instructions and prayers, which he had, and I hope were not bestowed in vain."

Lorrain, according to Lorrain, was irresistible. Like the doctor whose famous elixirs were advertised on the back of his broadsheets, he never had a failure.

These advertisements are a good deal more interesting than the text itself. In addition to the patent medicines—prepared from "secret recipes" and guaranteed to cure everything from gallstones to the King's Evil, three shillings a bottle—there were lengthy book lists. These included books of sermons (most of them by Lorrain himself), Latin grammars and other text-books, and lighter reading with such titles as *History of Cuckolds for Two Hundred Years Past;* and *Secret Memoirs of the Duke and Dutches of Orleance, intermixed with Amorous Intrigues,* by the Countess of D'Aunoy; and *Bumography; or, a Touch at the Lady's Tails*—" being a lampoon privately dispers'd at Tunbridge Wells in the year 1707, by a Water-Drinker."

Lorrain's industry was prodigious. He heard the prisoner's confession the day before the execution, and rode with him to Tyburn. The very next day, first thing in the morning, his broadsheet was on sale in the gutters of London, containing a full description of the prisoner's behaviour right up to the moment when "the cart drew away and he was turned off." It was high-speed journalism, so we mustn't be too critical of the quality. Sometimes as many as fifteen or twenty prisoners were hanged on the same day—but not before the Ordinary had got his copy. On such occasions as these Lorrain issued a sort of omnibus broadsheet, with a separate account of each man, suitably condensed. That the work was telling on him may be seen from the last sentence of one of these composite productions: "This is the best account, which in this hurry, and under this great fatigue, I can now give of these dying persons."

Why all this haste? That is easily explained. In those days of cut-throat competition among publishers even this was not quick enough. In the foreground of Hogarth's "Execution of the Idle Apprentice" stands a woman crying her wares, which are decipherable as copies of *The Last Dying Speech and Confession of Thomas Idle.* Thomas Idle, we observe, is sitting in the cart reading a Bible, looking very much alive, while the Ordinary, whose broadsheet won't be out for another twenty-four hours, is still collecting copy. This was typical. Pirate publishers, the forerunners of the Catnach Press, got their hacks to work as soon as a man was condemned, to make sure that their broadsheets would be printed in time for distribution at Tyburn, where they were sure of a ready sale. A condemned prisoner could always buy a copy of his last words and read it on the way to the gallows.

This literary piracy had a bad effect on Lorrain's sales.

Besides being out first, the "unofficial" biographies were written in a racy style, and without any of the turgid moralizings which he felt bound to put in his own accounts. They contained few facts and much fiction, but were always interesting. Moreover, some of the more enterprising publishers adorned their broadsheets with crude illustrations.

As a result of this unscrupulous competition Paul Lorrain was moved to put the following notice in his broadsheets:

"Whereas some persons take the liberty of putting out sham-papers, pretending to give an account of the malefactors that are executed; in which papers they are so defective and unjust, as sometimes to mistake even their names and crimes, and often quite misrepresent the state they plainly appear to be in under their condemnation, and at the time of their death "—not surprising, as the latter had to be guesswork— " to prevent which great abuses, these are to give notice that the only true account of the dying criminals is that which comes out the next day after their execution, about eight in the morning, the title whereof constantly begins with these words, *The Ordinary of Newgate, his Account of the Behaviour, Confessions, and Last Speeches of the Malefactors,* etc. In which paper (the better to distinguish it from counterfeits) are set down the heads of the several sermons preach'd before the condemned; and after their confessions and prayers, an attestation under the Ordinary's hand, that is, his name at length; and at the bottom the Printer's name."

At least we must admire the Ordinary's frankness for his admission that the synopsis of his sermon was included in the broadsheet only "the better to distinguish it from counterfeits."

The Ordinary in Hogarth's "Idle Apprentice" looks a very decent type, holding the Book in one hand and pointing to Heaven with the other. Compare this picture with the eyewitness description of an execution given by Anthony Storer, in one of his letters to George Selwyn:

"There were two clergymen attending on him, one of whom seemed very much affected. The other, I suppose, was the Ordinary of Newgate, as he was perfectly indifferent and unfeeling in everything he did and said."

Paul Lorrain died in office in 1719, leaving an estate of £5,000. The vacant post was the subject of keen competition, eventually being gained by the Reverend Thomas Purney, whom one outspoken contemporary journal described as " a young sucking divine of twenty-four years of age."

Purney was well qualified to enter Newgate, though scarcely as Ordinary. As a youth he was caught stealing a silver flagon and some books from the local rectory. The rector did not give him in charge, but preached a little sermon to the lad, in which he prophesied that if young Tom did not have a change of heart he would end his days in Newgate.

Shortly after this Paul was sent to Cambridge, and later ordained. His first post was as a curate in Newmarket, which was quite the wrong place for a young man of his temperament. He soon became a well-known figure on the racecourse and in the taverns and brothels of the town, and had to leave in disgrace. These qualifications, apparently, supported by a comfortable sum of money put up by his father as a bribe, were sufficient to get him the coveted post of Ordinary of Newgate.

Purney's output was not so prodigious as Paul Lorrain's, but his publications were more attractive. He had a better idea of what the public wanted. Taking a leaf out of the books of the pirate publishers—sometimes literally—he adorned his broadsheets with rough woodcuts. He kept Lorrain's title—*The Ordinary of Newgate, his Account of the Behaviour*, etc.— but abridged his prefatory sermons and gave more space to the details of the lives of the malefactors. His descriptions were certainly colourful. Realizing that the truth was often dull, he made full use of his imagination. Here is an extract from his biography of a highwayman-murderer:

" This monster of wickedness came behind him, and with a big stick cruelly struck the old gentleman in the hinder part of the head, which beat him down, broke his skull, and he never spoke more; yet his barbarity stopped not there, for he redoubled the blow, and though he was fully dispatched, yet did this vile man cut his throat from ear to ear, and let all the blood in his body run out; and so artful was he to prevent discovery that he mixed water with the blood which he put into the chamber pot, that it might not coagulate, and threw it down thro' a grate into a sink before the door; then stripped both the dead body and himself stark naked, to prevent any spots of blood being seen upon his clothes, and carried the corpse upon his naked back round the garden, and threw it into the bog-house."

One of the bitterest disappointments of Purney's career came from Jonathan Wild, whose story will be told in a later chapter. Wild and he were old friends, and had split many a bottle between them; so when the Great Man was finally caught the Ordinary looked forward to a really first-rate story. But Wild spurned his old pal, and entrusted his soul to an outside chaplain. However, Purney still had his public to consider. He used his imagination even more than usual, and twenty-four hours after the execution the Ordinary's account of Wild's behaviour and dying confession was being hawked in the streets as usual.

Mention must be made of one more Ordinary of Newgate. This was the Reverend John Villette, who came into office in the latter part of the eighteenth century. In addition to bringing out the usual broadsheets, he compiled an anthology of the works of his predecessors of the previous fifty years, and published it, together with reports of the trials, in four fat volumes bearing the title *The Annals of Newgate; or, the Malefactor's Register*. In presenting this work to the public Villette broke all records for hypocrisy, even among Ordinaries. On the title-page the book was described as " calculated to expose the deformity of vice, the infamy and punishments naturally attending those who deviate from the paths of virtue; and intended as a beacon to warn the rising generation against the temptations, the allurements, and the dangers of bad company." In his preface the author went farther. " The utility of a work of this kind," he wrote smugly, " cannot but be acknowledged by every impartial reader. Parents, guardians, and those entrusted with the care and tuition of youth will doubtless be stimulated to recommend these volumes to their perusal and attention." In the book itself youth is spared no details. In addition to highway robbery and murder, the author gives very full reports of cases of bigamy and incest, while cases of rape are described with a good deal more physical detail than the Press allows itself to-day.

But it is ungrateful of us to be so critical of Villette. His book is lavishly illustrated, and has provided us with many of our own plates.

CHAPTER TWENTY

The Road to Tyburn

HIGHWAYMEN did not have to spend long in that noisome place, Newgate. Not long enough, from their point of view. They had just time to receive the last homage of their admirers, to give the Ordinary enough facts and fiction for his chapbook biography—and perhaps to indulge in a little quiet meditation on a misspent life. When they left Newgate their destination was always the same: the Triple Tree of Tyburn.

Right up to the end of the highwayman era there was only one punishment for the crime. Whatever the circumstances, once the jury had given their verdict the judge had no more power to award a lesser sentence than he has on a case of murder to-day. There was a right of appeal—but the sentence was rarely commuted. Highway robbery was a felony, and all felonies except petty larceny (defined as the theft of articles valued at less than twelve pence) were capital offences.

The educated highwayman could not even claim " benefit of the clergy." This privilege, which dated from the twelfth century, was originally confined to clergymen, but later was extended to include all persons who could read. In 1547 it was still further extended to include all peers of the realm, whether they could read or not. Those whose crimes came within the categories for which the benefit could be granted were required to prove their literacy by reading out a passage from the Bible. The passage chosen was invariably the first verse of the fifty-first Psalm—which got the name of the " neck-verse "—and sympathetic chaplains frequently prompted the prisoners. As it was the chaplain who decided whether or not the man's claim was just, many total illiterates gained this benefit. But not highwaymen. Their offence was not " clergy-able." Not only was the benefit of the clergy confined to those cases of thefts of property valued at less than £5, but physical intimidation was an instant disqualification.

The punishment inflicted on those who were granted the privilege could scarcely be called beneficial. The prisoner was branded with a large " T," standing for " thief," with a red-hot iron " in the most visible part of the left cheek, next the nose." Not until the beginning of the nineteenth century, when the number of capital offences was drastically reduced, was this ancient " privilege " abolished.

This by the way. To return to that three-mile stretch that we have called the road to Tyburn: it began at Newgate, from where the cart or carts, according to the number of men to die, left between ten and eleven in the morning. The procession stopped outside St Sepulchre's for the condemned to hear the bellman's final proclamation and to receive his floral wreath. Then, the bouquet in his hands, he was driven down Snow Hill, up to High Holborn (no Viaduct in those days), and thence by St Giles's and up the Oxford Road, as it was called, to arrive at his destination at about midday.

Several eyewitness descriptions of the ride are extant, the most objective—and therefore the best—being that of François Misson, a French Huguenot who found refuge in England and wrote a brilliant book of impressions and observations at the close of the seventeenth century. This is his version of the Tyburn pilgrimage:

" They put five or six in a cart (some gentlemen obtain leave to perform the journey in a coach) and carry them, riding backwards with the rope about their necks, to the fatal tree. The executioner stops the cart under one of the cross beams of the gibbet, and fastens to that ill-favoured beam one end of the rope, while the other is wound round the wretch's neck. This done, he gives the horse a lash with his whip, away goes the cart, and there swing my gentlemen kicking in the air. The hangman does not give himself the trouble to put them out of their pain; but some of their friends or relations do it for them. They pull the dying person by the legs, and beat his breast to despatch him as soon as possible. The English are people that laugh at the delicacy of other nations who make it such a mighty matter to be hanged; their extraordinary courage looks upon it as a trifle, and they also make a jest of the pretended dishonour that, in the opinion of others, falls upon their kindred.

"He that is to be hanged or otherwise executed first takes care to get himself shaved and handsomely dressed, either in mourning, or in the dress of a bridegroom. This done, he sets his friends at work to get him leave to be buried, and to carry his coffin with him, which is easily obtained. When his suit of clothes, or night-gown, his gloves, hat, periwig, nosegay, coffin, flannel dress for his corpse, and all those things are bought and prepared, the main point is taken care of, his mind is at peace and then he thinks of his conscience. Generally he studies a speech, which he pronounces under the gallows, and gives in writing to the sheriff or to the minister that attends him in his last moments, desiring that it may be printed. Sometimes the girls dress in white, with great silk scarves, and carry baskets full of flowers and oranges, scattering these favours all the way they go. But to represent things as they really are, I must needs own that if a pretty many of the people dress thus gaily, and go to it with such an air of indifference, there are many others that go slovenly enough, and with very dismal phizzes."

As Misson observed, the choice of dress for the occasion was left to the condemned man's own discretion. Some of the gentlemen highwaymen had their tailors hard at work right up to the eve of the execution; others went more suitably attired in a plain shroud. The only article of clothing that was *de rigueur* was the neckwear, which was gratuitous, and put on by a warder before the man left Newgate. The provision of the coffin was the man's own financial responsibility, and it was almost a point of honour among highwaymen to get hold of one somehow.

Different in style, but none the less valuable, is Dean Swift's description of the ride, given in his famous satire—

GOING TO BE HANGED
1727

As clever Tom Clinch, while the rabble was bawling,
Rode stately through Holborn to die in his calling,

He stopt at the George for a bottle of sack,
And promised to pay for it when he came back.
His waistcoat and stockings and breeches were white;
His cap had a new cherry ribbon to tie't.
The maids to the doors and the balconies ran,
And said, " Lack-a-day, he's a proper young man!"
But, as from the windows the ladies he spied,
Like a beau in the box, he bow'd low on each side!
And when his last speech the loud hawkers did cry
He swore from his cart " It was all a damn'd lie!"
The hangman for pardon fell down on his knee;
Tom gave him a kick in the guts for his fee;
Then said, " I must speak to the people a little,
But I'll see you all damn'd before I will whittle!
My honest friend Wild (may he long hold his place)
He lengthen'd my life with a whole year of grace.
Take courage, dear comrades, and be not afraid,
Nor slip this occasion to follow your trade;
My conscience is clear, and my spirits are calm,
And thus I go off without prayer book or psalm;
Then follow the practice of clever Tom Clinch,
Who hung like a hero, and never would flinch."

" Clever Tom Clinch " has been identified with a highwayman named Thomas Cox, who was hanged at Tyburn thirty-six years before Swift wrote his satire—and therefore thirty-four years before Jonathan Wild. Cox was the younger son of a gentleman of Dorsetshire, and on at least one occasion he showed a ready wit. This was when he stopped Thomas Killigrew, the Court Jester, and demanded his purse.

" Are you in earnest, friend? " asked Killigrew.

" Yes, by God, I am," was the reply; " for though you can live by jesting, I can't! "

Swift's line " Tom gave him a kick in the guts for his fee " is founded on fact, although the hangman was not the immediate object of the prisoner's displeasure. It is recorded that when the cart drew up under the gallows Mr Smith, the Ordinary, asked Cox if he would care to join in a few final prayers; at which the highwayman " swore a great oath to the contrary, and kickt him and the hangman, too, off the cart."

The reference to the hawkers crying his " last speech " is, of course, an allusion to the current practice referred to in the last chapter. The bit about stopping at the "George" (some versions give the "Bowl") for a drink, and promising to pay "when he came back," is also authentic. As was recorded earlier, Captain Philip Stafford first made this crack on the way to Reading, and it became a part of the Tyburn tradition. The crowd expected it, and most highwaymen played to the gallery to the last. What the landlord of the inn thought about it is not known, but presumably it was a good advertisement. A similar custom existed in other parts of the country, and it is said that one Yorkshireman "was hanged for leaving his ale"—the story being that he declined a drink on the way to Knavesmire and was hanged just a minute before a reprieve arrived!

As a variation of the "last drink" theme, there is a little story of a certain Jack Witherington, highwayman, an associate of Claude Duval. On the way up Holborn Hill he asked the driver of the cart to stop, as he wished to speak to the Sheriff's Deputy, who was in charge of the procession. The request being granted, he addressed the Deputy as follows:

"I owe, sir, a small matter at the Three Cups Inn, a little farther, for which I fear I shall be arrested as I go by the door; therefore, I shall be much obliged to you if you will be pleased to carry me down Shoe Lane, and bring me up Drury Lane again to the place for which I am designed."

The Sheriff's Deputy regretted that it was not in his power to alter the itinerary in this way, but assured Witherington that "if such a mischance should happen, he would bail him." Whereupon "Jack, as not thinking he had such a good friend to stand by him in time of need, rid very contentedly to Tyburn."

Another anecdote is told of one Dick Hughes, who rode to Tyburn in 1709. His wife waited for him at St Giles's Circus, and the cart stopped to allow her to say farewell to her husband. The conversation between the pair was reported as follows:

MRS HUGHES. My dear, who must find the rope that's to hang you—we or the Sheriff?
DICK. The Sheriff, honey; for who's obliged to find him tools to do his work?
MRS HUGHES. Ah, I wish I had known so much before!

'Twould have saved me two pence, for I have been and bought one already.

DICK. Well, well, perhaps it mayn't be lost; for it may serve a second husband.

MRS HUGHES. Yes, if I've any luck in good husbands, so it may.

Fierce controversies have raged over the exact site of Tyburn gallows, but it is now generally agreed that it was at some point on the intersection of Edgware Road and Oxford Street. An equally fierce and equally barren controversy has raged over the etymology of the word "Tyburn" itself. According to Dr Fuller, " Some will have it from Tie and Bourne, because the poor Lollards for whom this instrument (of cruelty to them, though of justice to malefactors) was first set up, had their necks tied to the beame, and their lower parts burnt in the fire. Others will have it that it is called from Twa and Burne; that is, two rivulets, which it seems meet near to the place." The experts prefer the latter—they would!

The approximate site of Tyburn is marked by a tablet on the railings of Hyde Park opposite Marble Arch. The date of the first erection of the gallows is unknown. The first recorded execution took place in 1196, the victim being a man named William Fitzosbert, alias Longbeard. At that time Tyburn was not the only place used for hangings, nor did it acquire a monopoly for many centuries afterwards. Cornhill was a favourite spot in the Middle Ages, and later rivals included a place named The Elms, the location of which has never definitely been decided, and Smithfield. We read of executions taking place at Smithfield—where John Cottington was hanged in 1656—very late in the seventeenth century.

The original gallows at Tyburn consisted of two poles with a cross-beam, but by the sixteenth century the accommodation was found to be insufficient to meet the demand. A new gallows was erected, with three solid uprights and the same number of cross-pieces, from which no fewer than twenty-four men could be hanged at the same time. A triangular stone let in the roadway marks the site of one leg of this gallows. It remained there until 1759, when it was dismantled, the beams taking on a new lease of life as supports for beer-barrels in a neighbouring tavern. After that a movable gallows was used, being taken from Newgate and assembled before each separate execution. There were three reasons for this change in procedure: the owners of houses overlooking the spot objected to the sight of the gallows; the structure was an obstruction to the increasing traffic on the roads; and by the end of the eighteenth century there was a welcome falling off in the incidence of executions.

The crowds that attended the executions were enormous. Tyburn Fair, as it was popularly known, was London's favourite entertainment. People came from the outlying districts specially to see the show, taking the kiddies for a treat and making a day of it. Tickets for the grand-stand, sold at 2s. 6d. each, were usually all gone well in advance, and late-comers had to pay heavily on the black market. The windows of houses overlooking the scene were also let out, and there was free standing room for all. At least, for all within reason. The record "gate" at Tyburn was 200,000—though it must be admitted that the occasion was exceptional. The condemned man was a full-blown Marquis; he was not a highwayman, however, but a mere murderer, so we shall have to leave him out of our account.

It must be remembered that repugnance to public executions is a comparatively modern affectation. Before we condemn the mob that attended them it would be well to consider the views of the men of culture of the time. Dr Johnson, for instance. This is what he wrote to Sir Walter Scott in 1783, when suggestions were made to do away with Tyburn Fair:

"The age is running after innovation, and all the business of the world is to be done in a new way; men are to be hanged in a new way; Tyburn itself is not safe from the fury of innovation."

In reply to the suggestion that it would be better to have executions carried out in privacy he went on, "No, sir, it is *not* an improvement; they object that the old method drew together a number of spectators. Sir, executions are intended to draw spectators. If they do not draw spectators, they don't answer their purpose. The old method was most satisfactory to all parties: the public was gratified by a procession; the criminal was supported by it. Why is all this to be swept away?"

It hasn't been, Doctor. The spirit lives on. We are more civilized than you were, so we just queue up all night to see "sex-murderers" in the dock.

The novelist Samuel Richardson, who wrote on Tyburn forty years before Dr Johnson, had what is called a more enlightened outlook. This was how the scene appeared to him:

"I mounted my horse and accompanied the melancholy cavalcade from Newgate to the fatal Tree. The criminals were five in number. I was much disappointed at the unconcern and carelessness that appeared in the faces of three of the unhappy wretches; the countenance of the other two were spread with that horror and despair which is not to be wondered at in men whose period of life is so near, with the terrible aggravation of its being hastened by their own voluntary indiscretion and misdeeds. The exhortation spoken by the bellman from the wall of St Sepulchre's churchyard is well intended; but the noise of the officers and the mob was so great, and the silly curiosity of people climbing into the cart to take leave of the criminals made such a confused noise, that I could not hear the words of the exhortation when spoken. . . .

"All the way up to Holborn the crowd was so great as at every twenty or thirty yards to obstruct the passage; and wine, notwithstanding a late good order against this practice, was brought to the malefactors, who drank greedily of it, which I thought did not suit well with their deplorable circumstances. After this the three thoughtless young men, who at first seemed not enough concerned, grew most shamefully wanton and daring, behaving themselves in a manner that would have been ridiculous in men in any circumstances whatever. They swore, laughed, and talked obscenely, and wished their wicked companions good luck with as much assurance as if their employment had been the most lawful.

"At the place of execution the scene grew still more shocking, and the clergyman who attended was more the subject of ridicule than of their serious attention. The Psalm was sung amidst the curses and quarrelling of hundreds of the most abandoned and profligate of mankind, upon them (so stupid are they to any sense of decency) all the preparation of the unhappy wretches seems to serve only for a subject of a barbarous kind of mirth, altogether inconsistent with humanity. And as soon as the poor creatures were half dead, I was much surprised to see the populace fall to hauling and pulling the carcases with so much earnestness as to occasion several warm rencounters and broken heads. These, I was told, were the friends of the persons executed, or such as, for the sake of tumult, chose to appear so; as well as some persons sent by private surgeons to obtain bodies for dissection. The contests between these were fierce and bloody, and frightful to look at; so I made the best of my way out of the crowd, and with some difficulty rode back among the large number of people who had been upon the same errand as myself. The face of every one spoke a kind of mirth, as if the spectacle they had beheld had afforded pleasure instead of pain, which I am wholly unable to account for. . . .

"One of the bodies was carried to the lodging of his wife, who not being in the way to receive it they immediately hawked it about to every surgeon they could think of; and when none would buy it they rubbed tar all over it, and left it in a field scarcely covered with earth."

The last paragraph of Richardson's description suggests that the next of kin had the right to claim the body, but in this matter they had to face keen competition from Surgeons' Hall, where corpses for dissection were normally in great demand. On one occasion it was very nearly vivisection. The man's name was William Duell and he was hanged for rape in 1740. His body was brought to Surgeons' Hall, " but after it was stripped and laid on the board, and one of the servants was washing it, in order to be cut, he perceived life in him and found his breath to come quicker and quicker, on which a surgeon took some ounces of blood from him; in two hours he was able to sit up in his chair, and in the evening was again committed to Newgate, and his sentence, which might be again inflicted, was changed to transportation."

This was not the only case of inefficiency on the part of

Jack Ketch. The very first man to be hanged on the triangular gallows—a Dr Storey—made a miraculous come-back just as the hangman was " rifling among his bowels." Another remarkable escape occurred when one John Smith, after hanging for five and a quarter minutes, what time Jack Ketch " pulled him by the legs and used other means to put a speedy period to his life," was saved by the sudden arrival of a reprieve.

In an earlier chapter some idea was given of the various means by which prison staffs supplemented their incomes at the expense of the prisoners. From Jack Hall's description of the " Common Side " in Newgate it is easy to understand why there was such a brisk trade in the sale of privileges. But tipping did not stop at Newgate. Despite what Misson said about the hangman not troubling to put his charges out of their pain, we have it on a pretty good authority that it was not uncommon for Jack Ketch to visit the condemned man the day before the execution and offer to make it quick—for a consideration. It is said that one condemned prisoner, John James by name, was asked for twenty pounds for this favour. He pleaded poverty, and the hangman came down to ten, and finally five. That was his bottom price; and if John James couldn't pay, he said, " he would torture him exceedingly."

But hangmen had to live, and highwaymen had to die. And disposing of highwaymen was a simple matter compared with the ceremony attached to the execution of traitors. A man convicted of high treason had to be drawn and quartered as well. The drawing part of it came before the hanging; the prisoner was denied the luxury of a cart, but had to be dragged at the tail of a horse all the way from the prison to the gallows. (In later times this piece of savagery was observed in the letter rather than the spirit, and he had a fairly comfortable ride on a sort of sledge, or hurdle.) Arrived at the gallows, he was hanged in the normal way—but " not till he be dead." Then he was cut down and disembowelled while still alive, his entrails being burned " before his eyes." Finally his head was chopped off and his body carved into four parts, both head and quarters being " at the disposal of the Crown." Here is a contemporary account of such an execution:

" After the traitor had hung six minutes he was cut down,

and having life in him, as he lay upon the block to be quartered, the executioner gave him several blows on his breast, which not having the effect designed, he immediately cut his throat; after which he took his head off; then ripped him open and took out his bowels and heart, and then threw them into a fire which consumed them. Then he slashed his four quarters and put them with the head into a coffin. His head was put on Temple Bar and his body and limbs suffered to be buried."

That man got off lightly. The executioner generously put him out of his misery before starting with the disembowelling, and only his head was stuck up for public exhibition. Normally the quarters were also posted in various conspicuous parts of the town.

The above treatment did not apply to traitresses. They were just burnt alive. The official explanation for this discrimination was that " the decency due to the sex forbids the exposing and publicly mangling their bodies."

Among the traditions of Tyburn Day was the custom of the condemned man fixing the rope to his halter with his own hands. This was a privilege rather than a right, and Jack Ketch was not obliged to grant it. Understandably enough, the practice was less generally observed than the custom of stopping for a not-so-quick one at the George or the Bowl. We have, however, records of some remarkable instances of fearlessness at the gallows. There is not room for more than one here, but the Ordinary's description of the last moments of James or Valentine Carrick is a fairly typical example.

Carrick was the son of an Irish gentleman, who fought in Spain as an officer under the Earl of Peterborough. Women were his undoing. Coming to London, " when he had any money he entertained a numerous train of the most abandoned women of the town, and had also intrigues at the same time with some of the highest rank of those prostitutes." These ladies made heavy inroads on his fortune, and before long he took to the road to replenish it. After various adventures on Finchley Common, Hounslow Heath, and Bagshot Heath, he was apprehended after holding up the Hon. William Young, Esq., in Lincoln's Inn Fields.

Carrick's behaviour at Newgate, it is said, was " singular

and indecent," and the reader is not expected to ask for details. He was visited by " throngs of people," and the gaolers instituted an admission fee. This greatly tickled young Carrick. " You pay, good folks, for seeing me now," he remarked, " but if you had suspended your curiosity till I went to Tyburn you might have seen me for nothing!"

At Tyburn Carrick was as bold and gay as ever. " He gave himself genteel airs," wrote Mr Purney, " in placing the rope about his neck, smiled and bowed to everybody he knew round him, and continued playing a hundred little tricks of the same odd nature, until the very instant the cart drove away." Another report of his last moments says that " instead of praying with the rest of the criminals, he employed that time in giggling, taking snuff, making apish motions to divert himself and the mob."

In Hogarth's representation of the execution of the " Idle Apprentice " we see the hangman on one of the cross-pieces of the gallows puffing away at his pipe. From that point he reached down and fixed the rope as the cart came underneath. Then he left his post and, at a signal from the Sheriff's Deputy, drove the cart away. In addition to his fee he was entitled to the dead man's clothes. Sometimes the condemned man anticipated the Sheriff's Deputy and gave the signal himself; and we have a story of an occasion when one fellow " flung down his handkerchief for the signal for the cart to move on, and Jack Ketch, instead of instantly whipping on the horse, jumped on the other side of him to snatch up the handkerchief lest he should lose his rights. He then returned to the head of the cart and jehu'd him out of the world."

The last execution at Tyburn took place—in spite of Dr Johnson—on November 7, 1783. From then on the place of execution was changed to the Old Bailey. But although the procession was done away with by this, executions were still open to the public, and the Old Bailey became as popular a resort as Tyburn had been. However, the execution itself was a much speedier affair. In the *Gentleman's Magazine* for 1788 we find the following:

" 23 Ap. This day, the malefactors ordered for execution on the 18th were brought out of Newgate, about eight in the morning, and suspended on a gallows of new construction. After hanging the usual time, they were taken down, and the machine cleared away in half an hour. By practice the art is much improved, and there is no part of the world where villains are hanged in so neat a manner and with so little ceremony."

The "gallows of new construction" was the famous "trap," although it was not such an innovation as would appear from this report. An account of the execution of Earl Ferrers twenty-eight years earlier states that "he then mounted a part of the scaffold raised eighteen inches higher than the rest; and, the signal being given by the Sheriff, that part of the floor sunk under to a level with the rest, and he remained suspended in the air."

The last public execution in this country took place in 1868.

CHAPTER TWENTY-ONE

Jonathan Wild the Great

HISTORY, says Carlyle, is the lives of Great Men (his capitals). Certainly the history of crime in the first part of the eighteenth century is the life of Jonathan Wild the Great, as Henry Fielding ironically called him. Wild was not a highwayman; but during his fifteen-year reign as King of the Underworld the lives and deaths of many highwaymen were in his hands. For that reason he must be the central figure of this chapter.

The Jonathan Wild set were a grim collection of ruffians. Therefore, lest it should be thought that humour had entirely deserted the road during this period, we shall preface the chapter with an anecdote about a highwayman who succeeded in escaping from the clutches of this master criminal.

Ned Wicks was his name, and the incident for which he became famous took place on Hounslow Heath. Here he held up Lord Mohun, who was attended by a groom and a footman. His lordship showed the greatest reluctance to part with his money, and addressed the highwayman in a very threatening manner. Ned was not one to be intimidated, but he was very impressed by the peer's flow of language.

"My lord," he said, with more respect than when he had first addressed him, "I perceive you swear perfectly well extempore. Come, I'll give your honour a fair chance for your money; that is, he that swears best of us two shall keep his own and his that loseth."

The peer readily accepted the challenge, and flung down a purse of fifty guineas. Ned put up the same amount, and the groom was appointed stake-holder and umpire. Then the contest began.

It is very disappointing that not one of the chroniclers has reported any of the ensuing dialogue. All we are told is that the contest lasted fifteen minutes, at the end of which both the peer and the highwayman had exhausted their vocabularies. The groom was asked for his verdict.

He hesitated for a moment before passing judgment. He wanted to be honest, but at the same time he could not afford to risk offending his employer.

"Why, indeed, your honour swears as well as ever I heard a person of quality in my life," he told Lord Mohun. "But to give the strange gentleman his due," he continued, "he has won the wager, if it was for a thousand pounds!"

So much for the Swearing Highwayman, as Ned Wicks has been called. Now—Jonathan Wild the Great.

Jonathan was born at Wolverhampton in 1682, the son of a wig-maker. He served an apprenticeship to a buckle-maker in Birmingham, where he married while still in his teens. He was about twenty-one when he deserted his wife and child and came to London. Here he served for a time as a gentleman's gentleman, then went back to buckle-making, got into debt, and landed up in the Poultry Compter.

Wild spent four years in the Compter, but it was not a waste of time. He got introductions to representatives of every criminal trade in London, and received instruction from each. He also contracted what the *Newgate Calendar* calls a "close familiarity" with a prostitute named Mary Milliner. The pair were released about the same time, and for a time Wild lived as the woman's pimp. That was only to tide him over for the moment, however. Before long he had saved enough out of Mary's earnings to enable him to take a house in Cripplegate, and there he started up in business as a fence.

The Law relating to receivers of stolen goods had scarcely changed since the days of Moll Cutpurse. Like the Roaring Girl, Wild saw at once that the best way of doing business was to sell stolen goods back to their original owners. Accordingly, by advertisements and other means he invited persons who had been robbed to step into his office and give him a full description of the missing articles; then he would do his best to get them back—at a price, and provided that no awkward questions were asked. He charged a consultation fee of five shillings, and usually charged half the market value of the goods returned. With most of the thieves with whom he dealt he had an agreement whereby they split the proceeds between them on a fifty-fifty basis—but of course the thieves had to rely on Wild's word that they were getting a square deal.

This was Moll Cutpurse all over again. But Wild was not content to remain a mere fence for long, a humble go-between for robbers and robbed. He had great ambitions. In fact, he wanted to rule the Underworld.

Early in his career as a receiver Wild was fortunate in ingratiating himself with the City Marshal, Charles Hitchin. The latter was a notorious blackmailer, and had a large-scale protection racket already organized before he became associated with Wild. The two helped each other. At least, that was the agreement; in actual fact Wild used Hitchin as long as he was useful—which was until the Marshal was brought to book and dismissed from office. After that he had to fend for himself. Wild had no time for failures.

Meanwhile, Wild was becoming more and more powerful in the Underworld itself. With what Hitchin had told him added to his and Mary Milliner's knowledge, he knew enough to be able to put the screws on most of the thieves with whom he had dealings. Before long they were taking orders from him. From being a humble receiver he rose to master of the thieves, and detailed them off for various " jobs " as he thought fit.

Wild had a brilliant gift for organization. He divided London and the surrounding country into districts, and appointed different gangs to each. He classified the criminals into different types, encouraging them to specialize, and assigning them work according to their abilities. He had special squads of pickpockets for theatres, and others for similar work in churches during divine service, which required a different technique. He had his shop-lifts, his housebreakers, his footpads—yes, and his highwaymen.

With such an organization Jonathan Wild had little difficulty in driving the other fences out of business. Soon he found it unnecessary to solicit customers. People who had been robbed went to his office and paid their five shillings fee just as they had gone to Moll Cutpurse's shop in the Strand a century before.

But that was only one side of Wild's activities. At the

same time he was posing to the general public as a sort of private detective. From time to time he would go to the authorities with information against some criminal, and give evidence for the prosecution in Court. A prisoner was never acquitted if Wild was in the witness-box. After he had secured several convictions for the Crown in this manner, therefore, the authorities began to go to Wild to ask for assistance. Thus he had got himself into a position where robbers, robbed, and the agents of the Law were all asking for his help. Outwardly he maintained an appearance of a public-spirited citizen, and advertised himself in the Press as " Thief-Catcher General of Great Britain and Ireland." And for each conviction he got a reward of £40.

The men Wild got arrested in this manner were at first mainly criminals operating outside his circle—for he was determined to break up every gang in London that would not accept his directorship. Later, however, he used his reputation as a thief-catcher to enforce discipline within his own ranks. If one of his men tried to cheat him by keeping back some of his stolen goods—and Wild always knew if he did, for he had the list from the man who had been robbed—or was insubordinate in any way, then Wild would make an example of him. He could do so with impunity. He had never stolen a penny himself, and receiving was not illegal. No one ever had anything on him.

Within a few years of his leaving the Poultry Compter, Jonathan Wild had achieved his ambition, and was uncrowned King of the Underworld. He had broken every other important criminal organization in London, and his sway over his own subjects was absolute. His profits were enormous. He moved from Cripplegate to bigger premises just by the Old Bailey, whose shadow served as a warning to all his employees—for that was what the thieves had come down to. His commands were obeyed without question. As a symbol of authority he carried a silver staff the head of which was a crown. Even highwaymen attended Jonathan Wild's levées, as they were called.

About the time Wild moved his office he parted company with Mary Milliner, but not without providing her with a comfortable pension. His new mistress, a girl called Molly, was a Tyburn widow, and with her he lived in grand style. He was attended by a footman in livery, and dined in state. "His table was very splendid, he seldom dining under five dishes, the reversions whereof were generally charitably bestow'd on the Common Side felons."

Then, in 1718, Parliament passed an Act "for the farther preventing robberies, burglaries, and other felonies." Under this Law, which was said to have been directed specifically against Wild—a high tribute to his success—it became a felony for anyone to solicit or accept a reward for the return of stolen goods unless information was given regarding the identity of the thieves.

Wild had no difficulty in getting round this. He simply abolished the five-shilling consultation fee—a relic of his poorer days—and called his place of business an Enquiry Office. By this means he was able to appear more public-spirited than ever. He took no money. He was just there to help, he said. If people who had been robbed came to him he would do his best to put them on to the track of their property and of the criminals responsible. In actual fact what he did was to advise clients to send a servant to such-and-such a place (usually a street corner) at such-and-such a time, and on handing over a stated sum of money to one of Wild's men they would get the property back there and then.

So Jonathan Wild continued to prosper. Soon he had to open a branch office; and to get rid of unsold articles he started an export branch, with an agent in Ostend. For this he bought a sloop and enlisted a Captain Roger Johnson in his service. Goods were taken to Belgium and sold, and the sloop brought back contraband articles on the homeward trip. Once Johnson was caught by the Customs Officers, and detained in a riverside watch-house. At once Wild mobilized a party of his men and sent a mob down to the place to create a disturbance and rescue the Captain.

Wild continued to make occasional prosecutions against criminals who were guilty of breaches of discipline, and posed more than ever as the worthy citizen. Indeed, we have it on record that he actually had the audacity to petition the Cor-

poration for the Freedom of the City to be conferred on him
"for services rendered." But his petition was not approved.

That was in 1724, and in the same year the first cracks
appeared in Wild's organization. For nearly fifteen years he
had ruled by fear, and although none dared defy him openly,
he had more enemies than anyone else in London. He was
one of the first gangsters to have a personal bodyguard. Some
of the magistrates were gunning for him, too. It was about this
time that we read of Wild appealing to the Earl of Dartmouth
to protect him against "persecution" from the Bench. But
when the first blow was struck it came not from the authorities
but from a man whom Wild thought he had successfully got rid
of. It all began when Jack Sheppard and Blueskin decided to
flout their master's authority. . . .

Sheppard was a jack-of-all-dishonest-trades, highway robbery
included. His exploits on the road have not been recorded
very fully; but we must give some account of his amazing
achievements in prison-breaking.

Born in Spitalfields in 1702, the son of a carpenter, Jack was
befriended as a boy by a Mr Kneebone, a woollen-draper in
the Strand. The latter got him apprenticed to a carpenter
named Owen Wood. Jack was then fifteen, and he remained
with Mr Wood for four years. During this time, however, he
took to frequenting a pub in Drury Lane called the Black Lion,
where he got in with bad company: namely, Elizabeth Lion,
alias Edgeworth Bess, and Poll Maggot. These two ladies
initiated the young man into the art of picking pockets, and it
was not long before he was equally expert in the higher art of
picking locks.

After a brief apprenticeship in crime Jack Sheppard joined
forces with a well-known highwayman and housebreaker
named Joseph Blake, alias Blueskin. Blueskin came of a good
family and had had a liberal education; but he had turned
highwayman at the early age of seventeen, and at one time
was associated with Valentine Carrick. He had soon come
within the orbit of Jonathan Wild, and so he introduced Jack
to the great man.

Sheppard and Blueskin together robbed an attorney named
Pargiter on the Hampstead road, knocking him down and

rolling him into the ditch before asking him to deliver. In this and other adventures Jack showed a greater aptitude than his more experienced colleague, and after a little while we find Blueskin serving under the younger man's leadership in a gang which included Tom Sheppard (who got to Tyburn just before Jack) and two ruffians who went under the picturesque names of Hell and Fury. The gang operated under Wild's orders, but it seems that Sheppard retained more independence than was allowed to most gang-leaders.

The first time Sheppard saw the inside of a prison was when he went to visit Edgeworth Bess, who had been confined to St Giles's Round House over a little matter of some stolen plate. At the Round House Jack stopped for a chat with the beadle, knocked him over the head, took his keys, and set his mistress free. "This heroic act," says one of his biographers, "got him so much reputation among the fair ladies of Drury Lane that there was nobody of his profession so much esteemed by them."

It was Jack who was caught next time, and he was committed to the same Round House. He did not stay long enough to have any visitors. He made a hole in the roof and escaped via the churchyard.

Shortly after this Jack had a bit of very bad luck. He went for a walk one evening in Leicester Fields (Leicester Square) with a friend named Benson. As they were strolling along Benson took a sudden fancy to a handsome watch which was sticking out of a gentleman's pocket, and his fingers wandered. But he "missed his pull," and the gentleman gave the alarm. Benson got away, and Jack was left to take the rap.

For once he was innocent, but that did not save him from being lodged in St Anne's Round House, and the same evening Edgeworth Bess came to visit him. No sooner had she set foot inside the place, however, than she was detained on suspicion of being an accomplice. The following morning the pair were brought up before a magistrate, and committed to New Prison. Being taken for man and wife, they were given a cell together; and as Jack's reputation for prison-breaking had preceded him, the cell was the strongest in the place, known as Newgate Ward.

Not strong enough to hold Jack, though. Visitors called, among them Blueskin. The pair shook hands—and that night Jack got to work with a file. First his manacles, then his fetters; then to the window. He removed two of the bars, and looked out. There was a thirty-feet drop to the courtyard. Thereupon—it sounds like a school story, but it's true—he tore up their blankets and sheets and knotted them into a rope, tying one end to the remaining bar in the window. Escape was easy for him now—but what about Bess? Women's clothes in those days were ridiculously unsuited for prison breaking, and Bess could not possibly get through the small opening with all that stuff on. Fortunately it was summertime, and there was no moon; so she made the descent in her undies. Jack followed, and in the courtyard she made herself respectable again. They were not out of the wood yet, though. The wall surrounding the prison was twenty-two feet high, and apparently unscalable. But at the gate there were enough bolts and locks to give Jack a foothold, and he and Bess made good their escape.

Sheppard's latest success went to his head. Back in command of his gang, he dared to defy Jonathan Wild and break away from the great man's circle. He and Blueskin found a small-time fence named William Field, who offered them prices a good deal higher than the Director-General would give. Of course Wild's spies soon discovered the defection, and from that moment Sheppard's gang was doomed. Wild's union was the closest of closed shops, and no rival concerns were tolerated.

The affair for which Sheppard was caught was a particularly wretched business, as it was the house of his former benefactor, Mr Kneebone, that he burgled. Kneebone naturally went to Wild's Enquiry Office, and the receiver promised to do his best for him. His agents had already informed him that Sheppard and Blueskin had done the job, so Wild sent for Field and invited him to turn King's evidence. Wild's invitations were not refused lightly, and Field gave in. The same day Sheppard and Blueskin were arrested and taken to Newgate.

Newgate was a harder nut to crack than Round Houses

or New Prison, and Sheppard and Blueskin went up for trial at the Old Bailey. The case was pretty well conducted by Wild. Field's evidence was damning, and the pair were sentenced to death. Wild arrogantly went to visit them in prison—and nearly lost his life. Blueskin, under pretext of wanting to say something to him in confidence, suddenly whipped out a penknife and slit Wild's throat "from ear to ear." The injury was severe, and it was rumoured that Jonathan Wild was dead. Without waiting for it to be confirmed Dean Swift picked up the pen and dashed off a satirical elegy on the great man (*Blueskin's Ballad*). But Wild lived, and Blueskin died on the scaffold.

Meanwhile, Jack was planning to get out. Edgeworth Bess and Poll Maggot went to visit him, but he was allowed to speak to them only through the hatch leading to the Condemned Hold. But Bess took Jack his favourite present—a file—and managed to edge it under the wicket with her foot. Then, under cover of conversation, Jack started to work on the spikes on top of the wicket. When they were sufficiently loose to be broken off he sent Bess to keep the gaoler company in his lodge, which she did so well that the latter never looked out all the time Poll Maggot was helping Jack over the wicket.

An escape from Newgate was something out of the ordinary, and Jack retired to the country. But London drew him, and within a week or so he was back again in his old haunts. After less than a month's freedom he was caught on Finchley Common. This time the authorities put him into the Stone Room of Newgate, heavily ironed and chained to the floor. Every visitor was watched closely, and no files reached Jack this time. But he was not done yet. He had had previous experience in picking locks, and a crooked nail was enough for him to get rid of his chains. He wriggled out of his handcuffs, and, with his fetters still on, tackled the only possible exit from the room: the chimney. Removing an iron bar from across the opening, he went up, and got into a cell called the Red Room, the door of which had not been unlocked for seven years. Jack got it open in less than seven minutes, broke through a wall to get to the prison chapel, and finally escaped via the roof.

Jack Sheppard was famous. He had done what no one had ever succeeded in doing before—escaping from Newgate twice. But how vain he was! Ignoring the advice of his friends, he went back to his old haunts in Drury Lane, dressed in a brand-new suit and equipped with a silver-hilted sword. As a celebration he invited Bess and Poll to dine with him, and chose for the purpose a public-house in Newgate Street. On their way they passed the prison—and it was with great difficulty that Poll persuaded him to let her pull down the blinds of the coach. They ate, drank, and were so merry that the news of the party soon reached the authorities. When Jack was arrested again he was too drunk to try to resist.

Jack did not escape a third time. Special irons had been forged to receive him, and he was not left unguarded for a moment. He had an astonishing number of visitors, including many ladies and gentlemen from outside his profession. Artists came to paint his portrait, among them Sir James Thornhill, R.A., who decorated the dome of St Paul's Cathedral. Jack's daring exploits had won him the admiration of all. He remained cheerful to the end, and showed no sign of repentance. The Ordinary begged him to consider his soul, and offered him a Bible; to which Jack gaily replied, " that in his situation one file would be worth all the Bibles in the world." Of Edgeworth Bess, who was faithful to the end, he said, " A more wicked, deceitful, and lascivious wretch there is not living in England. She has proved my bane. God forgive her. I do."

Jack had no chance of getting a file, nor even a crooked nail; but he was still hoping. Somehow he managed to obtain a small penknife, and this he kept opened in his pocket, blade uppermost. He was planning to try to escape when in the cart on the way to Tyburn, cutting the rope with the knife, and jumping into the crowd. He was sure the crowd would be large, and equally confident that the people would help him. But unfortunately when the time came one of the gaolers made an examination of his pockets—and got a nasty cut on his hand in the process.

The crowd was indeed enormous, and Jack had not overestimated his popularity. He was only twenty-two at the time of his execution, and one mighty feminine groan went up as the cart drew away.

A very different end from that of Jonathan Wild. It would have been better for the latter if Blueskin had finished him off properly. He survived the attack on his life by only six months.

Sheppard's escapes from Newgate were all but forgotten when the news broke that Jonathan Wild had been arrested. At first no one believed it. Then, when the report was confirmed, bets were offered freely that he would be released within a week, and it was prophesied that whoever was responsible would suffer for this. But Wild was not released. He was kept in Newgate for three months, during which time the case against him was steadily built up. Then, on May 15, 1725, he appeared again in the Old Bailey—in the dock.

Wild faced two charges: stealing fifty yards of lace, valued at £40, and receiving the same and selling them back to the original owner " without discovering or apprehending, or causing to be apprehended and brought to justice, the persons that committed the said felony." Everyone knew it was a test case. If Wild was acquitted no one would ever be able to catch him.

He put up a brilliant defence. Although it was clear to the Court that he had ordered the robbery to be made, the evidence was insufficient, and on the first charge he was formally acquitted. But on the second, specifically framed under the Act of 1718, he was found guilty, and sentenced to death. In pleading for mercy Wild claimed that fifty-seven criminals had been brought to justice by his efforts. Reliable authorities estimate that the number of men he sent to the gallows was nearer a hundred and twenty.

When sentence was passed there was great rejoicing in the Underworld which Wild had disciplined and ruled. The reign of terror was over. Henceforth a criminal had only the authorities to fear, and he could sell his wares to whom he chose. Execution Day was looked forward to eagerly, and the gangsters prepared to turn out in force to give their late Chief a good send-off. Wild nearly cheated them of this pleasure, trying to poison himself with laudanum on the day before.

But the dosage was wrong, and he survived to make the journey in the cart. Our picture shows him being pelted with stones and mud on the way. He is shown as being alone in the cart, but according to another account he went down in a blaze of glory by picking the pocket of the Ordinary on the way to Tyburn. The Ordinary was the Reverend Thomas Purney, and the nature of the article Wild was said to have taken adds credence to the story; it was a corkscrew.

CHAPTER TWENTY-TWO

The Real Dick Turpin

THE first history of highwaymen was published in 1719. Written by a " Captain " Alexander Smith—who had no better claim to his rank than most of the heroes who figured in his book—it bore the grandiose title of *A Compleat History of the Lives and Robberies of the Most Notorious Highwaymen.* It is probably one of the most readable and least reliable history books ever written. Like ourselves, Smith collected his copy mainly from contemporary broadsheets and chapbooks; unlike ourselves, he brightened up the dull bits with a variety of anecdotes, usually smutty, and for the most part lifted from Boccaccio and Chaucer. How " compleat " the history was may be judged from the fact that in the year of its publication Jack Sheppard was earning an honest penny at Mr Wood's in the Strand; Jonathan Wild had just moved to the vicinity of the Old Bailey; Sixteen String Jack and Galloping Dick were not even born; and Dick Turpin was only thirteen years of age.

The second history on the subject appeared fifteen years later. It came from the pen of another " Captain," Charles Johnson, and bore the more modest title of *A General History of the Most Famous Highwaymen.* Johnson's modesty ended with the title. His book was an outrageous crib of Smith's, some chapters being copied almost word for word—Chaucer and Boccaccio and all; but that did not stop Johnson from attacking his forerunner in acrimonious tones for trifling errors of fact. Johnson's book is remarkable for the omission of any reference to Dick Turpin, who at that time had a price of fifty guineas on his head.

Perhaps our own title to this chapter is not very modest. There have been so many Turpins. . . . But we have conscientiously referred only to contemporary sources, so that the sordid truth about Dick Turpin is at least undisguised by the romantic lies that were told of him after his death. And there is no gainsaying that the truth was sordid; although perhaps modern critics, in a reaction against Ainsworth, have been unnecessarily hard on this popular hero. " A coarse, illiterate boor," was Edgar Wallace's summing up; while Violet Wilson, historian of the stage-coach, dismisses him as " a brutal and, it is hinted, cowardly ruffian."

Dick Turpin was born in 1705 at Hempstead, in Essex. The rival claim of the market town of Thaxted is unfounded. The confusion arose because Turpin's birthplace was given as Thaxted in a Royal Proclamation in 1737. We know that Turpin was born in Hempstead in 1705 because the parish register of St Andrew's Church is still extant, and contains the following entry for that year:

" Richardus Filius Johannis et Maria Turpin bapt. Sept. 25."

Dick was actually born in the Crown Inn—it was called the Bell then—of which his father was landlord. As a boy he was " put to school to one Smith a writing master." The point is important, because this education was later to cost him his life.

John Turpin was a butcher as well as a publican, and he got Dick apprenticed to the former trade. Dick served his apprenticeship in Whitechapel, and then opened a shop of his own at Waltham Abbey. He was then twenty-one. About this time he married the daughter of another innkeeper, Rose Palmer.

Dick made a good start in business, and his customers never found cause to complain of the quality of his mutton. It was unfortunate that his advent in Waltham Abbey coincided with an outbreak of sheep-stealing in the district; and still more unfortunate that one Farmer Giles—no, we aren't making up names—traced two of his beasts to Turpin's slaughterhouse. As a result of this incident Turpin went into sudden retirement. According to one account he jumped out of a back window while Farmer Giles was hammering on the front door.

The Butchers' Guild was a very upright body, and Turpin knew that his career in that trade was finished. Moving to the neighbourhood of Harwich, he tried his hand at smuggling. Dissatisfied with his share of the proceeds, he made his first essay as a highwayman by holding up other smugglers on the road, masquerading as a riding-officer. But this could not last long. Although he only attacked one at a time, smugglers were always as thick as thieves, and he became a marked man. So he left the district and took refuge in Epping Forest. Here he joined up with a gang of deer-stealers, later to become known as the " Essex Gang " or " Gregory's Gang." Gregory was the leader; his principal lieutenants were named Fielder, Rose, and Wheeler.

The gang did not stop at deer-stealing for long. They found housebreaking more profitable, and were responsible for a series of robberies of a particularly brutal nature. Their activities took them as far afield as Rippleside, Watford, and Croydon; once they robbed the churches at Chingford and Barking in the same night. But lonely farmhouses were their favourite game, and they usually waited till the menfolk were out and then tortured the housewives until they revealed where the money was kept. The gang were distinguished by their cruelty to persons and their wanton destruction of property. Here is an account of two typical outrages, both of which were later discovered to have been the work of the " Essex Gang." The source is the *London Evening Post*, of February 6, 1735.

" On Saturday night last, about seven o'clock, five rogues entered the house of the Widow Shelley, at Loughton in Essex, having pistols, etc., and threatened to murder the old lady if she did not tell them where her money lay; which she obstinately refusing for some time, they threatened to lay her across the fire if she did not instantly tell them, which she would not do. But her son being in the room, and threatened to be murdered, cried out, he would tell them if they would not murder his mother, and did; whereupon they went upstairs and took near £100, a silver tankard, and other plate, and all manner of household goods. They afterwards went into the cellar, and drank several bottles of ale and wine, ate the relicts of a fillet of veal, etc."

This story was later written up in more sprightly terms in the chapbook lives of Turpin. The latter was credited with having taken a leading part in the affair. The threat to lay the old lady across the fire came from him, his words being, " God damn your blood, you old bitch, if you won't tell us I'll set your arse on the grate."

Even more lurid accounts were given of the second outrage. We shall return to the circumspect report of the *London Evening Post*:

"On Tuesday night, about eight o'clock, five villains came to the house of Mr Lawrence, a farmer at Edgwarebury, near Edgware, in Middlesex, but the door being bolted they could not get in, so they went to the boy who was in the sheep-house, and compelled him to call the maid, who opened the door, upon which they rushed in, bound the master, maid, and one manservant, and swore they would murder all the family if they did not discover their money, etc.; they trod the bedding under foot, in case there should be money hidden in it, and took about £10 in money, linen, etc., all they could lay their hands on, broke the old man's head, dragged him about the house, emptied a kettle of water from the fire over him, which had fortunately only just been placed on it, and ravished the maid, Dorothy Street, using her in a most barbarous manner, and then went off."

Such, then, was the Essex Gang, of which Dick Turpin was a leading member. By Royal Proclamation fifty guineas' reward was offered for information leading to the apprehension of any member of the gang, and a free pardon thrown in for any of the gang who turned King's Evidence. The reward was later increased to a hundred guineas.

The ringleaders were finally caught in an alehouse in an alley in Westminster. There was a fight, and Fielder, Rose, and Wheeler were caught. For the second time in his life Turpin saved his skin by jumping out of the window. At the trial Wheeler turned King's Evidence, and his old comrades went to Tyburn. Gregory seems to have suffered the same fate, and that was the end of the Essex Gang.

After this Turpin resolved to keep clear of gangs. He also gave up housebreaking, and entered the more respectable profession of the road. Another of the gang, who had also escaped from justice, joined him, and the pair were soon in the news. A contemporary journal reported that on July 10, 1735, two gentlemen were held up between Wandsworth and

Barnes Common " by two highwaymen, supposed to be Turpin the Butcher and Rowden the Pewterer, the remaining two of Gregory's Gang, who robbed them of their money and dismounted them; made them pull off their horse's bridles, then, turning them loose, they rode off towards Roehampton, where a gentleman was robbed (as supposed by the same highwaymen) of a watch and £4 in money."

A fortnight later Turpin and Rowden were active in the same area. The *Grub Street Journal* of July 24 reports that " On Monday, Mr Omar, of Southwark, meeting between Barnes Common and Wandsworth, Turpin the Butcher, with another person, clapt spurs to his horse, but they coming up with him, obliged him to dismount, and Turpin, suspecting that he knew him, would have shot him, but was prevented by the other, who pulled the pistol out of his hand."

After this the Wandsworth district became too hot for the pair, and we next hear of them in another *Grub Street Journal* report dated October 16:

" We hear that for about six weeks past Blackheath has been so infested by two highwaymen (supposed to be Rowden and Turpin) that 'tis dangerous for travellers to pass. On Thursday Turpin and Rowden had the insolence to ride through the City at noonday, and in Watling Street they were known by two or three porters, who had not the courage to attack them; they were indifferently mounted, and went towards the bridge; so 'tis thought are gone the Tonbridge road."

At this point Rowden the Pewterer mysteriously disappears from our story. Our next story tells of a solo effort on the part of Turpin, in the neighbourhood of Twickenham. We have no newspaper report to quote here, and it must be admitted that the authenticity of the story is doubtful. But it seems worth repeating.

Turpin's victim was Alexander Pope. The poet declared that he had no money on him, and Turpin searched him. He found only a sheaf of papers, which he contemptuously tossed into a hedge. With a cry of alarm Pope dashed forward to retrieve them. Thereupon Turpin, thinking that perhaps he had overlooked something, snatched the papers back, intending to examine them more carefully at his leisure. Pope then fairly begged him to let him have them back, assuring Turpin that they would be of no value to him, and offering in exchange a small gold chain which the highwayman had indeed overlooked. Turpin accepted the chain and, after a brief hesitation, handed back the papers.

But for that, we are told, we might never have had the *Essay on Man*.

The story has a sequel. A certain Mrs Ballenden, who had heard of Pope's adventure, was herself stopped by Dick Turpin. When the highwayman told her his identity she immediately flung her rings in his face, saying angrily that he did not know real treasure from " silly gold."

Dick Turpin did not rob alone for long. One evening, on the road to Cambridge, he met a solitary traveller, " well mannered and appearing like a gentleman." Pistols out, he bade him stand. The other man obeyed—and then burst out laughing.

"What! Dog eat dog?" he exclaimed. "Come, come, brother Turpin, if you don't know me I know you, and should be glad to your company."

The name of this highwayman was, of course, Tom King.

King was already nearly as notorious as Turpin, and the pair immediately went into partnership together. They swore eternal fidelity, " until death do us part," and then decided to establish a sanctuary where they could take refuge when hard pressed. At Turpin's suggestion they chose a spot in Epping Forest between Loughton Road and King's Oak Road, in the middle of a large thicket. " Here they made a place large enough to receive them and their horses; and while they lay, quite concealed themselves, could see through several holes made on purpose what passengers went by in either road, and, as they thought proper, could issue out and rob them. In this cave they lived, ate, drank, and lay. Turpin's wife supplied them with victuals and frequently stayed there all night."

The partnership was soon in the news. The *Country Journal* of April 23, 1737, reporting the robbery of a party travelling to Epping, stated that " the famous Turpin and a new companion of his came up and attacked the coach, in order to rob it; the gentleman had a carbine in the coach, loaded with slugs, and seeing them coming, got it ready, and presented it at Turpin, on stopping the coach, but it flashed in the pan; upon which says Turpin, 'God damn you, you have missed me, but I won't you,' and shot into the coach at him, but the ball missed him, passing between him and a lady in the coach."

Three weeks after this Turpin committed his first known murder. His victim was one of the keepers of Epping Forest, who followed him and tracked him down to his hide-out. Turpin shot him outside his cave.

There is one story about Turpin and King which, although apocryphal, deserves mention if only because it shows our hero in a favourable light for once. From their cave the pair espied a carriage, and rode out to stop it. The passengers were a City merchant named Bradele and his two children. The merchant resisted, but under threats he surrendered first his money and then a watch which, he said, had been given to him by his father. King then demanded a ring which he was wearing, but Bradele declared that it was of even greater sentimental value than the watch. Turpin intervened, and persuaded his colleague to let the merchant keep the ring. Thereupon Bradele asked if the highwaymen would consider selling his watch back to him. Turpin and King had a hasty consultation, and finally agreed. The merchant asked how much it would cost him. "Six guineas," said Tom King. "We never sell for more, if it be worth six and thirty." Of course Bradele had no more money, but they trusted him. He agreed to leave the money at a coffee-house in the City—and, we are told, did so.

The partnership between Turpin and King came to an abrupt end in May 1737. Riding to London one Saturday evening, in company with a new associate named Potter, they had nearly reached the Green Man, in Epping, when Dick's horse began to tire. About the same time they met on the road a Mr Major, who was riding a fine racehorse named Whitestockings. Although they were within three hundred yards of the inn, Turpin boldly accosted Mr Major and forced him to change horses. It was a rash act, for Whitestockings, whose sire was the famous Partner, was a conspicuous grey colt well known in racing circles. As a crowning act of folly Turpin also stole Mr Major's whip.

No sooner had the three ridden off than Mr Major went to the Green Man and told Mr Boyes, the landlord, of his loss. "I dare swear 'tis Turpin has done it," said Boyes grimly. And at his advice Mr Major had handbills printed offering a reward for information leading to the recovery of the horse.

On the following Monday Mr Boyes received intelligence that the horse was in the stables of the Red Lion, in Whitechapel. He went up to town himself, proceeded to the stables, and recognized the horse. He summoned a constable, and with him waited in a hay-loft until eleven o'clock in the evening, when a man came in to get the horse. It was Matthew King, Tom's brother. Mr Boyes and the constable captured him at once. Matthew loudly declared that he had bought the horse—but unfortunately he was bearing the whip Turpin had stolen from Mr Major, which had the latter's name engraved on it. When Boyes pointed to this Matthew broke down completely. He knew nothing about the horse having been stolen, he said, but had just been sent to fetch it. Boyes and the constable thereupon offered to release Matthew if he would tell them where the persons who had sent him were waiting. Matthew—a coward if ever there was one—said there was "a lusty man in a duffel coat" waiting in Red Lion Street. Boyes went in the direction indicated, and saw Tom King. The latter recognized the landlord, and fired. He missed, and Boyes closed with him. "Dick, shoot him, or we are taken, by God!" shouted Tom.

Dick rode up, took aim, and fired. He missed Boyes—but his shot found a billet.

"Dick, you have killed me!" cried Tom King.

And so he had, although Tom lived for a week before he died of his wound in New Prison.

Such is the generally accepted account of the incident, although it is by no means the only one. According to some authorities Tom bravely urged Dick to get away while he could, and was faithful to the end; according to others, he cursed his old comrade and informed his captors where Dick was likely to take refuge (specifically the White House on Hackney Marsh—the cave in Epping Forest had apparently been discovered). Other reports, again, say that it was not Tom whom Dick shot, but Matthew—also by mistake. To confuse matters still further, Turpin was later reported by his executioner as having said that " he was a confederate with one King, who was executed in London some time since; and that once, being very near taken, he fired a pistol among the crowd, and by mistake shot the said King into the thigh, who was coming to rescue him." Of Tom King's execution, however, we have no record. A highwayman of the same name was hanged at Tyburn in 1753, but that was long after Turpin's own execution.

But there is nothing doubtful about the generally accepted version of the sequel. There is no more truth in it than there is in Ainsworth's tale of the ride to York. We are asked to believe that Turpin retired to the country, muttering " I have lost the best fellow I ever had in my life," and going into mourning. He did nothing of the kind. The date of Tom King's death is given as May 24, 1737. Here is an extract from the *London Magazine* of the same date:

" Sunday, May 22. Turpin, the butcher, who lately killed a man who endeavoured to take him on Epping Forest, this night robbed several gentlemen in their coaches and chaises at Holloway and the back lanes at Islington, and took from them several sums of money. One of the gentlemen signified to him that he had reigned a long time. Turpin replied, ' 'Tis no matter for that. I am not afraid of being taken by you, therefore don't stand hesitating but give me the coin.' "

A week later another London newspaper reported that " Turpin, the renowned butcher-highwayman, committed a robbery almost every day this month."

In the following month a Royal Proclamation was published in the *London Gazette*, stating:

" It having been represented to the King that Richard Turpin did, on Wednesday, the 4th of May last, rob on His Majesty's highway Vavasour Mowbray, Esq., Major of the 2nd Troop of Horse Grenadiers, and commit other notorious felonies and robberies near London, His Majesty is pleased to promise his most gracious pardon to any of his accomplices and a reward of £200 to any person or persons who shall discover him, so as he may be apprehended and convicted."

The Proclamation continued:

"Turpin was born at Thaxted, in Essex; is about thirty-five, five feet nine inches high, brown complexion, very much marked with smallpox, his cheek-bones broad, his face thinner towards the bottom, his visage short and pretty upright, and broad about the shoulders."

The Proclamation was repeated in the following month, and another newspaper report of the same period tells us that about this time our old friend Rowden the Pewterer was captured and sentenced to transportation for life—a remarkably light sentence for a highwayman. In August the *London Magazine* carried a leader bearing the heading "Common Sense Thoughts" complaining bitterly that "a fellow who is known to be a thief by the whole kingdom shall for a long time continue to rob us, and not only so, to make jest of us for being robbed, and shall defy the law and laugh at justice."

Then Dick Turpin disappeared.

Where he went to, and why, was a mystery. Some said he had gone north, others said west; some said he had died, others that he had retired from the road. But it was all conjecture. The only thing that was certain was that Turpin had ceased his patrol of the roads of London and Essex—as it turned out, for ever.

At this point we must break off in our story of Turpin and go northward ourselves. To Yorkshire—to Brough and Welton and Beverley. A man named John Palmer lived in these parts—a native of Lincolnshire, he said, and a horse-dealer by trade. He was never short of cash, and went hunting and shooting with the gentlemen of the county. He posed as a gentleman himself—although he was never quite convincing. And one day he showed himself in his true colours. It was in October 1738. A party was returning from the shoot, and Palmer, who was among them, spotted his landlord's gamecock in the street. On an impulse he raised his gun and took a potshot at it.

It was a senseless act, and another of the party told Palmer so, pretty sharply; whereupon Palmer snapped back angrily that if the man would just wait until he had charged his piece he would shoot him, too. Not very gentlemanly behaviour, and bound to make an unfavourable impression on the magistrate—for the landlord made a formal complaint to the authorities and had Palmer arrested. The magistrate at Beverley remanded him for the next General Quarter Sessions, and asked for sureties for his good behaviour.

John Palmer could not find any sureties.

Getting increasingly suspicious, the magistrate committed him to a house of correction pending his trial, and started investigations. The results were startling. From Lincolnshire came news that Palmer was wanted on charges of sheep-stealing; from other parts of Yorkshire it was learned that he was suspected of having stolen horses. The charge about shooting the gamecock was dropped, and Palmer was taken to York Castle. There he remained for four months, occupying the cell in which Will Nevison had spent his last days.

While in gaol Palmer wrote to his brother, telling of his plight, and begging him to come and bear witness to his character. But he omitted to pay the postage, and when the letter arrived at its destination Palmer's brother was asked for sixpence. Not recognizing the handwriting, he declined to accept the letter, and it went back to the local post-office. There, by an extraordinary accident, the writing on the envelope was recognized by someone else—by a Mr Smith, a teacher—the man who had taught " John Palmer " to write. . . .

Dick Turpin had come back to life. He had gone north, then, after all—and was in prison awaiting trial for having stolen a mare and a foal—for such were the charges which were finally brought against him. What a come-down for " the fellow who had struck terror all over the country," as the *London Magazine* had once described him! Mr Smith was positive it was Turpin's handwriting, and he journeyed to York to identify the prisoner—and to put in a claim for the £200 reward. He had not seen Dick for five years, but he had no difficulty in recognizing his former pupil. Nor was he the only one. Another witness at the trial was Mr Edward Saward, also of Hempstead, who said he had known Dick for twenty-two years.

Dick Turpin was found guilty of horse-stealing and sentenced to death.

In gaol his behaviour was " as jovial, merry, and frolicsome as if he had been perfectly at liberty and assured of a hundred years to come." He had numerous visitors, including scores who had journeyed from the south to see the former terror of their highways. One gentleman, on seeing Dick, swore that it was not Turpin at all, offering to wager anyone half a guinea that he was right. Whereupon Dick whispered to the gaoler, " Lay him the wager, and I'll go you halves! "

Dick Turpin was executed on Knavesmire on April 7, 1739—fifty-five years after Nevison. The following report appeared in the contemporary issue of the *Gentleman's Magazine*:

"The notorious Richard Turpin, and John Stead, were executed at York for horse-stealing. Turpin behaved in an undaunted manner; as he mounted the ladder, feeling his right leg tremble, he stamp'd it down, and looking round about him with an unconcerned air, he spoke a few words to the topsman, then threw himself off, and expir'd in five minutes. He declared himself to be the notorious highwayman Turpin, and confess'd to a great number of robberies, and that he shot the man that came to apprehend him on Epping Forest, and King, his own companion, undesignedly, for which latter he was very sorry. He gave 3 *l.* 10*s.* to five men who were to follow the cart as mourners, with hatbands and gloves to them and several others."

To judge by the manner of his execution, Turpin, whatever his faults, was no coward. Jumping off the ladder was a legal alternative to the "cart" method, and it made for a speedier death—but it required courage.

Turpin's obituary notices were disappointingly brief. The *London Magazine*, which had devoted leaders to him in his heyday, now dismissed him curtly as " a mean and stupid wretch." The gutter Press was kinder, but still gave him less space than was accorded to many second-rate highwaymen. The reason for this was—if we can judge by our own gutter Press—that he had a rather tame sex-life.

Such, then, as far as we can discover, was the real Dick Turpin. " A very commonplace ruffian, who owes all his fame to the literary skill of Ainsworth," is the verdict of the *Dictionary of National Biography*. A bit harsh, but true in the main. . . .

To blazes with the truth! Give us back our Ainsworth—our cocked hat and gold-braid jacket and jack-boots and, above all, our Black Bess flashing along in the moonlight! That may not be the real Dick Turpin, but it's the Turpin we want—and the Turpin that's going to live!

CHAPTER TWENTY-THREE

Gentlemen of the Road

DICK TURPIN was, as Edgar Wallace described him, " a coarse, illiterate boor." As such, he was typical of many of the highwaymen of the eighteenth century. But the age of what Harrison Ainsworth calls " night-errantry " (he puts it in italics so that we shan't miss the point) was not over by any means. The early years of the Brunswicks were distinguished by quite a number of " gentlemen highwaymen " with varying claims to the title. They did not take to the road out of political necessity, like the Royalists under the Commonwealth. They were for the most part sons of gentlefolk in straitened circumstances who inherited a taste for extravagance but little else.

These gentlemen did little to raise the tone of the road. Whatever manners their poor but proud parents had taught them were quickly forgotten. Naturally they had to mix professionally with men of the Turpin type; but instead of giving the latter a few sorely needed lessons in chivalry and courtesy, they soon became assimilated, and often rivalled their humbler-born colleagues for coarseness and brutality.

One of the worst examples of these so-called gentlemen highwaymen was William Parsons, youngest son of a baronet and nephew of the Duchess of Northumberland. He could not even plead poverty as an excuse. His father treated him generously, and he could not have had a finer education; for in William Parsons the profession was honoured by what we believe to be its one and only Old Etonian.

Parsons's undoing was a common complaint in those days: a passion for cards. To pay his debts he pilfered shamelessly from his family and their friends, on one occasion concluding a visit to his illustrious aunt by taking a gold-mounted miniature from her dressing-table. His father sent him into the Navy as a midshipman, but he did not last long at sea; he was caught cheating at cards, and had to quit the service. Old Sir William then got him an administrative job in West Africa, but he wasn't there long either. To pay his debts he forged a letter from his aunt guaranteeing him for up to £70. As a result of this the Duchess altered her will, under which young William had been sole beneficiary. When she died she left £25,000.

Back in England, Parsons married a girl with a dowry of £4,000, which he quickly ran through, and then entered the Army as an ensign. He was soon up to his old tricks, and after getting out of several nasty scrapes he finally landed up in gaol on a charge of forgery. He was tried at Maidstone Assizes and sentenced to transportation to the Virginian slave-plantations—a light sentence for the crime in those days. In Virginia he was noticed by Lord Fairfax, who was grieved to see a man of his birth and education so come down in the world. Lord Fairfax did Parsons a number of kindnesses, for which the young man repaid him by stealing one of his benefactor's finest horses. With that he began his career as a highwayman—on the roads of Virginia.

It is a pity that we have no record of Parsons' exploits in the colony, but at least they were successful enough to enable him to pay his fare home. He got back to England just after the death of his aunt. Her fortune had passed to his sister, who was as yet unmarried. Parsons plotted for a friend of his—a discharged footman—to try to win her hand, and if necessary to marry her by force, but the scheme was found out before it could be put into practice. So he went back to the road. Hounslow Heath was his favourite haunt, and it was on this happy hunting ground that he was finally caught. He was tried, convicted, and sentenced, and all the efforts of his noble family failed to secure him a pardon. He was hanged at Tyburn at the age of thirty-four.

Baronets' sons were the exception rather than the rule, although there were one or two instances of high-spirited young gentlemen staging a hold-up "for the fun of it." An interesting case of this sort happened during a parliamentary election at Chelmsford, where four young sparks of good family got very drunk and held up a farmer. They were caught, tried, and sentenced to death. Now one of these young gentlemen—

Morgan by name—was engaged to Lady Elizabeth Hamilton, daughter of the Duke, and a person of considerable influence at Court. She went to see the King (George II) and begged for her fiancé's pardon.

His Majesty refused. He expressed the surprisingly advanced opinion for his time that the young men's social status in no way mitigated their offence, but, on the contrary, made it all the worse, for they could not plead that they were driven to the highway by financial necessity, as so many of his subjects were. But Lady Betty would not take no for an answer, and she pestered the King every morning until the eve of the day appointed for the execution. This time she put everything she had got into it, and the sight of so much beauty in so much distress made George relent. " I will spare his life," he promised, " upon condition that he be not acquainted therewith till he arrives at the place of execution."

So it happened that when the four men arrived in their carts at Tyburn, Lady Elizabeth was there to snatch her beloved from the jaws of death. Silas Told, who was acting as a sort of missionary to Newgate at the time, and who tells this story, ends up his account with the words " and, truly, I was well pleased upon the occasion."

The reader will be no more pleased than I am when he learns that the King's clemency did not extend to Morgan's companions. All three were hanged while the lucky one was being driven away in Lady Elizabeth's carriage. The moral being, presumably, that you can't dabble in highway robbery and get away with it unless you're engaged to a Duke's daughter.

George I had also had to listen to pleas for mercy on behalf of condemned highwaymen. One of these was on behalf of John Hartley, who was convicted of having robbed a tailor of the sum of twopence and the clothes he was wearing. Hartley does not seem to have cut a very dashing figure in this escapade, but he did not suffer from a lack of girl friends. No fewer than six young ladies, all dressed in white, paraded at St James's Palace, and promised the King that if he would pardon Hartley they would draw lots among themselves to decide which of them would become his—Hartley's, not the King's—wife. But George I told them that " he thought hanging would be better for him than marriage," and Hartley died a bachelor. Hartley was not really a gentleman highwayman, but he has been brought into this chapter to show that highwaymen in the eighteenth century had not lost any of their old romantic appeal to the ladies.

Reading through the reports of trials during this period one is struck by the crop of parsons' sons who ended up at Tyburn. There seems to be no special reason for this filial backsliding, except that the clergy generally had a higher social status than most people of their income group; and that their sons, taught the importance of keeping up appearances but given small allowances to do it on, were more interested in getting the good things of this world than waiting for the distant riches of the next.

Nicholas Horner was the son of the Vicar of Honiton, Devonshire, and began life as an attorney's clerk in London. An early-acquired taste for drink and gambling made him seek more lucrative employment, and he took to the road. He made a bad start, being caught on his very first venture, and was tried and sentenced to death. However, influential friends of his father managed to get the sentence commuted to seven years' exile, and the same friends got him a job in India. There he remained till the seven years were up, by the end of which time both his parents had died. On his return to England he received £500 left by a forgiving father. That soon went on drink and gambling. Then, undaunted by his former ill-luck, he went back to the road.

In the course of a variety of adventures Horner once robbed a man of a paltry six guineas. "Sir, you love money better than I do, to thus venture your neck for it," said the victim. Horner did not take exception either to the nature of the remark or to the man's bad grammar. He simply launched into a lengthy exposition of his own personal philosophy, which is worth repeating even if it is of doubtful authenticity.

"I follow the way of the world, sir," he said, "which now prefers money before friends or honesty; yea, some before the salvation of their souls; for it is the love of money that makes the unjust judge take a bribe, the corrupt lawyer to plead an evil cause: the physician to kill a man without fear of hanging, and the surgeon to prolong a cure. 'Tis this that makes the tradesman tell a lie in selling his wares, the butcher to blow his veal, the tailor to covet so much cabbage, the miller to cheat in his corn-grinding "—remember Duval's parentage?—" the baker to give short weight, and to wear a wooden cravat for it, the shoemaker to stretch his leather, as he does his conscience, and the gentlemen of the pad, such as myself, to wear a Tyburn tippet, or old Storey's cap on some country gallows. So good-day to you, sir, and thank you, and never despise money in a naughty world!"

Old Storey's cap on some country gallows was Horner's final headgear, for he was hanged at Exeter shortly after.

Our next parson's son is Paul Lewis, of Hurstmonceaux, Sussex. His father got him a commission in the artillery, but Paul suffered from the same disease as young William Parsons. With his creditors on his heels he deserted from the Army, and went into the Navy as a midshipman. He rose to the rank of lieutenant before he was again forced to quit, and as there was no R.A.F. in those days he joined the regiment of the road. Like Horner, he was caught on his very first engagement, but by faking an alibi he managed to get himself acquitted. But he did not last long. He was soon back in Newgate, and his reverend father journeyed up to see him. The account of the last interview is graphically described in the *Newgate Calendar*:

" Such was the baseness and unfeeling profligacy of this wretch that when his almost heart-broken father visited him for the last time, in Newgate, and put twelve guineas into his hand to defray his expenses, he slipped one of the pieces of gold into the cuff of his sleeve by a dexterous sleight, and then, opening his hand, showed the venerable and reverend old man that there were but eleven; upon which he took from his pocket, another, and gave it to him, to make up the number intended. Having then taken a last farewell of his parents, Lewis turned to his fellow prisoners and exultingly exclaimed; ' I have flung the old fellow out of another guinea.' "

The last of our parsons' sons is a character of such interest that he will almost certainly extend this chapter beyond its allotted length. No matter. James Maclaine is almost worth a chapter to himself.

Maclaine was actually dubbed the "Gentleman Highwayman" in his lifetime, and his conquests among ladies of fashion rivalled those of Duval himself. His love-life—but perhaps we had better begin with his birth.

James Maclaine was a Scot born at Monaghan, the son of a Presbyterian minister. His elder brother, Archibald, followed in father's footsteps and became pastor of the English congregation at The Hague. James himself had a good education, and was soon "a perfect master of writing and accompts." The latter qualification was to be especially useful, as his father intended him to go into a business house in Rotterdam, where he would be near enough to his brother for any spiritual guidance he might need. But the old minister died when James was only eighteen, leaving him enough money to have a good time on, but not to keep him for the rest of his life. James got through the lot in a year. When he woke up to find it had all gone he had to take a job as a butler to a gentleman of Cork. But a butler's pay was not enough for a man of James's tastes, and he had to augment it by the sale of any odd trifles his employer left lying about. James was soon out of a job.

Shortly after that he left Ireland, and, in the words of the *Dictionary of National Biography*, "entered domestic service in London and fell under the influence of fast women." (Other authorities say the women were loose.) Soon after, however, a woman who was neither, but the respectable daughter of a horse-dealer "of the Golden Fleece in the Oxford Road" (*i.e.*, Oxford Street), fell under his influence, and accepted his hand. He accepted a dowry of £500, and set up as a grocer in Welbeck Street. Business was bad, and his wife died; so he decided to try to repeat his former success on a larger scale. Posing as a gentleman of quality and substance, and engaging a bankrupt apothecary named Plunkett as a "footman," he set off in search of romance and a dowry in the fashionable watering-places of Bath and Tunbridge Wells. But James was handicapped by a lack of capital, and the ladies weren't to be hurried. Plunkett suggested that they should try to recoup their fortunes on the road.

There they did pretty well—thanks to Plunkett. Maclaine

was pretty hot stuff with the ladies, but a damned bad highwayman. On their first outing—on Hounslow Heath—he almost messed the whole thing up by losing his nerve at the critical moment. His lack of courage was conspicuous throughout his career, and it is a wonder that Plunkett put up with him as a partner for so long. But, of course, Maclaine was still after a rich bride. He nearly got one, too—with " a doe of £40,000 "—but the girl was tipped off just as she was about to say yes.

Nothing daunted, James kept on trying, and he put up a fine show in public. He took rooms in St James's Street, opposite the fashionable White's Club, at two guineas a week—high rent in those days—and another suite in Chelsea. Plunkett didn't do badly for himself, either, taking apartments in Jermyn Street. James passed himself off as an Irish squire, and he became a well-known figure in the West End. His tailor's bills must have cost Plunkett many a pang. His favourite rig-out comprised a crimson damask banjan, a silk waistcoat with lace trimmings, black velvet breeches, white silk stockings, and yellow morocco slippers. Phew!

Maclaine and Plunkett made a number of valuable coups, including a big haul from an official of the East India Company. Their best-known exploit was when they held up Horace Walpole, who naturally tells us all about it. It happened in Hyde Park on a moonlight night in 1749, when Walpole was returning from Holland House. He does not tell us how much he had to hand over, but mentions that Maclaine's pistol " going off accidentally, razed the skin under my eye, left some marks of shot on my face, and stunned me. The ball went through the top of the chariot, and, if I had sat an inch nearer to the left side, must have gone through my head." In a later account, written after Maclaine's death, Walpole relates that " the whole affair was conducted with the greatest good breeding on both sides." Further, the following morning he received from the highwayman " two letters of excuses, which, with less wit than the epistles of Voltaire, had ten times more natural and easy politeness in the turn of their expression." In a postscript Maclaine offered to sell back any trifles Walpole might want, and suggested meeting him at Tyburn at midnight.

Walpole did not accept the invitation. Perhaps the time and place had something to do with it.

Shortly after this Maclaine paid a visit to his worthy brother in Holland. It was his last holiday. He had spent rather lavishly abroad, and the faithful Plunkett urged him on to fresh efforts on the road. The pair must have been pretty hard pressed for cash, for they actually undertook two jobs in one night. The first was at Turnham Green, where they held up the Salisbury stage-coach, taking, among other things, two portmanteaux containing clothes belonging to a Mr Higden. Then, going on to Hounslow Heath, the pair held up the Earl of Eglinton, whom they relieved of valuables, clothes, and a blunderbuss.

The loot was taken as usual to St James's Street, and at his leisure Maclaine got a pawnbroker to come and look at the clothes. But the losses had already been advertised, and the pawnbroker recognized some of the garments from their description. He went away to get some money, he said—and returned with a constable. Mr Higden's clothes were soon identified, as were the blunderbuss and " a remarkable coat " belonging to Lord Eglinton. Maclaine spent the night in Newgate.

On being charged the highwayman broke down and made a complete confession. When he came up for trial at the Old Bailey, however, he had recovered his nerve and delivered a polished speech in which he put all the blame on the absent Plunkett. (Plunkett, by the way, had disappeared, and was never caught.) He had taken Plunkett into his employment, said Maclaine, and lent him quite a lot of money. To repay his debts Plunkett had offered him these garments, which he said he had bought. Of course, went on Maclaine, it was quite obvious now that the villainous Plunkett must have been leading a double life, and had obtained those articles by highway robbery. But how could he have known that?

Of course Maclaine's confession was brought up as evidence against him, and he found it harder to explain this away. All he could say was that his arrest " caused a delirium and confusion in my brain, which rendered me incapable of being myself, or knowing what I said or did. I talked of robberies," he went on, " as another man would do in talking of stories."

The courtroom was packed with people of high station—mostly ladies. In his defence Maclaine called nine witnesses to vouch for his character. Our illustration shows one of them, Lady Caroline Petersham, making her little speech. Maclaine, immaculate as ever, despite his fetters, stands in the dock in the forefront.

The jury found him guilty without leaving court.

After the verdict was announced Judge Lediard asked the prisoner if he had anything to say.

" My Lord, I can go no further," replied Maclaine—and this sentence got him into the annotations of Gray's poems, under the *Long Story*—

> But soon his rhetorick forsook him,
> When he the solemn hall had seen,
> A sudden fit of ague shook him,
> He stood as mute as poor Maclean.

The case created a sensation at the time, and a full report was published in the *Gentleman's Magazine*, which also printed a letter from brother Archibald. It is a pretty sanctimonious, I-knew-this-would-happen sort of document. The Reverend Archibald explains how he was always warning " him whom I will call brother no more " about the dangers of an idle life, and ends by complaining that James " has, I fear, broken my heart, and will make me draw on the rest of my days in sorrow."

Horace Walpole himself tells us the rest of the story. After Maclaine's arrest, he says, " there was a ward robe of clothes, three and twenty purses, and the celebrated blunderbuss found at his lodgings, besides a famous kept mistress. As I conclude he will suffer, and wish him no ill, I don't care to have his idea, and am almost single in not having been to see him. Lord Mountford, at the head of half White's, went the first day: his aunt was crying over him : as soon as they were withdrawn, she said to him, knowing they were of White's, ' My dear, what did the Lords say to you? have you ever been concerned with any of them? ' Was it not admirable? what a favourable idea people must have of White's! and what if White's should not deserve a much better! But the chief personages who have been to comfort and weep over this fallen hero are Lady Caroline Petersham and Miss Ashe: I call them *Polly* and *Lucy*, and asked them if he did not sing, ' Thus I stand like the Turk with his doxies around.' "

The last sentence is an allusion to the concluding song in John Gay's *Beggar's Opera*, which had been such an enormous success when it was first produced some years previously. Polly and Lucy were two girl friends of the highwayman " hero " of the show, Captain Macheath.

While in his cell Maclaine was visited periodically by the Rev. Dr Allen, who found him truly penitent. He spun the clergyman a fine yarn. " Altho' most of those with whom he had lately conversed ridiculed all religion," reported Dr Allen, " yet the truths of Christendom had been so deeply rooted in his mind by a pious education that he never entertained the least doubt about them, even while he was engaged in course of the most flagitious wickedness." Dr Allen goes on to say that Maclaine burst into tears when he read his brother's letter, and behaved throughout his confinement in a very creditable way.

Compare this with Walpole's report:

" The first Sunday after his condemnation, three thousand people went to see him; he fainted away twice with the heat of the cell. You can't conceive the going there is to Newgate; and the prints that are published of the malefactors, and the memoirs of their lives and deaths set forth with as much parade as—as—Marshal Turenne's—we have no Generals worth making a parallel."

However, it is on record that Maclaine was bent over his prayer-book all the way to Tyburn, and he made no farewell speech to the huge crowd. His last words were addressed to the constable who had arrested him, and who now came to ask for his pardon.

" I forgive you, and may God bless you, and your friends," Maclaine told him. " May He forgive my enemies and receive my soul."

Now, what was the secret of this " Gentleman Highwayman's " fatal attraction? He danced no corantos—he hadn't even got a French accent! The *Dictionary of National Biography* tells us that "his features were good." Well, the old prints can't have been very flattering, can they? And here is the testimony of the Ordinary of Newgate:

"He was in person of the middle size, well limbed, and a sandy complexion, a broad, open countenance pitted with the small-pox; but though he was called the Gentleman Highwayman, and in his dress and equipage very much affected the fine gentleman, yet to a man acquainted with good breeding, and that can distinguish it from impudence and affectation, there was very little in his address or behaviour that could entitle him to the character."

Perhaps it was just that impudence and affectation that Lady Caroline & Co. fell for.

CHAPTER TWENTY-FOUR

The Arm of the Law

WITH rare exceptions all our highwaymen so far have ended their lives on the gallows. This, and the fact that most of them died young, might suggest that crime-detection was in an advanced state in the seventeenth and eighteenth centuries. Nothing could be farther from the truth.

There are two reasons why most of our chapters end at Tyburn. The first, and more important, is that our sources of information have perforce been limited to records of the Old Bailey and Newgate and contemporary Press reports of arrests, trials, and executions. Highwaymen who were unhung were also unsung. The second reason is that many highwaymen were their own worst friends. In general the knights of the road were vain, boastful, and careless. Half the fun of robbing on the highway was bragging about it afterwards. Vanity and drink loosened their tongues, and the offers of rewards did the rest.

During the first part of the eighteenth century highwaymen generally were better armed and better organized than ever before. None of the roads were safe, by day or by night. Indeed, one enterprising coach-builder advertised a bullet-proof chaise "for the convenience of gentlemen travelling." It was the same all over the country, though the blackest spots continued to be on the roads leading into London.

London was always the Mecca of highwaymen, and in the first part of the eighteenth century many daring robberies were carried out in the streets of the capital itself. To this day Members of the House of Commons are reminded of the dangers to those of their forerunners who stayed for late sittings. "Who goes home?" is still the cry—only a bit of tradition now, with the bobby outside and another round the corner. It was very different in the old days. When the House rose

Members left in little groups, composed according to residential rather than political affiliations, and were escorted home by linkmen.

Until very recently London boasted a physical relic of highwaymen in the West End. This was the iron bar down the middle of Lansdowne Passage, leading to Curzon Street—now absorbed by Lansdowne Row. The bar was put up in 1768, following the escape of a highwayman who had held up a coach in Piccadilly. This bold fellow, whose name was never discovered, was pursued into Berkeley Street, and when capture seemed certain he urged his horse down the steps of the narrow passage and got away.

Such was the state of affairs two centuries ago. What was the Government doing about it? Nothing. The liability of the Hundreds remained the Law. There was no police force. Very occasionally troops were turned out to put down some particular gang that had overstepped the mark. It was by a detachment of Dragoons that " Captain " James Whitney was caught the first time, after a pitched battle near Barnet between his men and the soldiers. Later, a band composed mainly of deserters and disbanded soldiers had the audacity to pitch camp in Epping Forest, and used it as their headquarters until a detachment of their former comrades in arms was sent to break them up. But these were isolated cases, and soldiers were used for this work only when there was no alternative. Then, as now, good troops made bad policemen—especially when employed in connexion with offences against property.

Leaving out the troops, then, and the more dangerous reward-hunting informers, what were the highwaymen up against?

First of all, there were the constables. These were selected by local authorities from ordinary citizens, just as jurymen are appointed to-day. The duty was obligatory, and the term of office was one year. It was unpaid, and remained so until as late as 1792.

Clearly this was a highly unsatisfactory system from every point of view except that of the criminals. No physical or moral qualifications were demanded; and no sooner had a constable acquired some experience than he was replaced by a novice. Moreover, since he had to earn his living during his period of office, he could not be expected to regard it as a full-time occupation. Business-men often thought it worth their while to pay someone else to do the job for them—and of course such professional proxies were rarely of the mettle required for the office. Typical was Shakespeare's "simple constable" Elbow, who held his appointment for seven and a half years. When asked if there were no other citizens eligible he replied:

" 'Faith, sir, few of any wit in such matters; as they are chosen they are glad to choose me for them; I do it for some piece of money, and go through with all."

In the seventeenth century the constables were supplemented by paid watchmen. In *Jackson's Recantation* we got a pretty clear picture of the contempt in which these "silly old decreeped men" were held by the highwaymen. In London a permanent night watch—paid, but quite inadequately—was established in the reign of Charles II, the men being given the obvious nickname of "Charlies." This is how Fielding described the London watchmen in *Amelia* (1751):

"They were chosen out of those poor, old, decrepit people who are from their want of bodily strength rendered incapable of getting a living by work. These men, armed only with a pole, which some of them are scarce able to lift, are to secure the persons and houses of His Majesty's subjects from the attacks of young, bold, stout and desperate and well-armed villains. If the poor old fellows should run away from such enemies no one, I think, can wonder unless he should wonder that they are able even to make their escape."

Such, then, were the custodians of Law and Order in England in the middle of the eighteenth century. But a change was coming—and it was Henry Fielding himself who largely brought it about. Forced by lack of means to take non-literary employment, in October 1748 he obtained the appointment of Commissioner of the Peace for Middlesex (and later for Westminster). He took up office in Bow Street, where his predecessor, Colonel Sir Thomas de Veil, had set up his headquarters. De Veil, who had held office continuously since

1729, had made a start in the war against crime, and had personally done some very fine detective work.

With Henry Fielding went his blind half-brother, John, who became his assistant in 1751 and succeeded him in 1754. With John's help Henry set to work with surprising vigour and enthusiasm for a disgruntled, disillusioned dramatist. The chief obstacle to reform was, as usual, the Government—and especially the Treasury.

The method of appointing constables was one of the first things that engaged Fielding's attention. He quickly found that he could expect little help from these officers as long as they were amateurs and changed every year. He therefore kept the constables under observation, and at the end of their period of service he approached the best of them and persuaded some of these to remain in office for a further period. His loyalest supporter was Saunders Welch, High Constable of Holborn, whom Fielding described as "one of the best officers who was ever concerned in the execution of justice." After a year he had eighty constables working directly under him, and he drew up a list of rules for their guidance.

Had Fielding received the slightest support from the Government he would in this way have anticipated Sir Robert Peel by more than half a century, and constables would never have got the name of Bobbies. But the Government refused to finance a professional force, and Fielding could not expect the men to carry on without payment indefinitely. So this first unofficial police force had to be allowed to dissipate through lack of funds.

In 1751 Henry Fielding published a pamphlet entitled *An Enquiry into the Causes of the Late Increase of Robberies, etc., with some Proposals for Remedying this growing evil*. It was not a bestseller, and is frequently ignored by Fielding's bibliographers. Its importance in the history of crime was tremendous. It prompted the Government—always more generous with legislation than with financial aid—to bring in two important Bills in the following year. Both became law. The first was the Gin Act, which restricted the sale of gin; the second, an "Act for Better Preventing Thefts and Robberies," which drove half the fences in London out of business. This latter

Act carried the half-measure of 1718 to its logical conclusion. Receiving property known to be stolen became a criminal offence, as did advertising for stolen property " with no questions asked."

Meanwhile the Fieldings were doing some advertising themselves. In 1752 they started a periodical called the *Covent Garden Journal*, which always carried some such advertisement as the following:

" All persons who shall for the future suffer by robbers, burglars, etc., are desired immediately to bring or send the best descriptions they can of such robbers, etc., with the time and place and circumstances of the fact, to Henry Fielding, Esq., at his house in Bow Street."

But Henry Fielding was not content to remain in his house in Bow Street and wait for information to come in. He was out and about a good deal, as can be seen from the following extract from the *Gentleman's Magazine*. The date is March 6, 1753:

" About four this morning, Justice Fielding having intelligence that some highwaymen were to be at the masquerade, went into the gaming room, with the officers upon guard, and oblig'd all the company to unmask and give an account of themselves. It's suppos'd those fellows had notice of his coming before he could get up stairs, and so made off in the crowd, for none of them were taken."

That was the trouble. The fellows always seemed to have advance information. They were supported by large organizations—while Fielding had to rely only on a handful of unpaid inexperienced constables and the " old, decrepit " Charlies. He did his best. He often worked sixteen hours a day, and sometimes sat up all night examining suspected criminals. But crime continued to increase. The gangs round London got so bad that in August 1753 the Duke of Newcastle summoned Henry Fielding to his office and asked him to submit a plan.

Fielding's proposals were brief and pointed. He wanted a grant of £600. With this, he declared, he would " demolish the reigning gangs, and put the civil policy into such order that no such gangs should ever be able for the future to form themselves into bodies, or at least to remain any time formidable." He did not add that he would need continued financial assistance to be able to keep the civil policy in order.

The proposals gave no hint of how Fielding intended to accomplish his purpose. For this there were two reasons. In the first place, his plan could only work if it were put into practice under conditions of great secrecy; and, secondly, the means he was going to adopt were likely to be regarded with hostility and suspicion by both the authorities and the public at large. For Fielding proposed to establish not a police force, but an organization of detectives.

Detectives—or thief-takers, as they were called then—had been in bad odour ever since the days of Jonathan Wild the Great. At best the thief-taker was no more than a common informer. The idea of a police detective was a novel one; and the difficulties of making thief-taking an honourable profession seemed insuperable. How could men be found who would have both sufficient knowledge of the Underworld for them to be useful, and sufficient moral integrity for them to be trusted? The answer was that Fielding already had the men. He had been training detectives, in a small way, ever since 1749. They were few in number, but, as he said later, " all men of known and approved fidelity and intrepidity."

Thus was born the germ of the modern C.I.D.

Fielding remained at Bow Street only a few months longer, but he had the satisfaction of seeing his work partially completed. The Government gave him two-thirds of the money he had asked for, and at once he put his detectives on a full-time basis. The money was used partly for salaries and partly for the purchase of information about the gangs—for Fielding was a realist. The result was that many of the gangs were completely broken up and others forced to flee from the London district, and that winter the capital was freer from the ravages of highwaymen and burglars than it had been for many years.

By the beginning of 1754 Fielding's health was very bad, and his half-brother took over most of his work. In May Henry retired, and in the following month set off on his voyage to Lisbon, where he died in October.

During his period of office at Bow Street Henry Fielding had found time to write *Amelia*, from which we quoted earlier in this chapter. It is often erroneously stated that he also made use of his time to collect copy for his satire *Jonathan Wild the Great*; but this was published five years before he took office. All the same, it is indicative of Fielding's interest in "thief-taking" even before his professional connexion with criminals.

John Fielding, who succeeded Henry at Bow Street, carried on the good work with amazing success for a man who had never seen a criminal. Nature compensated for his blindness by giving him exceptional powers of hearing, and he was reputed to know more than three thousand thieves by the sound of their voices. Like his half-brother, he frequently went out on cases himself. His work, indeed, was the logical development of Henry's ideas.

Following upon the success of the thief-takers in the previous winter, the Duke of Newcastle's grant of £400 became a regular annual allowance. Thus London had a permanent professional detective organization before it had a police force. These detectives—or Bow Street Runners, as they came to be known—were kept constantly on call, and undertook the investigation of cases outside London when their assistance was requested. They became a force akin to our Special Branch. Unlike the Special Branch, however, their services were not entirely free. The Government grant was too small for Fielding to pay any but very small salaries, which the Runners regarded more as a retaining fee than an income. Thus, when a man who had been robbed called in the Runners he was expected to pay the cost of the investigation. The usual charge made by a Runner was a guinea a day plus fourteen shillings for expenses.

Another of Henry's innovations which was carried on by John was in the matter of public relations. The *Covent Garden Journal* died shortly before Henry, and John used mainly the columns of the *Public Advertiser*. Here is a typical notice, which appeared in October 1754:

"Whereas many thieves and robbers daily escape justice for want of immediate pursuit, it is therefore recommended to all persons who shall henceforth be robbed on the highway or in the streets, or whose shops or houses shall be broke open, that they should give immediate notice thereof, together with as accurate a description as possible, to John Fielding, Esq., at his house in Bow Street, Covent Garden; by which means, joined to an advertisement containing an account of the things lost (which is also taken in there), thieves and robbers will seldom escape, as most of the pawnbrokers take in this paper and by the intelligence they get from it assist daily in discovering and apprehending rogues."

The *Public Advertiser* and other journals were used for official advertisements containing lists of stolen property until 1786, when a publication called the *Hue and Cry* appeared. Each issue of this was limited to four pages, the contents being taken up by accounts of police-court proceedings, reports of all crimes in the London area, lists of stolen goods, and descriptions of " wanted " men and of all deserters from H.M. Forces. Later the name of this journal was changed to the more prosaic *Police Gazette*.

John Fielding was not a professional writer, but in the year following his brother's death he brought out a remarkable pamphlet entitled *A Plan for Preventing Robberies within Twenty Miles of London*, on which he and Henry had been working for some time.

The *Plan* was aimed directly against the highwaymen who infested the roads leading into London. It was based also on the indisputable axiom that little help could be expected from the Government. If crime was to be suppressed, it could be done only by private enterprise. The Fieldings therefore proposed that the co-operation should be sought of twenty gentlemen with country houses within twenty miles of London. When any of these heard news of a highway robbery he should immediately send a messenger to Bow Street with a written account of the incident, including exact time and place, name of person robbed, description of robber or robbers, articles stolen, and other similar details. The messenger should be instructed also to warn all turnpike-keepers, publicans, and stable-keepers whom he passed on the way.

Payment for the services of the messengers would be made out of a Pool, to which each of the twenty gentlemen was to be invited to contribute two guineas. Before collecting payment the messenger would be required to produce a chit signed by Fielding acknowledging receipt of the message. On receipt of the information, whatever other action was taken, a notice would be placed in the *Public Advertiser*, cost for this also being paid out of the Pool. Meanwhile, investigations would be started by one of the Bow Street Runners.

This *Plan*, which was greeted with derision by many, proved an unqualified success. Fielding found enough "country gentlemen" to co-operate, and shortly after the scheme was put into practice one highwayman was arrested in London less than forty-eight hours after committing a robbery in Essex. Eventually the plan was adopted by the Government, and the Treasury was prevailed upon to make an annual grant of £200 for the Pool with an additional £60 for cost of notices in the *Public Advertiser*.

In 1761 John Fielding was knighted for these services. But it was the establishment of the Bow Street Patrol that was his crowning achievement. This was the first professional police force, and it was kept in being, in some form or another, until the formation of the Metropolitan Police in the following century. It was a great achievement when Fielding persuaded the Government to grant the enormous sum of £4,000 a year for the policing of the whole of London and a good deal of the surrounding country, but somehow he managed it.

The original establishment of the Patrol was sixty-eight men, who were split up into thirteen roughly equal parties, each commanded by a "conductor." Eight were "country parties," detailed to patrol the roads leading into London; the remaining five were "town parties," assigned to areas within the capital. The parties assembled every evening to mount duty, and maintained the Patrol until well after midnight. They paraded at Fielding's office first thing every morning to make their report.

Payment was five shillings per night for conductors and half that sum for the rank and file. Each conductor was armed with a carbine, a pair of pistols, and a cutlass; each man was issued with a cutlass. Discipline was high. Strict rules and regulations were drawn up and frequent inspections carried out. The force became known as the Foot Patrol, or Night

Patrol. The name of " Robin Redbreasts " was never applied to them, though it has been several times since. They wore no red waistcoats; indeed, they were not uniformed at all.

The Foot Patrol was primarily a preventive force, and later came to be used in the daytime for keeping the peace on public occasions, attending the King to Parliament, and other similar activities.

Some indication of the value of the Patrol can be gathered from the following paragraph from *Jackson's Oxford Journal*, dated January 14, 1764:

" Information has been sent to His Majesty's Justice of the Peace for this county that several gangs of thieves have lately left London to avoid Sir John Fielding's parties. . . ."

To Sir John Fielding also goes the credit for the establishment of the first Mounted Police. This was the Horse Patrol, for which he got another, smaller grant out of the Government. The men were paid four shillings a night, plus expenses, and the limited funds kept their numbers small. The Patrol was well armed, and for the first time the forces of Law were able to meet the highwayman on equal terms. But the Government never regarded the Horse Patrol as a permanent force. Not long after its inception Sir John was pleading " for the continuance of the Horse Patrol for a short time longer, as a temporary but necessary step in order to complete that which had been so happily begun." Of course Sir John knew that it was no temporary step, but to have said so would have been fatal. As it was, the Government refused to listen, and eventually the Horse Patrol was allowed to lapse.

The setting up of these various forces by the Fieldings was a beginning, and it led to a sharp decrease in the incidence of crime in London. However, the highwaymen continued for many years afterwards, although in steadily diminishing numbers. As late as 1771 Horace Walpole—who seems to have been a special mark for highwaymen—was held up in the streets of London. He tells the story in one of his letters to the Countess of Ossory:

" Lady Browne and I were going to the Duchess of Montrose at seven o'clock. The evening was very dark, and in the lane under her park-palings a black figure on horseback passed the chaise. I suspected it was a highwayman, and so did Lady Browne. I had the presence of mind to stuff my watch under my arm. He said, ' Your purse and watches.' I gave him my purse; it had nine guineas. It was so dark that I could not see his hand, but I felt him take it. He then asked for Lady Browne's purse, and said, ' Don't be frightened, I will not hurt you.' She gave it to him, and was going to add her watch, but he said, ' I am much obliged to you. Good night,' pulled off his hat and rode away."

Sir John Fielding died in 1780, just after his house had been burned down in the Gordon Riots. The importance of his work was not appreciated in his lifetime, nor has it been since his death. He came in for some sharp criticism from his contemporaries. Inevitably he was accused of peculation, and specifically for accepting a bribe of fifty guineas a year from two newspapers in consideration of the use of their columns for police advertisements. Another charge against him was that he gave criminals limited encouragement before suddenly having them arrested; this, of course, could be justified on the grounds that by so doing he was able to round up accomplices and confederates who would otherwise not have been detected. A further complaint against the methods of the magistrate was that he not only admitted reporters to his police court, but actually supplied them with pen and ink—which "cruelly exposed the criminals." There is something humorous about this complaint, made in an age when the normal punishment for stealing a sheep was a public execution.

Bow Street remained London's police headquarters after Sir John Fielding's death, and in 1805 the residing magistrate, Sir Richard Ford, re-established the Horse Patrol. A Government grant of £8,000 a year was obtained, and the first establishment numbered fifty-two men and two inspectors. The men were drawn mainly from the ranks of ex-cavalrymen. They had the distinction of being the first uniformed police in the country, wearing blue jackets, blue trousers, and red waistcoats.

In 1822 Sir Robert Peel established a Day Patrol of uniformed policemen, complete with red waistcoats. It was probably these who got the nickname of " Robin Redbreasts."

Incidentally, it is interesting to note that the Bow Street magistrate who supplied Peel with information and recommendations was William Fielding, Henry's son.

The story ends—so far as London is concerned—in 1829, when Peel's Metropolitan Police Act brought all the various forces under one administration and laid down proper regulations and conditions of service. County police followed soon after.

Beyond that we need not go. For in 1829 the highwayman was dead—for ever.

There is an obvious moral to be drawn from this chapter. The only real deterrent from crime is an adequate police force.

Thus a nation gets the amount of crime it deserves.

CHAPTER TWENTY-FIVE
William Page and the Weston Brothers

THE decline and fall of the highwayman was not a sudden process. First—thanks to the Fieldings—went the gangs. The profession in the latter half of the eighteenth century was almost entirely in the hands of robbers who worked singly or in pairs. Their numbers diminished steadily; but in boldness and other traditional characteristics they were worthy of the greatest of their ancestors. The highwayman of old was famous for the "brave show" he put up at Tyburn; as with the individual, so with the profession as a whole; highwaymen died out as the highwayman died—game to the last.

Historical generalizations are not only usually false, but are liable to the more serious danger of being dull. The story of highwaymen in the last fifty years of the eighteenth century will therefore be given in the form of biographies of the six leading characters: three in this chapter, and a chapter each for the others.

William Page was a farmer's son, but you wouldn't have thought it. As a boy he was sent to London to learn the haberdashery business under a cousin; but he had thoughts above underwear. "He was such a consummate coxcomb," says his biographer, "that he was perpetually employing tailors to alter his clothes to any new fashion he had seen"—and telling them to send their bills to his cousin. The latter objected, and that was the end of that. But not quite. William was so determined to be in the fashion that he got a lantern, hid it under his bed, and when every one else was asleep sat up in bed and altered his clothes himself. But he had to buy the cloth, and an apprentice did not get much pocket-money. One day £15 was missing from the till, and William was caught out. The same day he found himself in the street.

Farmer Page was furious when he heard of this, and refused to help the boy any further. To get a living William was reduced to taking a job as a livery-servant, which sorely wounded his pride. While serving in this employment he had his first sight of a highway robbery, his master being the victim. It made a deep impression on William. Within a matter of minutes his master had handed over more money than he paid William in a year. The highwayman rode off, followed by the envious eyes of William Page. It looked so easy, and was certainly very profitable—and how well the highwayman was dressed. . . .

William had no capital, but that did not deter him. He managed to borrow a pair of pistols and hire a horse, and sallied forth. £4 was his first night's earnings—enough to pay the hire of the horse and to buy the pistols. More daring, he rode out to Shooter's Hill, and held up the Canterbury stage-coach. From the passengers he collected money and valuables to the value of about £30. He straightway took lodgings near Grosvenor Square, ordered a new suit, and entered society. He soon got in with a gambling set, and the £30 did not last long. But there was plenty of money on the road. . . . He soon had £200 behind him, a doxy beside him, and one of the best wardrobes in town.

William Page was responsible for two innovations to his conservative profession. First, he taught himself cartography, and drew a map of the roads twenty miles round London. This map was discovered in his lodgings after he was arrested. Second, instead of riding out on horseback, he went to work in a phaeton and pair. As soon as he was out of town he would pick some secluded spot to park his phaeton, and then, after changing his clothes and putting on a new wig and mask, would saddle one of his horses and ride out on to the road. After a successful robbery he hurried back to where he had parked the phaeton, changed again, and drove back to town at his leisure.

This ingenious idea served Page well for some time, until one day, after robbing some travellers on the road near Putney, he went back to his hide-out and found the phaeton had disappeared. The loss of the vehicle and one of his horses was bad enough, but much more serious was the fact that he could not change out of his working clothes. He dismounted, and investigated. Following the track of the phaeton, he found that it had been taken by a party of hay-makers. Ironically, they were stopped on the road by the travellers whom Page had robbed, and were accused of having been the highwayman's accomplices. This gave Page an idea. He took off his working clothes, and threw them down a well; then, dressed only in his underwear, he showed himself publicly and claimed the phaeton as his, accusing the hay-makers of having robbed him and stripped him into the bargain. His charge was denied, but his own victims supported him, and all parties went before a Justice of the Peace. Page called the carriagemaker to support his claim to ownership, and as a result the hay-makers were committed for trial. However, with his phaeton back and his own activities still unsuspected, he declined to prosecute the men, and they were acquitted for lack of evidence. After that, though, he kept his phaeton for joyrides, and observed the convention of his profession by going to work on horseback.

Shortly after this Page met an old school friend named Darwell, whom he persuaded to join him on the road. It was a happy partnership, and in the course of three years the pair were said to have committed no less than three hundred robberies. They always divided their spoils on a strictly fifty-fifty basis; where there was an odd watch or piece of jewellery they tossed up for it. These were the best years of Page's life. He was able to live and dress like a gentleman, frequenting the fashionable watering-places of Bath and Scarborough, and losing most of his money on the gaming tables.

The end came in 1758, when one of Sir John Fielding's patrols caught Darwell on the Tonbridge Road, Page only just getting away. Taken to Bow Street, Darwell refused to reveal anything about his confederate; but the blind magistrate tempted him with promises of a pardon and intimidated him with threats of punishment, and in the end Darwell turned King's evidence. As a result of this Page was arrested in the Golden Lion, near Hyde Park. He was tried, sentenced, and executed in April of the same year.

There was rarely more than one highwayman in a family, and the case of the Weston brothers is of unusual interest.

George, the elder, was sent to London by his father—a Staffordshire farmer—to enter a merchant's office. He was so efficient that he soon rose to be chief clerk, with a salary of £200 a year. Unfortunately his tastes were nearer £2,000 a year, and he made up the balance by fiddling the books. His brother Joseph, who had joined him in town, helped to spend the money without contributing much to the exchequer himself. Inevitably the frauds were discovered, and the pair had to leave town in a hurry. After a short holiday in Holland, they returned to England and joined a party of strolling players. The pay was poor, though, and they left the company at Manchester. There the versatile George entered the teaching profession, and used his talents to such good purpose that within a very short time he was actually appointed High Constable. The temptations of this office were too much for him, and his tenure came to an abrupt end when he was discovered blackmailing innkeepers. The pair left Manchester, and after trying their hands at horse-stealing, confidence tricks, forgery, and smuggling, took up the profession of the highway.

George Weston always aimed high. He was not going to risk his neck for a gold watch or a few guineas. He proposed that they should hold up the Royal Mail; and Joseph—who seems to have accepted his brother's leadership in all things—agreed. The best account of the incident is contained in a notice issued by the G.P.O. on the day of the robbery, which shows that an official document does not have to be dull:

" General Post Office, Jan. 29th, 1781.

" The postboy bringing the Bristol Mail this morning from Maidenhead was stopped between two and three o'clock by a single highwayman with a crêpe over his face between the eleventh and twelfth milestones, near to Cranford Bridge, who presented a pistol to him, and after making him alight, drove away the horse and cart, which were found about seven o'clock this morning in a meadow field near Farmer Lott's at Twyford, when it appears that the greatest part of the letters were taken out of the Bath and Bristol bags, and that the following bags were entirely taken away. . . ."

A list of the destinations of thirty-five mail-bags follows. The notice continues:

"The person who committed this robbery is supposed to have had an accomplice, as two persons passed the postboy on Cranford Bridge on horseback prior to the robbery, one of whom he thinks was the robber; but it being so extremely dark, he is not able to give any description of their persons.

"Whoever shall apprehend and convict, or cause to be apprehended and convicted, the person who committed this robbery will be entitled to a reward of TWO HUNDRED POUNDS, over and above the reward given by Act of Parliament for apprehending highwaymen; or if any person, whether an accomplice in the robbery or knowing thereof, shall make discovery whereby the person who committed the same may be apprehended and brought to justice, such discoverer will upon conviction of the party be entitled to the same reward of TWO HUNDRED POUNDS and will also receive His Majesty's most gracious pardon.

"By command of the Postmaster-General."

The haul was estimated at being worth about £15,000, all in banknotes and bills. As the Westons knew, descriptions of these would soon be circulated, and speed in disposal was essential. But George had his plans all ready. Returning to London after the robbery, he dressed himself as a naval officer, while Joseph put on servant's livery. Then they hired a post-chaise and set off north.

The first news of them came from Nottingham, where one of the bills was changed shortly before its description reached the bank. The G.P.O. received similar information from banks in other towns. The thieves were conducting a grand tour of the country at high speed, getting rid of notes and bills at every town they passed through.

The Post Office authorities called in Bow Street, and the Runners went after them, following one of the strangest paper-chases in criminal history. They nearly caught the pair at Lincoln, but lost the trail soon after. They picked it up again later, only to find that it led all the way back to London.

In London the case was entrusted to an experienced Runner named John Clarke. He found the coachman who had driven the pair on part of their journey, and tracked them down as far as the Red Lion, in Bishopsgate. There the trail ended. But on the following day Clarke's attention was drawn to a naval uniform which had been found in the river near Chelsea Waterworks.

From the description given by the coachman and others the Bow Street detectives soon discovered the identity of the robbers, and fresh notices were issued. That the Bow Street men knew their job can be seen from the remarkably detailed descriptions given of the pair:

" George Weston is about twenty-nine years of age, five feet seven inches high, square-set, round-faced, fresh-coloured, pitted with smallpox, has a rather thick nose, his upper lip rather thick, his hair of lightest brown colour, which is sometimes tied behind, and at other times loose and curled; has much the appearance of a country dealer or farmer. One of his thumb-nails appears, from an accident, of the shape of a parrot's bill, and he is supposed to have a scar on his right hand, from a stroke with a cutlass.

" Joseph Weston is about twenty-three years of age, five feet nine inches high, slender made, of a fair and smooth complexion, genteel person, has grey eyes and large nose with a scar upon it; his hair is of a light brown colour, sometimes tied behind, at other times loose and curled; his voice is strong and he speaks a little through his nose; has a remarkable small hand and long fingers."

But the Weston brothers had disappeared.

They reappeared in Winchelsea, under the names of William Johnson and Samuel Watson. Posing as gentlemen of some means—which indeed they now were—they leased a large house called " The Friars." They ordered expensive furniture from Messrs Elliot & Co. of New Bond Street, and, with two " wives " whom they had picked up in town, set up house in the December following the robbery of the Royal Mail. Money talked, and they were soon admitted to local society. They behaved as respectable, law-abiding citizens; George, in particular, was so tremendously respectable that at Easter in the following year he received an honour unique among highwaymen: he was elected churchwarden.

But it was the same old George Weston. However much money he had he could always spend more. The account with Messrs Elliot was left unsettled, and the directors of that firm were alarmed to learn that their name had been given by " Mr William Johnson " as a reference to a jeweller. Messrs Elliot invoked the assistance of the Law, and two of the Sheriff's officers were sent down to arrest the pair. They met the brothers on the road near Rye, and explained their business. Seeing how the affair was going to end, George knocked down one of the officers with the butt-end of his riding-whip, and then produced a pair of pistols. The officers did not press their business any further after this, and the Westons made good their escape. They rode fast back to " The Friars "—so fast that they found time to pack a few belongings before setting off for the safest hiding-place in the country—London.

Winchelsea had lost one of her churchwardens for ever.

It had been good fun while it lasted, and George and Joseph were prepared to start life again with new aliases. But the notices issued from Bow Street over a year previously had not been forgotten. The Sheriff's officer whom George had knocked down had observed a peculiar deformity about the latter's thumb. The nail was shaped like a parrot's bill. . . .

John Clarke was informed, and on April 17 he tracked them down to a hotel in Wardour Street. The landlord tipped the Westons that the Runner was after them, and they made a hasty departure. No sooner were they in the street than Clarke gave the alarm. The brothers were chased through Soho, and finally, after a bit of gunplay, overpowered and captured.

The trial for the robbery of the Royal Mail began in May, but was postponed owing to the sudden death of the chief witness for the prosecution—the postboy. George and Joseph remained in Newgate, where they were visited by their " wives," who brought them gifts of money, food, drink, clothes—and pistols and a file. They rid themselves of their fetters, overpowered the warder, and made a bolt for it. Outside the gaol they separated. George made for Smithfield Market, but was rearrested almost immediately. Joseph, seeking to escape via Cock Lane, was held up by a porter, whom he shot and wounded in the cheek, but who clung on to him until help arrived. The pair were taken back to Newgate.

The trial was resumed in July, and over a hundred witnesses were called. Most of these were recipients of stolen bills from various parts of the country. However, the vital evidence of the postboy was lacking, and the case could not be proved. The accused were formally acquitted—and then immediately rearrested. On the same day they were tried for forging endorsements on the stolen bills, and on this indictment George was capitally convicted. Joseph was again acquitted; but without rising the Court tried him again, this time under the Black Act, for having fired at and wounded the porter in Cock Lane. He too was found guilty and sentenced to death. The pair were hanged together at Tyburn on September 3, 1782. They had a full obituary notice in the *Gentleman's Magazine*, while the *Annual Register* described them as " two most notorious villains, who for some years have defrauded the country by various artful contrivances."

The Weston brothers belong to the select band of highwaymen who found their way into the pages of Victorian fiction. In their case, very august pages—namely, in Thackeray's *Denis Duval*. But Thackeray did not cast them for a heroic rôle. He had no time for romantic highwaymen. Indeed, he joined forces with the pedantic historians attacking Harrison Ainsworth. (As a novelist himself he ought to have known better.) Five years after the publication of *Rookwood* Thackeray brought out his *Catherine*, written, as he said, " to counteract the injurious influence of some popular fiction of the day, which made heroes of highwaymen, and created a false sympathy for the crime." It counteracted nothing, and was a flop. There was no such high moral purpose about *Denis Duval*, although the Weston brothers are shown as a pretty pair of villains. They were saved from complete disgrace only by the death of the author before the work was finished.

CHAPTER TWENTY-SIX

Sixteen String Jack

DR SAMUEL JOHNSON was not noted for any tenderness towards highwaymen, and his views on the punishment of criminals generally have already been quoted. Yet to one highwayman—a contemporary of his—he paid a remarkable tribute. In a eulogy of Thomas Gray he declared that the poet " towered above the ordinary run of verse as Sixteen String Jack above the ordinary footpad."

Sixteen String Jack was born John Rann, of poor but industrious parents, in a village near Bath. He was a likely-looking boy, and at the age of twelve was taken into service by a lady who was taking the waters at the spa. He proved a good worker, and she took him to London with her. There he rose to the station of officer's batman, and then to post-chaise driver. He was now about twenty, and had developed a taste for two things: good clothes and bad women. Both were too expensive for a coachman, so he sought other employment.

Picking pockets was one way of making a living, but it did not appeal to John Rann for long. He was cut out for the road, and he soon equipped himself with a horse, a couple of pistols, a crêpe mask—and a superb suit of clothes. John became Jack, and how he got his nickname is told in a contemporary description:

" He was about five feet five inches high, wore his own hair, of a light brown colour, which combed over his forehead, remarkably clean, and particularly neat in his dress, which in two instances was very singular, that of always having sixteen strings to his breeches knees, always of silk (by which means he acquired his fictitious name) and a remarkable hat with strings, and a button on the crown. He was straight, of a genteel carriage, and makes a very handsome appearance."

Later the story was added that the sixteen strings symbolized the number of times Jack had been arrested and acquitted, but this is not supported by the facts. Official records reveal that he was in custody seven times in all—but only six of the cases resulted in acquittal. He first fell into the clutches of the Law in 1772, when he was committed to Bridewell on a charge of robbing a post-chaise on Hounslow Heath. The case was not proved, and he was formally acquitted. He continued his vocation undisturbed until December of the following year, when, in company with three other highwaymen—William Davis, alias Scarlet, David Monro, and John Saunders—he held up the Hampstead stage-coach and robbed a Mr Simmonds of one guinea three shillings and sixpence. The robbery was reported to Bow Street, and, despite the smallness of the sum stolen, the investigation was placed in the competent hands of John Clarke, the Runner who had gained fame by tracking down the Weston brothers. Clarke had had his eye on Jack and his companions for some time, and he knew where to look for them: namely, in a disorderly house in Long Acre, where they were arrested the following evening. But at the trial the evidence was again inconclusive, none of the passengers being able to swear to the identity of the highwaymen.

Jack appeared in dock twice in the following spring, and was acquitted on both occasions. The main reason for this series of acquittals was that he never dealt direct with a fence. Added to the fact that he took exceptional pains about his disguise, this meant that the prosecution could neither produce witnesses to swear to his identity nor bring evidence to show that the stolen property had passed through his hands. Jack's intermediary was a girl named Eleanor Roche, former milliner and mistress of an ex-officer of the Guards. Jack and Eleanor took lodgings together, and it was a happy combination. They lived extravagantly, and what Jack could not get by riding the roads Eleanor picked up by walking the streets.

In May 1774 Jack came the nearest to being convicted so far. Working alone on this occasion, he held up a Mr John Devall near Nine Mile Stone on Hounslow Heath, and robbed him of his watch and seven guineas. The robbery took place in the early hours of the morning; later in the day Mr Devall's watch was offered to a pawnbroker named Allam by a girl called Catherine Smith. Allam asked her where she had got it, and dissatisfied with her answer, informed Bow Street. A Runner was sent out, and two days later Jack Rann and Eleanor Roche were arrested in their lodgings.

Jack put up a fine show when he was brought before the magistrate, but of course it was wasted on Sir John Fielding. " His irons were tied up and decorated with blue ribands, and he had a bundle of flowers affixed to the breast of his coat full as large as a common birch-broom." Catherine Smith, on examination, asserted that she had been given the watch by Eleanor Roche and told to dispose of it through a pawnbroker. She further deposed that the watch had been given to Eleanor by Jack Rann. The accused both denied the whole story. " I know no more of the matter than you do," Jack told Sir John—adding, " nor half so much neither! "

Sir John thought otherwise, and the pair were committed for trial—Jack for highway robbery, and Eleanor for receiving stolen goods. No charge was brought against Catherine Smith.

The trial was held in the Old Bailey in the following July. The evidence of the prosecution was entirely circumstantial. Mr Devall identified his watch, but could not swear that the accused was the man who had accosted him. The evidence of the other important witness—Catherine Smith—was unreliable. According to Jack she was trying to frame him on account of a previous quarrel, and from her manner in Court it was clear that there was bad blood between her and Eleanor. In the end the jury gave Jack the benefit of the doubt, and he and Eleanor were acquitted. They celebrated by dining at Vauxhall, and before retiring for the night Jack collected two watches and three purses from travellers on the road.

Four months later Jack was arrested again—on a charge of housebreaking! Of course he was innocent; a highwayman of his calibre would not have stooped to such a low form of crime. It was a humiliating affair, the more so as it was not a Runner, but one of the " silly decreeped old " Charlies who arrested him. The watchman saw Jack climbing into the window of a house about midnight, and pulled him out by the legs, refused to listen to his explanations, and detained him for the night. The next morning Jack was brought up before Sir John Fielding again, and had to explain that he was only

paying a social call when the watchman intercepted him.
He had a supper invitation with a girl named Doll Frampton,
and had been unavoidably detained by business. When he
got to her house Doll, assuming that he would not come, had
already retired; so Jack, thinking to give her a pleasant
surprise, decided to let himself in. Doll Frampton was called,
and supported Jack's story with brazen immodesty. Sir John
dismissed the case—but not before giving a general warning
to Jack about his conduct in the future.

Jack laughed that one off, and hurried back to his lodgings
to make his peace with Eleanor, who was nothing like so
lenient about the affair as the magistrate had been. To make
amends Jack took her on the following Sunday to the fashionable Bagnigge Wells. They travelled in a carriage, Jack being
"elegantly dressed in a scarlet coat, tambour waistcoat, white
silk stockings, laced hat, etc., and publickly declared himself to
be a highwayman." The party was lively. "Having drank
pretty freely, he became extremely quarrelsome, and several
scuffles ensued, in one of which he lost a ring from his finger;
and when he discovered his loss he said it was but an
hundred guineas gone, which one evening's work would
replace." In spite of the smallness of the sums mentioned in
the robberies for which Jack was arrested, there was probably
a good deal of truth in his boast.

For the time being, however, he was not in a mood for work,
and he and Eleanor enjoyed themselves in and out of town,
living on a grand scale. Of course they got into debt; and
one of Jack's creditors had him arrested for a matter of fifty
guineas, and the highwayman found himself in the Marshalsea
Prison.

He did not stay there long. He had plenty of admirers, and
Eleanor looked the other way while his casual girl-friends
had a whip-round, which soon realized the amount required
for his freedom. Scarcely was he out, however, when other
creditors made their demands, and two Sheriff's officers
arrested him in an alehouse in Tottenham Court Road. The
sum was even smaller, and Jack's friends opened a subscription
list on the spot. The debt was paid, and Jack gave the Sheriff's
men a bit of his mind. "You have not treated me like a

gentleman," he said. "When Sir John Fielding's people come after me, they use me genteelly; they only hold up a finger, beckon me, and I follow them as quietly as a lamb."

But Jack was not one to bear malice for long. " Lend me five shillings," he said to the officers, " and I will treat you to a bowl of punch." And so he did; and they parted firm friends.

Tired of being pressed by creditors, Jack decided to do a bit of dishonest work again, and saddled his horse. He soon earned enough to clear the most urgent of his debts. The Bow Street men were after him, but he always managed to elude them. Once, stopping at a turnpike, he asked the tollman if anyone had been asking about him. The tollman replied that he could answer that better if he knew who he was, which upset Jack a good deal.

"What, do you not know me?" he said incredulously. " I am Sixteen String Jack, the famous highwayman. Have any of Sir John Fielding's people been this way?" he rapped out peremptorily.

"Oh, yes, they have," said the frightened tollman. "Some of them have just gone through."

"If you see them again, tell them I am gone towards London," Jack instructed him—and rode off in the opposite direction.

Jack never tried to conceal his identity except when actually on business. Shortly after this he went to the Barnet races, and appeared on the course "dressed like a sporting peer of the first rank. He was distinguished by the elegance of his appearance (his waistcoat, blue satin, laced with silver) and was followed by hundreds from one side of the course to the other, whose looks expressed their pleasure and satisfaction to behold a genius of whose exploits the world had talked so freely."

Yet in his heart he knew it could not last. Once, at an execution at Tyburn, he pushed his way through a large crowd until he came to the ring formed by the constables round the gallows. He asked if he might be allowed to stand within the ring to get a better view—"for," he explained, "perhaps it is very proper that I should be a spectator on this occasion."

The point of the remark was that it was a highwayman who was being hanged.

Shortly after this Sixteen String Jack took a partner named William Collier, and in September 1774 the pair held up Dr Bell, chaplain to Princess Amelia, on the Uxbridge Road at about half-past three in the afternoon. The doctor had no more than eighteenpence in cash, and a plain watch in a tortoiseshell case. If Jack had had any sense he would have let him keep his property and ride on; but he took both the money and the watch, and handed the latter over to Eleanor for disposal through the usual channels.

Eleanor sent her servant, Christian Stewart, to a pawnbroker named Cordy in Oxford Street. The pawnbroker accepted the watch, but his suspicions were aroused. He got in touch with the maker, a Mr Grignion of Covent Garden—and was informed that the watch had been made for Dr Bell. Cordy at once went to Bow Street. There it was quickly discovered that Christian Stewart was servant to Eleanor Roche, and after that it did not take much deduction for the authorities to realize who was responsible for the robbery. John Clarke went out to get his man.

The Runner called at Jack and Eleanor's lodgings on the same evening, but the pair were out. However, he found inside two pairs of riding boots which bore traces of recent use. A watch was set for the night, and the next morning two horses were brought round to the lodgings. Jack Rann and William Collier went out to saddle them—and were promptly arrested by Clarke. Eleanor Roche and Christian Stewart were taken into custody at the same time.

Once again Sixteen String Jack appeared before the blind magistrate of Bow Street, who committed him for trial at the Old Bailey. When the case opened Jack appeared very confident. Indeed, the day before the trial he had ordered " a genteel supper " to celebrate his acquittal, and sent invitations to his friends.

The first witness for the prosecution was Dr Bell. He stated that he had been stopped by two men " of a mean appearance," who might have been Jack Rann and William Collier, but he could not swear to it. Looking at Jack in the dock, dressed in a magnificent suit of pea-green, with buckskin breeches and ruffled shirt, the Court found it difficult to reconcile the dandy with the man of Dr Bell's description.

Then John Clarke was called, and the prisoner lost some of his confidence. But so far the case for the prosecution was entirely circumstantial, and Jack was still optimistic.

The last witness was a man named William Hills, servant to Princess Amelia. He declared that he had seen the accused going up the hill at Acton about twenty minutes before Dr Bell was robbed. He was positive about their identity, for the pair were not masked at the time, and he remained unshaken under cross-examination.

Hills's evidence was damning. The jury did not take long to come to their verdict, and both Rann and Collier were sentenced to death. Collier was given a recommendation for mercy, and his sentence was later commuted. Eleanor Roche, charged with receiving, was sentenced to fourteen years' transportation. Christian Stewart was acquitted.

While awaiting his execution in Newgate Jack lived " a very gay and expensive life "—as well he could afford to. He had numerous visitors, including " a great number of the girls of the town," and shortly before his execution he gave a farewell dinner in his cell, which was attended by seven of them, and at which Jack was the life and soul of the party.

Jack Rann went to Tyburn bravely, dressed in yet another brand-new suit (pea-green, of course), and with his sixteen strings fluttering gaily at his knees.

CHAPTER TWENTY-SEVEN

Jerry Abershaw and Galloping Dick

ACCORDING to that mine of information the ostler in *Romany Rye*, Jerry Abershaw was " a capital rider, but decidedly inferior to Richard Ferguson, generally called Galloping Dick." The pair rode together, and were the last highwaymen of note in the eighteenth century. In their lifetime Jerry was probably the more famous. At the time of his execution, according to the *Newgate Calendar*, he was " an old offender "—and so he was, although only twenty-two years of age.

Jerry was born at Kingston in 1773, and his first job was driver of a post-chaise. He could not have kept it for long, however, for when he was only seventeen he was the ringleader of a small band of highwaymen. It was not a gang in the old sense of the word, but rather a professional association of individual operators. Putney Heath and Wimbledon Common were their happiest hunting grounds, and their committee rooms were in the Bald Faced Stag Inn, near Beverley Brook. Abershaw's own favourite hide-out was in a house in Clerkenwell near Saffron Hill known as the " Old House in West Street "—a very old house indeed, with sliding panels and secret passages and hidden trap-doors, which, it is said, had once afforded asylum to Jack Sheppard.

Details of Jimmy's career are remarkably sparse, scarcely any of his actual exploits having been recorded. He was more reticent than most of his fellows, and even omitted to make a dying confession. In one respect he was remarkable; he had neither a wife nor, as far as we can discover, a doxy. That is not to say that he had no sex-life; but he seems to have confined it to occasional visits to ordinary prostitutes. Doubtless this avoidance of entanglements contributed greatly to his continued success at a time when his profession was in a worse state than at any previous stage in its history.

For five years Jerry robbed on the highway without once being arrested—in spite of the fact that the best brains of Bow Street were after him. He achieved a speedy notoriety. One evening, it is recorded, he was suddenly taken ill on the road, and carried by his companions to the Bald Faced Stag. He was put to bed, and one of the men went to Kingston to fetch a doctor.

The doctor came and treated Jerry, and was about to leave when the highwayman stopped him.

" You had better have some one to go with you," he said, " as it is a very dark and lonesome journey."

The doctor thanked him for the offer, but assured him he could take care of himself. Jerry, who knew what he was talking about, repeated his warning, but the doctor brushed it aside.

" I thank you," he said, " but I fear no man on the road—no, not even Jerry Abershaw himself! "

This amused Jerry highly, and afterwards he never lost the opportunity of telling the story.

Here we must leave Jerry for a time, and take up the story of Galloping Dick. He was born about the same time, at a village in Hertfordshire. His father was a gentleman's servant, and in consequence not often at home. As a result, says Dick's biographer, " he could not bestow that strict attention to the education and morals of his son which his own conduct gave every proof he would otherwise have done." Whether it would have had any effect on Dick is a different matter.

Dick's father did his best to keep an eye on the boy, though. When he was fifteen Dick was given a job as stable-boy in the same establishment. In this employment he was a great success, showing a natural love of horses; and when, a year later, the postilion was taken ill, young Dick was decked out in livery and given this responsible job. His father shared in his pride, but it was short-lived. The regular postilion recovered, and back to the stables went Dick.

However, it was not for long. A lady who was friendly with the family happened to be in need of a postilion, and Dick was recommended for the job. He acquitted himself to the entire satisfaction of his mistress, and everything was going well until the good lady discovered him, as his biographer puts it, " in an improper situation with one of her female servants." Dick was dismissed on the spot.

After this he had several other jobs as postilion, but was always getting into trouble of some sort—usually the same sort. Then his father died, leaving him the savings of a lifetime: £57. Dick promptly threw up his job and set himself up as a gentleman. In particular, he " bought mourning and frequented the theatres." One evening, at Drury Lane, he found himself sitting next to a very attractive girl, and he was soon up to his old games. So, however, was she. She readily granted her favours, and still more readily accepted his presents. For the first—and last—time in his life Dick made a fool of himself over a woman. He knew that Nancy was attended by a number of other men, including some noted highwaymen, " who, in turn, all had their favoured hours." Sometimes her engagement book was overcrowded, and the men met in the hall. Among them was the famous Jerry Abershaw.

Dick could not keep pace with men of such wealth, and within a very short time his father's savings had all gone. He had never let his Nancy know his lowly station in life, and kept up his pose of a gentleman of means. When he woke up to find his pockets empty, therefore, he said nothing to the girl, but took employment as a postilion at an inn in Piccadilly. His wages were low, and only rarely was he able to pay visits to Nancy.

It was while he was in this employment that Dick saw his first highway robbery. He was driving a gentleman along the Great North Road one day when the chaise was stopped by two masked highwaymen. There was a strong wind blowing, and a gust suddenly blew the crêpe off the face of one of them. Dick recognized the man at once. He had met him at Nancy's. And Jerry Abershaw—for it was he—knew he had been recognized. Before either could say anything, however, there were sounds of horses approaching, and the two highwaymen galloped off.

As soon as they were clear of any pursuers the highwaymen had a hasty conference. Jerry told his companion that he had been recognized, and they decided to wait at an inn where Dick was expected to stop for water for his horses. A little later the chaise drew up, and Jerry sent the waiter to ask Dick to come inside. The highwaymen talked with guineas, which was Dick's favourite language. He accepted their bribe and promised to keep silence; and he further accepted an invitation to supper the same evening.

Before the appointed time, however, Dick had to go to Nancy's lodgings to get rid of his new wealth. His call was not expected, and Nancy was already engaged. Dick waited; but when she came down she revealed that she had found out that he was only a postilion, and requested him not to call again. In fact, she slammed the door in his face.

"Nettled to the soul," Dick went off to keep his supper appointment with Jerry and his companion. Good food and wine cheered him up a bit, and the evening passed off merrily. It was only natural that Dick should be criticized for wasting his time as an ill-paid postilion when there were better jobs on the road; and equally natural that Dick should accept the offer of enrolment under Jerry's leadership.

However, it was not Jerry's plan that Dick should leave his employment at present. He could play a more useful part by using it to obtain information about travellers, such as when and where they were going, and whether they were likely to be worth robbing. It was not a heroic rôle, but the money promised to be good, and Dick agreed.

The scheme worked well for some time. Dick got information about travellers on chaises other than his own, and was never suspected of complicity. He might have kept his position for a long time if it had not been for the money. It was more than he had ever had in his life—and now he had no Nancy to spend it on. He had plenty of affairs, however, including two with publicans' wives, but none of them were as mercenary as Nancy. So he spent freely on drink and cards, and got so irregular in his appearances at his place of employment that he was finally dismissed as unreliable.

Just about this time—in July 1795—Jerry Abershaw was arrested. On information received at Bow Street officers were sent to apprehend him in the Three Brewers inn, Southwark. Jerry knew the game was up, and when the officers informed him of the nature of their errand he produced his pistols.

He looked little more than a boy, and the officers took the gesture for mere bravado. They rushed forward to close with him, and Jerry fired the pistols simultaneously. Both men fell; one, with a bullet in his body, never rose again; the other, wounded in the head, later recovered to give evidence at Jerry's trial.

For Jerry did not remain free for long. He was brought before the magistrate at Bow Street, and committed for trial at Croydon Assizes. The trial was very short, and the jury took only three minutes to make up their minds. However, before sentence was passed Counsel for the defence discovered a flaw in the indictment, and began a lengthy legal argument. The point was debated for nearly two hours, at the end of which the judge said he would have to adjourn the case and seek a ruling from higher legal authority. Here Counsel for the prosecution intervened. He said he was willing to waive the point for the time being, as there was another indictment against the prisoner which, he said, depended on the evidence of a single witness, and would therefore not occupy much of the Court's time. The judge agreed, and the case proceeded. Again the jury brought in a verdict of guilty.

Up till this point Jerry had sat throughout the proceedings with a bored expression, but now he protested violently. According to the reporter, he "began, with unparalleled insolence of expression and gesture, to ask his Lordship if he was to be murdered by the evidence of one witness."

The judge solemnly picked up his black cap—whereupon Jerry, with a look of contempt, mimicked his Lordship by putting on his own hat at exactly the same moment.

Jerry's behaviour in prison was unusual. No tearful ladies came to make their farewells—not even Nancy. But former confederates brought him food and drink, including some black cherries. Jerry used these for painting on the walls of his cell sketches depicting some of the robberies he had committed. One of these cherry-juice pictures showed him stopping a post-chaise and pointing a pistol at the driver's head;

from his mouth were issuing the words, " Damn your eyes, stop! "

Jerry was hanged on August 3 on Kennington Common. He went to the gallows with his shirt open at the neck and a flower in his mouth. On the way, according to the *Oracle and Public Advertiser*, " he kept up an incessant conversation with the persons who rode beside the cart, frequently laughing and nodding to others of his acquaintances whom he perceived in the crowd, which was immense." When the hangman adjusted the noose Jerry kicked off his shoes, laughingly explaining to the crowd that he wanted to disprove a prophecy made by his mother when he was a child—" that he would die in his shoes!"

After the execution Jerry's body was gibbeted at Putney Bottom, and on the following Sunday literally thousands of people left London to go and see it. In Bow Street Police Office information was received of a plan to cut down the body and bury it secretly, and a well-known Runner was sent with a strong party to keep an all-night vigil under Jerry's swinging heels.

Dick Ferguson, meanwhile, deprived of his job and his leader, had become an active highwayman himself. And a very successful one he was, too. His skill in the saddle saved him from capture many times. On one occasion, when he and two companions were robbing two gentlemen on the Edgware Road, they were interrupted by the sudden appearance of three other travellers, and were hotly pursued. Dick's companions were caught, and later tried and executed; but he got away. When his friends congratulated him on his escape he asserted he could " gallop a horse with any man in the kingdom." It was from this remark that he got his nickname.

" To follow him through the various exploits in which he was afterwards engaged would require volumes to enumerate," says his biographer, and leaves it at that. This is a pity, for Galloping Dick practised his profession for nearly five years after Jerry's death. He was finally caught by the Bow Street Runners, and charged at Aylesbury for having committed a highway robbery in Buckinghamshire. He was convicted at the Lent Assizes, 1800, and executed shortly after. His "official" biography ends with a neat little epitaph:

"Galloping Dick took a hasty road to perdition. Happy had it been for him had he chosen the safe path of virtue, and run a good race."

CHAPTER TWENTY-EIGHT

The Last of the Highwaymen

"ENGLAND, sir, has reason to be proud of her highwaymen! They are peculiar to her clime, and are as much before the brigand of Italy, the contrabandist of Spain, or the cut-purse of France—as her sailors are before all the rest of the world. The day will never come, I hope, when we shall degenerate into the footpad, and lose our *night errantry*."

The day had already come when Harrison Ainsworth put those words into the mouth of Dick Turpin, and the highwayman never rose again. Long afterwards, it is true, neo-highwaymen appeared in various guises—bushrangers, car-bandits, train-robbers, etc.; but in other countries, mainly in other continents. In England there were only footpads; and, with the emancipation of women, these in turn degenerated to the lowest form of criminal—the bag-snatcher.

The Age of Highwaymen only just intrudes on the nineteenth century. In criminal records we read of one Richard Smith, who was executed in 1803 " for robbing coachmen on the highway "; but he can scarcely be classed as a real highwayman, for his method—ingenious enough—was to order a postchaise, tell the coachman to drive out to some lonely place, and there rob his own driver! Similarly, the case of Henry Clarke, who in 1810 robbed the Bath mail-coach of banknotes worth £1,825, does not come within the scope of our story, for the robbery was committed while the coach was standing in the yard before the journey began. But there were a few genuine highwaymen in the nineteenth century, the most interesting of whom were John Beatson and William Whalley.

This was the nearest to a father-son partnership of which we have records. William Whalley was John Beatson's adopted son. Which of the pair first thought of going on the road is uncertain, but they entered the profession at the same time.

Beaston started on the road unusually late in life, for according to official records he was already seventy years old. Whalley's age is given as twenty-seven.

The career of this pair was very brief, being confined to a single robbery. Shortly after midnight on July 20, 1801, they held up the Royal Mail near East Grinstead. After intimidating the postboy and turning the horse loose, they took their booty to a field some miles away and sorted the mail in the privacy of standing corn. They took only banknotes. A month later, when the corn was reaped, letters and bills were found scattered over the field.

Although they took no bills of exchange, the banknotes were identifiable and had to be got rid of as quickly as possible. Returning to London, the pair spent as quickly as they could, mainly on jewellery, tendering notes of £10 and over and collecting gold as change. They passed a week in town, and then bought a horse and gig with the intention of going to Ireland. At Knutsford, in Cheshire, they made the fatal mistake of attracting attention to themselves by ill-treating their horse. They had scarcely left the town when the London mail came in, bearing handbills with notices of the robbery and descriptions of the men concerned. The descriptions seemed to tally with this pair of strangers who had alienated the horse-loving folk of Knutsford, and a Post Office Surveyor went after them. He caught them up at Liverpool. They were arrested, and a search of their belongings disclosed £1,700 in banknotes together with gold and jewellery to the value of over £1,000. The numbers of the notes tallied with those stolen, and after being conveyed to London and examined at Bow Street the pair were committed for trial at Horsham. Before their trial they succeeded in escaping from Horsham Gaol, but were rearrested in a sewer in the town.

The trial took place on March 29, 1802. In addition to the postboy, thirty London shopkeepers gave evidence, and the case was never in doubt. The trial was interesting for the behaviour of the elder of the accused, who confessed his guilt but swore that his adopted son had played no part in the robbery, and that he did not know that the banknotes were stolen. William Whalley told the same story, but it did not save him.

They were hanged at Horsham on April 7, before a crowd of 3,000.

Robert Peel is sometimes credited with having dealt the highwaymen their death-blow, but by the time he brought in his Metropolitan Police Bill (1829) the highwayman had long been in his grave. Footpads lingered on; but gone for ever were the colourful figures with the prancing steeds and black crêpe masks and pistols gleaming in the moonlight.

Various reasons have been given for the decline and ultimate disappearance of the highwayman, and those of the amateur criminologist George Borrow deserve attention. His ostler in *Romany Rye* specifies three: " the refusal to license houses which were known to afford shelter to highwaymen; the inclosure of many a wild heath in the country; and particularly the establishing in the neighbourhood of London of a well-armed mounted patrol." The last was undoubtedly the main factor. The decline of the highwayman dates from 1748, when Henry Fielding took up office at Bow Street. He and his blind half-brother, by laying the foundations of both a police force and a detective organization, made the roads as unsafe for highwaymen as they had been for travellers earlier in the century.

There were other reasons not mentioned by Borrow. The coming of the railways is often cited as one, but that is an anachronism. The banking legislation introduced at the end of the eighteenth and beginning of the nineteenth centuries, which went some way to relieving travellers of the necessity of carrying large sums of gold or notes, had some effect. A less obvious reason was the extreme conservatism of the highwaymen. One of the most striking features of their history is their poverty of invention and reluctance to depart from the recognized conventions of the road. The innovators, such as Jonathan Simpson with his skates and William Page with his phaeton, were remarkable because they were rare. Highwaymen did not move with the times; had they done so, England would have been the birthplace of the later train-robber.

Such, briefly, were the main reasons for the decline of highwaymen. There is one notable omission from our list, which will surprise nobody who has taken an interest in the annals of crime: the effect of punishment as a deterrent.

The so-called deterrent value of punishment is strikingly shown up in our illustration of "Highway Murder" (facing page 65), depicting a woman being strangled in full view of an occupied gibbet. Yet it is not altogether strange that this fallacy persisted throughout the highwayman era. Even in our own enlightened times people are still heard to prattle childishly about capital punishment being necessary for the protection of society for precisely the same reason. The prattlers talk as if the deterrent effect of the punishment were a manner of opinion, whereas in reality it is a matter of fact. This naïve argument reveals an ignorance of the history of crime.

In no branch of crime is the absurdity of the "deterrent" theory more clearly revealed than in the history of highwaymen. Our story began with the execution of Thomas Dun of Dunstable, who had no trial and was punished with exemplary severity. Soon after the beginning of the nineteenth century the maximum punishment for highway robbery was imprisonment. During the hundred years when highwaymen were most numerous and most daring (1650–1750) the punishment was invariably hanging, with the bodies of the worst offenders being gibbeted; during that period the incidence of highway robbery was slowly ascending. In the latter half of the eighteenth century it became increasingly common for sentences to be commuted to transportation; this remission of severity coincided exactly with the first waning of the highwaymen. At the beginning of the nineteenth century British Law recognized two hundred capital crimes. The early stages of the legislation under which that number was eventually reduced to four synchronized with the final disappearance of the highwayman.

It is not suggested that the diminishing severity of the Law and the decline of the crime were cause and effect; the reasons for the disappearance of the highwayman have already been given. Our point is simply that severity of punishment failed completely as a deterrent; the history of every other crime reveals an equally complete failure; and scientific reasoning from historical data proves that capital punishment is equally valueless as a deterrent from murder to-day.

Epitome

"HE followed a liberal profession, one which required more accomplishments than either the bar or the pulpit, since it presumed a bountiful endowment of qualifications—strength, health, agility, and excellent horsemanship, intrepidity of the first order, presence of mind, courtesy, and a general ambidexterity of powers for facing all accidents and for turning to good account all unlooked-for contingencies.

" The finest men in England, physically speaking, throughout the last century, the very noblest specimens of man, considered as an animal, were the mounted robbers who cultivated their profession of the great roads. When every traveller carried firearms the mounted robber lived in an element of danger and adventurous gallantry."

This handsome eulogy came not from a romantic novelist, but from Thomas de Quincey. Although over-generous, it is at least accurate in its emphasis on the physical requirements of the highway profession. Only the very fittest survived on the road.

More interesting, if less easily stated, were the mental and moral qualities of the highwayman. Here it is impossible to make any such sweeping generalizations. Group character, be it national, regional, familiar, financial, or vocational, can never be more than a very rough mean of the characters of a moderate majority of the individuals of the group. There were highwaymen who were courteous, like Captain Hind; others brutal, like Thomas Wilmot; some robbed only the rich, and gave to the poor, like Dick Dudley; others would slit a poor man's throat for a few shillings, like John Withers; some, again, were gangsters, like " Captain " James Whitney; others, again, were rugged individualists, like the Golden Farmer. To complicate matters still further they came from all strata of society, and included University graduates and illiterates.

However, there were some general characteristics common to most highwaymen, as there are in all professions; innate characteristics, which served as Nature's entrance examination, and characteristics acquired by conditioning on the road. Macaulay in his *History of England* has a brief but interesting note which calls attention to some of both classes of characteristics:

"It was necessary to the success and even to the safety of the highwayman that he should be a bold and skilful rider, and that his manners and appearance should be such as suited the master of a fine horse. He therefore held an aristocratical position in the community of thieves, appeared at fashionable coffee houses and gaming houses, and betted with men of quality on the race ground. Sometimes, indeed, he was a man of good family and education. A romantic interest therefore attached, and perhaps still attaches, to the names of freebooters of this class. The vulgar eagerly drank in tales of their ferocity and audacity, of their occasional acts of generosity and good nature, of their amours, of their miraculous escapes, and of their manly bearing at the bar and in the cart."

Leaving aside horsemanship and other physical qualities, probably the most general characteristic of highwaymen was courage. It showed itself in various forms. Sometimes it was purely physical, an indifference to danger born of unintelligence; sometimes it was moral courage, even heroism, as in the valiant spirits who suffered the torture of the Press. More often, though, it was just a bold, gay, devil-may-care love of danger and excitement. Only rarely did it turn out to be a pose, however; throughout their history highwaymen showed the greatest courage when it was of least material avail: under the gallows at Tyburn.

Allied with bravery was bravado. The highwayman was nearly always a braggart, and was vain rather than conceited. Conscious of his position in the aristocracy of the criminal classes, as Macaulay happily phrases it, he usually dressed and behaved according to his conception of a gentleman. Love of fashion and finery, however, were often a primary motive rather than an acquired trait, as in the case of William Page.

The highwayman's chivalry and courtesy were not, it must be admitted, as characteristic as the romantic novelists would have us believe. Perhaps Harrison Ainsworth spoiled us, made us unprepared for the truth; yet in what other crime do we find any chivalry and courtesy at all? Dick Turpin was a ruffian, Claude Duval only a successful lecher; but we still have our Captains Hind and Dudley, and our Captain Howard too—his affair with Lady Fairfax and her daughter was only a political rape—and quaint old characters like Old Mob. As for generosity—true, there were no real Robin Hoods, but whoever heard of a mean highwayman? Utterly improvident, they got rid of their money almost as quickly as they earned it. Not many took up works of charity, admittedly; the ladies took most, and the publicans the rest. But there was no one like a highwayman for standing drinks all round.

Mention was made in an earlier chapter of the comparatively small number of murders committed by highwaymen, in spite of the fact that robbery alone was almost always punished by the death sentence. Murder frequently meant gibbeting as well; and although this was regarded as a pretty bad disgrace in the seventeenth and eighteenth centuries, it is beyond belief that the thought of such posthumous indignity should have had a restraining effect. (Of the efficacy of deterrents in general we have already spoken.) Highwaymen, then, were not killers. In general, they avoided all physical violence, resorting to the use of their pistols only when trying to escape arrest.

Perhaps the greatest characteristic of the highwayman—the one that makes him most likable, even lovable—was his sense of humour. Again, it was not common to all; and again, it varied in expression. At the bottom of the scale we have the rough-and-ready types with rough-and-ready humour, expressed chiefly by practical jokes at the expense of their victims. But many of them were more subtle, and some of their best wit was uttered spontaneously when Jack Ketch was tying the rope round their necks. And all, without exception, laughed. You never heard of a mournful highwayman.

The evidence of contemporary literature, from Shakespeare to John Gay and after, leaves no illusions about the popularity of highwaymen. That, at least, was not a posthumous appendage, as Ainsworth's critics would have us believe. If further proof were needed, an extract from the very reliable travel-book of the Abbé J.-B. le Blanc, who visited England in 1737, is sufficient:

"I continually met Englishmen who were not less vain in boasting of the success of their highwaymen than of the bravery of their troops. Tales of their cunning and generosity were in the mouths of everybody and a noted thief was a kind of hero."

The reasons for this popularity are not hard to find. If Robin Hood was a wish-fulfilment, the highwayman who robbed the rich was at least half that wish come true. Social conditions in England during the highwayman era put the common people on the side of many sorts of criminals—notably smugglers. There was one Law for the poor and scarcely any Law for the rich.

We can find no better conclusion for this rough analysis of the character of the highwayman than the opinion on the matter of one who was a highwayman himself. We quote from the *Memoirs of the Right Villanous Jack Hall* (1708), " penned from his own mouth some time before his death," from which extracts were given in our chapter on Newgate.

" His [the highwayman's] life has, generally, the most mirth and the least care in it of any man's breathing, and all he deals for is clear profit: he has that point of good conscience that he always sells as he buys, a good pennyworth, which is something rare, since he trades with so small a stock. The fence and he are like the devil and the doctor, they live by one another; and, like traitors, 'tis best to keep each other's counsel."

(The expression "fence," incidentally, is one of the oldest words in criminal slang still extant.)

" He has this point of honesty, that he never robs the house he frequents, and perhaps pays the debts better than some others; for he holds it below the dignity of his employment to commit so ungenteel a crime, and loves to pay nobly. He has another quality, not much amiss, that he takes no more than he has occasion for, which he verifies this way: he craves no more while that lasts. He is a less nuisance in a commonwealth than a miser, because the money he engrosses by his villany all circulates again, which the other hoards as though 'twere only to be found again at the day of judgment."

The last sentence shows a prescience in the science of economics surprising for a highwayman; Jack Hall seems to have anticipated the late Lord Keynes's famous "parable of the bananas" by over two centuries!

"He is the tithe-pig of the family, which the gallows, instead of the parson, claims its due. He has reason enough to be bold in his undertakings, for, tho' all the world threaten him, he stands in fear of but one man in it, and that's the hangman; and with him, too, he is generally in fee; however, I cannot affirm he is so valiant that he dares not look any man in the face, for in that point he is now and then a little modest. Newgate may be said to be his country house, where he frequently lives so many months in the year, and he is not so much concerned to be carried thither for a small matter, if 'twere only for the benefit of renewing his acquaintance there. He holds a petty larceny as light as a nun does auricular confession, though the priest has a more compassionate character than the hangman. Friendship is a vertue oftener found among theeves than other people; for when their companions are in danger they venture hardest to relieve them. Every man in this community is esteemed according to his particular quality, of which there are several degrees, though it is contrary often to public government; for here a man shall be valued purely for his merit, and rise by it too, though it be but to a halter, in which there is a great deal of glory in dying like a hero, and making a decent figure in the cart to the two last staves of the fifty-first psalm."

Later, the writer of these *Memoirs*—who was even then preparing for his own execution—lets us into the secret of the philosophy of the "brave show" put up by highwaymen at the gallows. They put on their best suits, powdered wigs, and nosegays, Hall tells us, " so that one would take 'em for bridegrooms going to espouse their old Mrs Tyburn. The great comfort of having it said, ' There goes a proper handsome man,' somewhat ameliorates the terrible thoughts of the meagre tyrant death; and to go in a dirty shirt were enough to save the hangman a labour, and make a man die with grief and shame at being in that deplorable condition."

Bibliography

IT is doubtful whether the bibliography of this book will serve any purpose other than to demonstrate the author's industry. It is equally doubtful whether bibliographies are meant to serve any other purpose. There is, however, no doubt at all that the omission of a bibliography would be severely criticized.

1. *Periodicals*

Periodicals come first, because the main sources of this book have been newspapers, journals, and broadsheets of the sixteenth and seventeenth centuries. The following have been consulted most frequently:

> *Annual Register.*
> *Country Journal.*
> *Covent Garden Journal.*
> *Daily Gazetteer.*
> *Gentleman's Magazine.*
> *Grub Street Journal.*
> *London Daily Post.*
> *London Evening Post.*
> *London Gazette.*
> *London Magazine.*
> *North Country Journal.*
> *Public Advertiser.*
> *Whitehall Evening Post.*

The most interesting of the broadsheets are the publications of the Newgate chaplains, especially those of the Reverend Paul Lorrain and the Reverend Thomas Purney. The title never varies; it is always in the form *The Ordinary of Newgate, his Account of the Behaviour, Confessions, and Last Speeches of the Malefactors.* The British Museum copy of Purney's *Account* of Jonathan Wild, distinguished by an exceptionally pornographic advertisement on the back, was unfortunately destroyed by enemy action during the 1939-45 War, and it is doubtful if any other copy is extant.

2. Books

Over two hundred books have been consulted, very few of which are available outside the Reading Room of the British Museum. There is no point in listing any but the most important. For example, Stow's *History of England* was consulted only for verification of minor data, while the little that Lord Macaulay had to say about highwaymen, in his book of the same title, has been quoted almost in full. Similarly, many old guide-books have been used for checking topographical details.

The best books are the chapbooks which appeared regularly after the execution of every well-known highwayman. Most of them are obviously embroidered, and only contemporary ones are of any value at all. Those published after 1800 (*e.g.*, by the Catnach Press) must be treated only as fiction.

The classics of highway literature are the *Recantation of an Ill-led Life* by James Clavel, Gentleman (1627), *Jackson's Recantation* (1674)—which should be read in conjunction with *The Confession of the Four High-way-men*, published in the same year—and the *Memoirs of the Right Villanous Jack Hall* (1708). The information in these is first-hand and first-class, although in the latter two the style is somewhat esoteric.

Other recommended chapbooks are:

The Life and Death of Gamaliel Ratsey (1605).
The English Gusman (1652). This is the best of several biographies of Captain James Hind.
The Life and Death of Mary Frith (1660).
Bloody News from Yorkshire (1674).
The Yorkshire Robber (1684).
The Jacobite Robber (1693).

The Trial of Richard Turpin (1739). Thoroughly reliable, although the same cannot be said for the *General History* prefixed to the fourth edition.

Life and Death of Jack Sheppard (1724).
The Life of Jonathan Wild (1725).

Dr William Pope's *Memoirs of Du Vall* (1670) was reprinted in its entirety in the Harleian Miscellany (1744-46), Volume III. The same collection includes Samuel Butler's "Pindarick Ode" to the memory of Duval.

Of the more general books on highwaymen the best-known are "Captain" Alexander Smith's *Compleat History . . . of the Most Notorious Highwaymen* (1719) and "Captain" Charles Johnson's *General History of the Most Famous Highwaymen* (1734). Both are thoroughly unreliable. Smith's is an anthology of chapbooks liberally seasoned with spicy tales from Chaucer and Boccaccio, while Johnson's is just a copy of Smith's with still more seasoning. A new edition of Smith's book, edited but unspoiled by A. L. Hayward, was published by Messrs. Routledge in 1926. Johnson's work is especially recommended for those with a taste for pornography.

Other general works include:

Lives of the Most Remarkable Criminals (1735). This has also been edited by A. L. Hayward and republished by Messrs. Routledge (1927).
The Tyburn Chronicle (1768).
The Annals of Newgate; or, the Malefactors' Register, by the Reverend John Villette (1776).
Celebrated Trials, by George Borrow (1825).
The Newgate Calendar, by Andrew Knapp and William Baldwin (1826).
Chronicles of Crime, by Camden Pelham (1841).

A brilliant selection from all the above, including Smith and Johnson, was made by J. L. Rayner and G. T. Cook and published by the Navarre Society in 1926 under the misleading title *The Complete Newgate Calendar* (five volumes).

Good books on life in Newgate and death at Tyburn include:

The London Spy, by Edward Ward (1696).
A Glimpse of Hell (1705).
History of the Press Yard (1717).

Memoirs of François Misson (English translation, 1718).

An excellent modern work is Charles Gordon's *The Old Bailey and Newgate* (T. Fisher Unwin, 1903).

Two good books have been written on the history of Bow Street. P. H. Fitzgerald's *Chronicles of the Bow Street Police Office* (Chapman and Hall, 1888) is largely anecdotal, while G. Armitage's *History of the Bow Street Runners* (Wishart, 1932) is more serious. The pamphlets written by the Fieldings, the titles of which were quoted in Chapter XXIV, are well worth reading; and there is additional information in the biographies of Henry Fielding by Lawrence and Austin Dobson.

Of twentieth-century literature on highwaymen generally two books are exceptionally valuable. The first is Charles G. Harper's *Half-hours with the Highwaymen* (Chapman & Hall, 1908), largely biographical, very well informed, and always readable; the other is G. S. Maxwell's *Highwayman's Heath* (Middlesex Chronicle, 1935), a scholarly but unpretentious history of Hounslow Heath.

Finally, there is that monumental starting point in every literary research, the *Dictionary of National Biography*.

3. Fiction

The best highwayman fiction is still W. Harrison Ainsworth—in particular, *Rookwood*, *Jack Sheppard*, and *Talbot Harland*. Lord Lytton's *Paul Clifford* is more prosy. Thackeray's *Catherine* and *Denis Duval* are hostile. Fielding's *Jonathan Wild* tells us a lot about Fielding and little about Wild; *Amelia*, written while the author was at Bow Street, is more interesting. There is an interesting chapter on highwaymen in George Borrow's *Romany Rye*.

4. Poetry and Drama

Samuel Butler's *Ode to Duval* has already been mentioned. Tennyson's *Rizpah* is a brilliant commentary on the popular feeling towards gibbets. Swift's satirical *Clever Tom Clinch* is notable for its exactness of observation.

Highwaymen were popular stage-characters in the seventeenth and eighteenth centuries. *The Beggar's Opera*—which Sir John Fielding asked Garrick not to revive owing to the danger to public morals—is the best-known. Other plays of interest are Anthony Munday's *Sir John Oldcastle*, Middleton and Dekker's *Roaring Girle*, Farquhar's *Beaux' Stratagem*, and, of course, Shakespeare's *Henry IV, Part I*.

INDEX

Abershaw, Jerry, 258–263
"Act for Better Preventing Thefts and Robberies," 234
Act of Oblivion, 52
Acton, 88, 257
Ainsworth, W. Harrison, 66, 135–137, 139, 142, 143, 208, 215, 219, 220, 250, 265, 271
Albemarle, Duchess of (Nan Clarges), 114–115
Albemarle, Duke of (General Monck), 75
Alchemist, The, 27
All the Year Round, 140
Allam, pawnbroker, 252
Allen, Rev. Dr, 229
Allen, Thomas, 43–45
Amelia, 233
Amelia, Princess, 256–257
Amends for Ladies, 58
Annals of Newgate, 180
Annual Register, 69, 70. 250
Ashe, Miss, 229
Atkinson, Isaac, 30, 31, 32
Atrocity stories, 77
Aubrey, John, 25
Aylesbury, 263

Bagnigge Wells, 254
Bagshot Heath, 37, 109, 116, 146, 152, 192
Bald-Faced Stag Inn, Beverley Brook, 258, 259
Ball, Thomas, 169
Ballenden, Mrs, 212
Banbury, 114
Banking legislation, 267
Barbican, the, 55
Barking, 209
Barnes Common, 211
Barnet, 85, 232, 255
Barons, highwaymen and, 14, 15
Bath, 120, 225, 245, 246; the Bath mail, 265
Bayes, Richard, 136
Beaconsfield, 146
Beatson, John, 265–266

Bedford, 16, 18, 19, 27; Sheriff of, 18; Gaol, 20, 48
Beggar's Opera, The, 22, 229
Belch, Sir Toby (in *Twelfth Night*), 58
Bell, Dr, 256–257
"Benefit of the clergy," 182–183
Benson, pickpocket, 201
Berkeley Street, 232
Beverley, 216
Beverley Brook, 258
Bilerecay, 137
Bird, Jack, 79–80
Bishopsgate, 248
Black Act, 250
Black Bess, 135, 137, 138, 139, 142–143, 219
Blackheath, 38, 104, 113, 211
Black Horse Inn, Broadway, 142
Black Lion Inn, Drury Lane, 200
Blacket, Mary, 60–61
Blake, Joseph ("Blueskin"), 200–203, 205
Bloody News from Yorkshire, 130
"Blueskin" (Joseph Blake), 200–203, 205
Blueskin's Ballad, 203
Bobbies (policemen), 234
Boccaccio, Giovanni, 32, 207
Bocking, 137
Borrow, George, 267
Bowl Inn, Holborn, 186, 192
Bow Street, 233–242, 245, 247, 249, 252, 253, 255, 256, 259, 262, 263, 267; Patrol, 63, 239; Runners, 70, 237–242, 247, 248, 261
Boyes, Mr, landlord, 214
Brace (or Bracy), John, 124
Bracey (or Bracy), Edward, 59–60, 130
Bracey (or Bracy), Joan, 59–60, 130
Bradele, city merchant, 213
Bradshaw, Jack, 65–66
Bradshaw, Sergeant, 47–48, 52, 65
Braintre, 137
Branding of criminals, 183
Bridewell, 169, 252

Index

Bristol, 59; the Bristol Mail, 70–72, 246–249
Broadway, 142
Brough, 216
Broughton, Squire, 111, 112
Browne, Lady, 240–241
Buckingham, Duke of, 34, 35
Burnworth, Edward ("Young Frazier"), 168–170
Burton, Daniel, 70–71
Burton, Elizabeth, 133
Butler, Samuel, 107

Cady, William, 146–147
Cambridge, 137, 212
Canterbury, 244
"Canting crew," 126, 129
Capital punishment, deterrent effect of, 267, 268
Carlyle, Thomas, 195
Carrick, James or Valentine, 192–193, 200
Catherine, 250
Catnach Press, 177
Chamberlain, John, 57
Chambers's *Cyclopaedia*, 68
Chandos Street, 104
Charles I, King, reign of, 28 *et seq.*
Charles II, King, 36, 41, 51, 119, 133, 139, 140, 141, 233
"Charlies," 233, 235, 253. *See also* Watchmen
Chaucer, Geoffrey, 14, 108, 207
Chelmsford, 137, 140, 221
Chelsea, 226; Waterworks, 248
Cheney, Tom, 40
Chester, 38
Chingford, 209
Chronicle of Scotland, 14
Civil War, 35 *et seq.*
Clarges, Nan (Duchess of Albemarle), 114–115
Clarke, Henry, 265
Clarke, John, 248, 252, 256–257
Clavel, John, 28–30, 32, 33, 81, 82, 92
Clavel, Sir William, 28, 29
Clergymen, highwaymen and, 24, 36, 46–47, 75, 78–79, 182–183, 189–190, 224, 228. *See also* Ordinary of Newgate
Clerkenwell, 258
Clinch, Tom (Thomas Cox), 184–185
Cock Lane, 250

Colebrook (Colnbrook), 87
Collet, James, 78–79
Collier, William, 256, 257
Commonwealth, 35 *et seq.*
Compleat History of the Lives and Robberies of the Most Notorious Highwaymen, A, 207
Confession of the Four High-way-men, The, 81, 87, 88
Constables, 232–233, 234, 235
Cordy, pawnbroker, 256
Cornelius-à-Tieburgh, 118
Cosens, Madam, 153
Cottington, John ("Mulled Sack"), 39–41, 67, 187
Country Journal, 212
Covent Garden, 71, 72, 105, 162, 238, 265
Covent Garden Journal, 235, 237
Cox, Thomas, 185
Cranford Bridge, 246, 247
Cripplegate, 196, 198
Cromwell, Oliver, 37, 38, 40, 44, 45, 52
Croydon, 209; Assizes, 262
Curtis, Peter, 66
Cutpurse, Moll (Mary Frith), 55–59, 75, 196, 197
Curzon Street, 232

Dacey, Mr, 59–60
Dartmouth, Earl of, 200
Darwell, highwayman, 245
Davis, William (alias Scarlet), 252
Davis, William ("Golden Farmer"), 109–116, 151, 269
Day, John, 58
Day, Sir Thomas, 112
Day Patrol, Bow Street ("Robin Redbreasts"), 241
Defoe, Daniel, 137, 139–142, 144
Dekker, Thomas, 55, 58
Denis Duval, 250
Denville, Sir Gosselin (Jocelyn), 23–24, 27, 64, 75
Denville, Robert, 23
De Quincey, Thomas, 269
Derby, 133
Deserters, 145, 146, 154, 238
Detectives, 236, 237. *See also* "Thief-catchers"
Deterrents from crime, 91, 242, 267, 268, 271
Devall, John, 252, 253
De Veil, Colonel Sir Thomas, 233

Index

Dickens, Charles, 139–140, 143
Dictionary of National Biography, 98, 108, 219, 225, 229
"Dixie." *See* Jackson, Francis
Dover Road, 65
Dowe, Robert, 158
Doxies, 54, 59, 77, 85, 127, 129, 131, 229
Drury Lane, 186, 200, 201, 204, 260
Dudley, Captain Dick, 73–76, 79, 80, 269, 271
Duell, William, 190
Dun, Thomas, 16–20, 23, 77, 268
Dundee, Viscount, 146
Dunstable, 16, 20, 268
Duval, Claude, 77, 98–108, 123, 151, 186, 224, 225, 271

East Grinstead, 266
Edward I, King, 13
Edward II, King, 23, 64
Edgeworth Bess, 200, 201, 202, 203, 204
Edgware, 210
Edgware Road, 70, 187, 263
Eglinton, Earl of, 227
Elbow, constable (in *Measure for Measure*), 233
Elliot & Co., Messrs, 248, 249
Elms, The, 187
Encyclopædia Britannica, 135
Enfield, 45
England's Calamities discovered, 171
English Gusman, The, 52
Enquiry into the Causes of the Late Increase of Robberies, An, 234
Epping, 213–214
Epping Forest, 136, 209, 212, 213, 215, 218, 232
Essay on Man, 212
Essex, Earl of, 25, 36, 37
"Essex Gang," the ("Gregory's Gang"), 209, 210, 211
"Execution Bell" (St Sepulchre's), 158–159, 183, 189
"Execution of the Idle Apprentice," 177, 178, 193
Exeter, 117, 224; road, 109, 115

Fairfax, General, 35, 37, 38, 58
Fairfax, Lady, 37–38, 39, 40, 271
Fairfax, Lord, 221
Falstaff, Sir John, 22; (in *Henry IV, Part I*), 21

Fences (receivers), 56, 57, 196–197, 202, 234–235, 272
Fenny Stanton, 138, 140
Ferguson, Richard ("Galloping Dick"), 258–264
Ferrers, Earl, 194
Ferrybridge, 141
Field, Nathaniel, 58
Field, William, 202
Fielder, highwayman, 209, 210
Fielding, Henry, 195, 233–237, 238, 240, 242, 243, 267
Fielding, Sir John, 233–241, 243, 245, 253, 254, 255
Fielding, William, 242
Fighting Cock Inn, St George's Fields, 170
Finchley Common, 66, 113, 163, 167, 192, 203
Fitzosbert, William ("Longbeard"), 187
Fitz-othes, or Fitzooth, Ralph, 13
Fleet Street, 56, 116
Fletcher, Darcy, 132, 133
Foot Patrol (Night Patrol), Bow Street, 239–240
Footpads, and highwaymen, 28
Ford, Sir Richard, 241
"Foster, Sheriff," 144
"Fowler" (John White), 81, 88
Frampton, Doll, 254
"Frazier, Young" (Edward Burnworth), 168–170
Frith, Mary (Moll Cutpurse), 55–59, 75, 196, 197
Fry, Elizabeth, 158
Fuller, Thomas, 25, 26, 142, 187
"Fury," highwayman, 201

Gadbury, John, 118
Gad's Hill, 21, 30, 65, 137, 138
Gadshill (in *Two Gentlemen of Verona*), 22
Gaieties and Gravities, 143
"Galloping Dick" (Richard Ferguson), 258–264
Garnish, 160, 161
Gay, John, 22, 109, 229, 271
Gazette, 75
General History of the Most Famous Highwaymen, A, 207
Genesis, Book of, 13
"Gentleman Highwayman" (James Maclaine), 224–230

Gentleman's Magazine, 156, 161, 193, 218, 228, 235, 250
Genuine History of the Life of Turpin, 136, 141
George I, King, 222
George II, King, 222
George III, King, 64
George Inn, Holborn, 185, 186, 192
Gibbets, 68, 69, 70, 88, 91, 116, 268, 271
Giles, Farmer, 208
Gin Act, 234
Glimpse of Hell, A, 157
Gloucester, 143, 144
Godmanchester, 138
" Golden Farmer " (William Davis), 109–116, 151, 269
Golden Farmer Inn, 109
Golden Fleece, Oxford Road (Street), 225
Golden Lion Inn, near Hyde Park, 245
Gordon Riots (1780), 157, 241
Gravesend, 137
Gray, Thomas, 228, 251
Great Fire (1666), 156
Great Frost (1689), 147
Great North Road, 66, 260
Great Western Road, 64
Green Man Inn, Epping Forest, 136, 213–214
Gregory, highwayman, 209–210
" Gregory's Gang " (" the Essex Gang "), 209–211
Grignion, Mr, watchmaker, 256
Grosvenor Square, 244
Grub Street, 168
Grub Street Journal, 211
Guy Fawkes, 25
Guy of Gisborne, 15
Gwynne, Nell, 77–78

Hackney Marsh, 215
Hague, The, 51
Haines, highwayman, 69
Hal, Prince (in *Henry IV, Part I*), 21
Hall, Jack, 160, 161, 191, 272, 273
Hamilton, Lady Elizabeth, 222
Hamlet, 27
Hampstead, 252; Heath, 88, 89; road, 200
Hardcastle, Captain William, 133
Harper, Charles G., 98, 142, 143, 144

Harrison, Colonel, 48, 52
Harrow-on-the-Hill, 74, 88
Hartley, John, 222–223
Harwich, 208
Hawes, Nathaniel, 167–168
Hawley, 132
" Hell," highwayman, 201
Henry I, King, 16, 20
Henry III, King, 69, 155
Henry IV, King, 155, 170
Henry IV, Part I, 21
Henry V, King, 20
Hereford, Bishop of, 15
Hewson, Colonel, 40
Higden, Mr, 227
High Holborn, 183
Highways, 62–72
Highwaywomen, 54–61
Hillingdon, 111
Hills, William, 257
Hind, Captain James, 41, 42–53, 56, 73, 74, 77, 89, 151, 269, 271
History of England (Macaulay), 62, 98, 123, 270
History of the Press Yard, 164, 174
Hitchin, Charles, 197
Hogarth, William, 177, 178, 193
Holborn, 184, 189, 234; Hill, 186
Hole in the Wall Inn, Chandos Street, 104
Holland House, 226
Holliday, William, 129, 130
Holloway, 215
Honiton, 117, 223
Horndon, 137
Horne, Captain, 40
Horner, Nicholas, 223–224
Hornsey, 135
Horse Patrol, Bow Street, 240, 241
Horsham, 75, 266
Houghton, Hugh, 70–72
Hounslow, 69, 87, 88; Heath, 40, 58, 64, 74, 76, 102, 143, 151, 192, 195, 221, 226, 227, 252
House of Commons, 231–232
Howard, John, 157–158, 173
Howard, Captain Zachary, 36–38, 39, 41, 271
Hue and Cry, 238
Hughes, Dick, 186–187
" Hundreds," liability of, 62, 63, 112–113, 232
Hunt, Leigh, 98
Huntingdon, 44, 138
Huntingdon, Earl of, 13

Index

Hurstmonceaux, 224
Hyde Park, 187, 226, 245

Indicator, The, 98
Innkeepers, highwaymen and, 92, 95–97, 132, 133, 149, 150
Isle of Man, 51
Islington, 215

Jackson, Francis (" Dixie "), 81–97, 148, 174, 176
Jackson's Oxford Journal, 240
Jackson's Recantation, 81–97, 148, 174, 233
Jacobite Robber, The, 148, 151
James, King, 25, 26
James, John, 191
Jeffreys, Judge, 120
Jenks, Rowland, 156
Jermyn Street, 226
John, King, 13, 155
Johnson (John Brace or Bracey), 124
Johnson, " Captain " Charles, 207
Johnson, Captain Roger, 199
Johnson, Dr. Samuel, 188–189, 193, 251
Johnson, William (George Weston), 248–249
Jonathan Wild the Great, 237
Jonson, Ben, 27, 34
Journey to Exeter, 109

Keeper of Newgate, 72, 73, 76, 163–164, 170–172
Kennington Common, 263
Kéroualle, Louise de (Duchess of Portsmouth), 119, 120
Ketch, Jack, 20, 148, 162, 191, 192, 193, 271
Keynes, Lord, 273
Killigrew, Thomas, 185
King, Matthew, 214–215
King, Tom, 212–215
King's Oak Road, Epping, 212
Kingston, 258, 259
Knavesmire, the, 134, 186, 218
Kneebone, Mr, 200, 202
Knightsbridge, 70
Knutsford, 266
Kyll, Thomas, 136

Langland, William, 14
Lansdowne, Marquis of, 142

Lansdowne Passage, 232
Lansdowne Row, 232
Lauderdale, Duke of, 76
Lawrence, Mr, farmer, 210
Lawyers, highwaymen and, 18, 31, 75–76, 111–112, 120–121, 200–201
Le Blanc, Abbé J.-B., 272
Lediard, Judge, 228
Leicester Fields (Leicester Square), 201
Leicester Gaol, 131
Leonard, Kit, 169
Lepton, John, 142
Letters by Eminent Persons, 25·
Lewis, Paul, 224
Liber Albus, 170
Life and Death of Gamaliel Ratsey, 26, 27
Life and Death of Mary Frith, 55
Lincoln, 133, 247
Lincoln's Inn Fields, 192
Linkmen, 232
Lion, Elizabeth, 200
Liverpool, 266
London Evening Post, 209, 210
London Gazette, 102, 125, 133, 140, 147, 215
London Magazine, 215, 216, 217, 218
London Spy, The, 43
Long Acre, 252
" Longbeard " (William Fitzosbert), 187
Long Story, The, 228
Lorrain, Rev. Paul, 176–179
Lott, Farmer, 246
Loughton, 209; road, 212
Ludgate, 39
Lytell Geste of Robyn Hoode, A, 14

Macaulay, Lord, 62, 63, 76, 98, 123, 130, 134, 142, 270
Macheath, Captain (in *The Beggar's Opera*), 22, 229
Machyn's *Diary*, 64
Maclaine, Archibald, 225, 227, 228
Maclaine, James (the " Gentleman Highwayman "), 224–230
Madde Prancks of Merry Moll of the Bankside, The, 58
Maggot, Poll, 200, 203, 204
Maid Marian, 13, 14
Maidenhead, 86, 246
Maidstone, 221; gaol, 38
Major, Mr, 213–214

Marble Arch, 187
Marie Magdalene, 59
Marlborough, 86, 87
Marlow, Mr, 70–71
Marshalsea Prison, 254
"Matchet, The" (John Williams), 88
Mazarin, Duchess of, 78, 79
Meighen, Richard, 30
Memoirs of Du Vall, 98–108
Memoirs of the Right Villanous Jack Hall, 160, 272, 273
Metropolitan Police, 239
Metropolitan Police Act (1829), 242, 267
Middleton, highwayman, 23
Middleton, Thomas, 55, 58
Midhurst, 75
Milan, Duke of (in *Two Gentlemen of Verona*), 22
Milford Lane, 153
Milliner, Mary, 196, 197, 198
Mint, the, 169
Misson, François, 183, 184, 191
Mohun, Lord, 195, 196
Molly (Jonathan Wild's mistress), 199
Monck, General (Duke of Albemarle), 75
Monmouth, Duke of, 74
Monro, David, 252
Montrose, Duchess of, 240
Moorfields, 168
Morgan, highwayman, 222
Morley, 132
Morton, Judge, 105
Mounted Police (Horse Patrol), Bow Street, 240, 241
Mountford, Lord, 228
Mowbray, Major Vavasour, 215
Munday, Anthony, 14, 22
"Mulled Sack" (John Cottington), 39–41, 67, 187
"Mute, standing," 163–170

Nancy, prostitute, 260, 261, 262
"Neck-verse," 182
Nelson, Jane, 131, 141
Nevison, William, 77, 123–134, 217, 218
"Nevison's Leap," 141
New Prison, 201, 202, 214
Newark, 76, 133
Newcastle, Duke of, 235, 237
Newgate Calendar, 196, 224, 258

Newgate Prison, 155–162; the Keeper, 72, 73, 76, 163–164, 170–172; the Ordinary, 72, 82–84, 173–181, 182, 230; the Press Yard, 159, 163–170, 270; also mentioned, 51, 52, 58, 72, 74, 88, 106, 107, 130, 153, 183, 188, 189, 190, 191, 192, 193, 202–203, 204, 205, 224, 227, 228–229, 231, 249, 250, 257
Newgate Street, 204
Newmarket, 119, 179
"Nicks, Mr," 137–139, 140, 141, 142, 144. *See also* "Swift Nicks"
Night Patrol (Foot Patrol), Bow Street, 239–240
Nine Mile Stone, Hounslow Heath, 252
Northallerton Fair, 131
Northumberland, Duchess of, 220, 221
Nottingham, 133, 247
Noy, Attorney-General, 31

Oates, Titus, 108
O'Brien, Patrick, 77–78
Ogden, Will, 65–66
Old Bailey, 51, 147, 156, 159, 193, 198, 202, 205, 207, 227, 231, 253, 256
Oldcastle, Sir John (in Munday's *Life*), 22
"Old House in West Street," Clerkenwell, 258
"Old Mob" (Thomas Sympson), 117–122, 147, 271
Old Testament, 13
Omar, Mr, 211
Oracle and Public Advertiser, 263
Ordinary of Newgate, 72, 82–84, 173–181, 182, 230
Ossory, Countess of, 240
Oxford, 156; road, 67, 111
Oxford English Dictionary, 59
Oxford Road (Oxford Street), London, 183, 187, 225, 256

P——, Earl of, 37
Page, William, 243–245, 267, 270
Palmer, John, 216–217. *See also* Turpin, Dick
Palmer, Rose, 208
Pargiter, attorney, 200
Paris, Matthew, 69
Parkhurst, Walter, 81, 88

Index

Parsons, William, 220–221, 224
Peel, Sir Robert, 234, 241–242, 267
Peine forte et dure, 164, 170
Pepys, Samuel, 115
Peters, Hugh, 45–47, 52
Petersfield, 49
Petersham, Lady Caroline, 228, 229, 230
Philips, Joan (Joan Bracey), 59–60
Phillips, Thomas, 164, 165, 166
Piccadilly, 169, 232, 260
Picken, Joseph, 66–67
Piers Plowman, 14
" Pindarick Ode " (Samuel Butler), 107
Plan for Preventing Robberies, A, 238, 239
Plough Inn, Sandal, 133
Plunkett, highwayman, 225, 226, 227
Poellnitz, Baron von, 139
Police, development of, 231–242. *See also* Bow Street, Constables, *and* Watchmen
Police Gazette, 238
Pope, Alexander, 99, 211, 212
Pope, Dr William, 98–108
Popham, Sir John, 24–26, 28
Portledge Papers, 116
Portsmouth, 49
Portsmouth, Duchess of, 119, 120
Potter, highwayman, 213
Poultry Compter, 43, 74, 196, 198
Press Yard, Newgate, 159, 163–170, 270
Prince of Prigs, The, 53
Public Advertiser, 237, 238, 239
Putney, 244; Heath, 258; Bottom, 263
Purney, Rev. Thomas, 179–180, 193, 206

Raleigh, Sir Walter, 25
Ramsden, John, 133
Rann, Jack (" Sixteen String Jack "), 207, 251–257
Ratseis Ghoaste, 27
Ratsey, Gamaliel, 26–27, 28
Reading, 36, 52, 86, 186; road, 36
Recantation, Jackson's, 81–97, 148, 174, 233
Recantation of an Ill-led Life (Clavel), 29, 30, 33, 81
Receivers. *See* Fences
Records of York Castle, 141

Red Lion Inn, Bishopsgate, 248
Red Lion Inn, Whitechapel, 214
Red Lion Street, Whitechapel, 214
Reresby, Sir John, 133
Restoration, 58 *et seq.*
Reynolds, Captain, 35
Reynolds, Tom, 65–66
Richardson, Captain, 74
Richardson, Samuel, 189–190
Richmond, Duke of, 101
Rippleside, 209
Rizpah, 68
Roaring Girle, The, 55
Robin Hood, 13–15, 17, 18, 21, 22, 48, 74, 113, 151, 271, 272
" Robin Redbreasts " (Bow Street Day Patrol), 240, 241
Roche, Eleanor, 252–257
Rochester, Earl of, 74
Romany Rye, 258, 267
Rookwood, 135–139, 143
Rose, highwayman, 209–210
Round House, 201
Rowden the Pewterer, 211, 216
Royal Mail, robberies of, 70–72, 246–249, 265, 266
Rye, 249
Ryswick, Treaty of, 145

Saffron Hill, Clerkenwell, 258
St Alban's, 151
St Anne's Round House, 201
St George's Fields, 170
St Giles's, 106, 183, 201; Circus, 186
St. James's Street, 226, 227
St Martin's Church, Ludgate, 39
St Paul's Cross, 57
St Sepulchre's Church, Holborn, 158–159, 183, 189
Salisbury, 114
Sandal, 133
Saunders, John, 252
Saward, Edward, 217
Scarborough, 245
Scarborough, Earl of, 169
" Scarlet " (William Davis), 252
Scott, Sir Walter, 188
Selwyn, George, 178
Shaftesbury, 47
Shakespeare, William, 21, 22, 24, 58, 65, 233, 271
Shelley, Widow, 209
Sheppard, Jack, 66, 200–205, 207, 258
Sheppard, Tom, 201

Index

Sherwood Forest, 13–14, 17, 18
Shoe Lane, 186
Shooter's Hill, 30, 43, 65, 244
Shorthose, highwayman, 26, 27
Shotover Hill, 40, 67
Shower, Sir Bartholomew, 117, 118
Simmonds, Mr, 252
Simpson, Jonathan, 147–148, 267
"Sixteen String Jack" (Jack Rann), 207, 251–257
Slader, highwayman, 88
Sloth the priest (in *Piers Plowman*), 14
Smith, Mr, Dick Turpin's schoolmaster, 208, 217
Smith, "Captain" Alexander, 207
Smith, Catherine, 252, 253
Smith, Horace, 143
Smith, John, 191
Smith, Richard, 265
Smith, Rev. Samuel ("Samuel Swiftnicks"), 84, 85, 87, 89, 92, 93–94, 97, 174–176, 185
Smithfield, 41, 187; Market, 249
Snell, highwayman, 26, 27
Snow Hill, 183
Soho, 249
Soldiers, as highwaymen, 25, 35, 145
Southwark, 261–262
Spalding, 26
Special Branch, 237
Spiggot, William, 163–167, 168, 169
Stafford, Captain Philip, 35–36, 39, 186
Staines, 87
Statute of Winchester, 62, 63
Stead, John, 218
Stewart, Christian, 256–257
Stone Hold, Newgate, 161
Stone Room, Newgate, 203
Storer, Anthony, 178
Storey, Dr, 191
Stow, John, 155
Strand, 197, 200, 207
Strangeways, Major, 167
Street, Dorothy, 210
Sunday Trading Act, 63
Sunday travelling, 63, 93, 94
Surgeons' Hall, 190
"Swearing Highwayman" (Ned Wicks), 196
Swift, Dean, 184, 185, 203
"Swift Nicks," 75, 139, 140
"Swiftnicks, Samuel" (Rev. Samuel Smith), 83, 84

Sympson, Andrew, 24
Sympson, Thomas ("Old Mob"), 117–122, 147, 271

Talbot Inn, Newark, 133
Tangier Tavern, St Giles's, 106
Tankard, Thomas, 130
Tennyson, Lord, 68
Temple Bar, 192
Thackeray, W. M., 250
Thicket, the, Maidenhead, 86
"Thief-catchers" and "thief-takers" (detectives), 198, 236, 237
Thornhill, Sir James, 204
Three Brewers Inn, Southwark, 261–262
Three Cups Inn, Holborn, 186
Tilbury, 137
To the Memory of the Most Renowned Du-Vall, 107
Told, Rev. Silas, 222
Tonbridge road, 211, 245
Tottenham Court Road, 254
Tour through the Whole Island of Great Britain, 137, 139
Tracey, Walter, 32–34
Trial of the Notorious Highwayman Richard Turpin, 136
True and Honourable History of the Life of Sir John Oldcastle, 22
Tunbridge Wells, 225
Turnham Green, 31, 58, 227
Turpin, Dick, 66, 123, 135–137, 139, 141, 142, 143–144, 207–219, 220, 265, 271
Twickenham, 211
Two Gentlemen of Verona, 21
Twyford, 246
Tyburn, 182-194; also mentioned, 35, 40, 44, 47, 48, 60, 61, 67, 69, 76, 105–106, 107, 114, 148, 149, 152, 155, 159, 165, 166, 177, 199, 201, 204, 205, 210, 215, 221, 222, 223, 224, 226–227, 229, 231, 243, 250, 255, 257, 270, 273

Unemployment, and highwaymen, 145
Uxbridge Road, 256

Valentine (in *Two Gentlemen of Verona*), 21
Villette, Rev. John, 180–181
Virginia, 221

Index

Wager, Lewis, 59
Wakefield, 133; prison, 131
Wallace, Edgar, 208, 220
Walpole, Horace, 57, 226, 228–229, 240
Waltham Abbey, 208
Wandsworth, 210, 211
Ward, Edward, 43
Wardour Street, 249
Warwick, 48
Watchmen ("Charlies"), 63, 95, 233, 253
Watford, 209
Watling Street, 211
Watson, Samuel (Joseph Weston), 248
Welbeck Street, 225
Welch, Saunders, 234
Weller, Sam (in *Pickwick Papers*), 143
Welton, 216
Westminster, 210
Weston brothers, George and Joseph, 246–250
Wethersfield, 137
Whalley, William, 265–266
Wheeler, highwayman, 209–210
Whiston, James, 171
White, John ("Fowler"), 88
White House, Hackney Marsh, 215
White's Club, St James's, 226, 228

Whitechapel, 142, 208, 214
Whitestockings, horse, 213
Whitney, "Captain" James, 148–154, 232, 269
Whittle, William, 60–61
Wicks, Ned, 195–196
Wigley, John, 66
Wild, Jonathan, 169, 180, 186, 195–206, 207, 236
William the Conqueror, 13
Williams, John ("The Matchet"), 81, 88
Wilmot, Thomas, 77, 80, 269
Wilson, Violet, 208
Wimbledon Common, 258
Winchelsea, 248–249
Winchester, Bishop of, 79
Winchester, Statute of, 62, 63
Windsor Forest, 153
Wit for Money, 52
Witherington, Jack, 186
Withers, John, 145–146, 269
Wood, Owen, 200, 207
Worcester, 52
Worde, Wynkyn de, 14
Worthies of England, 25, 142
Wyntoun, Andrew of, 14

York Castle, 131, 133, 141, 217
York, the ride to, 135–144, 215
Yorkshire Robber, The, 134, 141
Young, the Hon. William, 192

MERTHYR TYDFIL PUBLIC LIBRARIES